MINE!

Michael Heller is Professor of Real Estate Law and former Vice Dean for Intellectual Life at Columbia Law School. One of the world's leading authorities on ownership, he is the author of *The Gridlock Economy*.

James Salzman is Professor of Environmental Law at UCLA School of Law. He has written more than ninety articles and nine books, including *Drinking Water*.

MINE!

From Personal Space to Big Data, How Ownership Shapes Our Lives

MICHAEL HELLER
AND JAMES SALZMAN

Atlantic Books
London

First published in the United States in 2021 by Doubleday, a division of Penguin Random House LLC, New York.

First published in hardback in Great Britain in 2021 by Atlantic Books, an imprint of Atlantic Books Ltd.

This paperback edition published in 2022.

10 9 8 7 6 5 4 3 2 1

A CIP catalogue record for this book is available from the British Library.

Paperback ISBN: 978-1-78649-781-9
E-book ISBN: 978-1-78649-780-2

Printed in the U.K. by Clays Ltd, Elcograf S.p.A.

Atlantic Books
An imprint of Atlantic Books Ltd
Ormond House
26–27 Boswell Street
London
WC1N 3JZ

www.atlantic-books.co.uk

What's Mine Is Yours

To Debora, Ellie, and Jonah
—MH

To Heather, Ben, Eleanor, Elizabeth,
Jamie, and Kate
—JS

CONTENTS

MINE!

WHO GETS WHAT AND WHY

Mine! This primal cry is one of the first words children learn. Toddlers in sandboxes shout it out during epic struggles over plastic buckets. For adults, the idea of ownership seems natural and beyond contest. You know what it means to own stuff, whether you're buying a new home or claiming the last slice of pie. *Mine* couldn't be simpler.

But a lot of what you know about ownership is wrong.

Once you understand how the rules actually work, you will see the drama taking place beneath our workaday concept of ownership. Governments, businesses, and ordinary people are constantly changing the rules on who gets what and why. Each of these choices creates winners and losers. And this has always been so. At its core, human society exists to help us deal with competing claims to scarce resources—whether food, water, gold, or sexual partners—so that we don't kill each other too often.

Even the Garden of Eden story turns on ownership. God instructs Adam and Eve that the Tree of Knowledge and its fruit belong to God alone. *It's mine. Don't touch.* But the first people pluck the apple, they are evicted from the Garden, and human history begins. Since then, ownership has been up for grabs.

The Knee Defender

James Beach is a large guy, over six feet tall. On a United Airlines flight from Newark to Denver, after takeoff the businessman lowered his tray table from the middle seat of row twelve and attached his Knee Defender. The Knee Defender is a simple plastic bracket available for $21.95 that clamps onto the metal tray table support and locks the seat in front. Its website claims the Knee Defender will "stop reclining seats on airplanes so your knees won't have to." Assured of his workspace, Beach opened his laptop.

The Knee Defender claims are real. When the passenger sitting in front of Beach tried to "sit back, relax, and enjoy the flight," her seat didn't budge. She complained to the flight attendant, who asked Beach to remove the clamp, but Beach was slow to comply. Outraged, the passenger slammed her seat back, popping out the Knee Defender and jolting Beach's laptop. He quickly jammed her seat back up and reattached the clamp. That's when she turned around and threw her drink at Beach. We'll never know how this might have escalated because the pilot took charge and changed course to Chicago for an emergency landing. Both passengers were removed from the plane, which then continued on to Denver, an hour and thirty-eight minutes late.

The same conflict keeps erupting—most recently with video. On an American Airlines flight from New Orleans to North Carolina, Wendi Williams reclined her seat. The man behind was in the last row, so he could not recline. Instead, he pushed the back of Williams's seat repeatedly, like an irritating metronome. Her video of this high-altitude fracas quickly went viral.

With each incident, the blogosphere boomed back and forth with hundreds of self-righteous accusations, all equally certain of the correct rule. Talk show host Ellen DeGeneres defended the recliners: "The only time it's ever okay to punch someone's seat is if the seat punches you first." Delta Air Lines chief executive Ed Bastian took an opposing view: "The proper thing to do is, if you're going to recline into somebody, you ask if it's OK first." Williams didn't ask.

So who's right?

Williams's view is simple: her armrest button reclines her seat. The wedge of reclining space therefore belongs to the front seat. This claim of attachment—it's mine because it's attached to something that's mine—is one of the oldest justifications for ownership, dating back thousands of years. Beach was relying on a different attachment story, a maxim coined in medieval England that "whoever owns the soil, owns up to Heaven and down to Hell." He claimed dominion over the vertical column of space attached to his seat—straight up to the luggage compartment and down to the crumb-coated carpeting. When the seat in front intrudes into that column, it's a trespass, a jarring affront to good order.

Attachment is the most pervasive ownership claim you've never heard of. It's why landowners in Texas can extract underground oil and gas, why farmers pumping groundwater are causing California's Central Valley to sink, and why Alaska can limit overfishing in the Bering Sea. Attachment translates two-dimensional boarding passes, land deeds, and territorial maps into three-dimensional control of scarce resources.

But attachment is not the only ownership claim in play for Beach and Williams. At the beginning of every flight, all seats are "in their full, upright, and locked position," as the flight attendant commands. At that moment, Beach had exclusive use of the space in front of him. He had first dibs on the wedge. *First come, first served* is another primitive and visceral basis for claiming *mine*. Kids assert it on the playground; adults invoke it up in the air. And recall that Beach actually took physical possession of the wedge when he locked the Knee Defender in place and opened his laptop screen. As we hear so often, *Possession is nine-tenths of the law.*

Air travel brings into sharp focus this clash of conflicting stories about ownership—*attachment, first-in-time,* and *possession.*

When we ask audiences about the Knee Defender conflict, most respond with versions of "It's obvious," "There's nothing to debate here." But when we press further and ask for a show of hands, generally people are split between Williams and Beach—and both groups look at each other with incredulity. In a 2020 *USA Today* poll with three thousand respondents, about half replied, "If it can recline, I'm reclining," and the other half said, "No, just don't do it." Everyone feels in the right, as did Williams and Beach. That's why Williams felt justified in posting her video and Beach didn't hesitate to shove the seat forward. *Don't mess with what's mine.*

Why are these conflicts breaking out now? There never used to be such rage around reclining. Until recently, airline seats had greater pitch, or space between seats—enough both for reclining and for lowering the tray table. No one thought to ask who controlled the wedge of space because it didn't much matter. But airlines have been shrinking the pitch, down from 35 inches not that long ago to about 31 inches today. On some planes, the pitch is just 28 inches.

There's a lot at stake for the airlines: one inch of pitch saved per row can add up to six extra seats per flight to sell. To grow profits, airlines are squeezing ever more passengers inside a fixed steel tube—at the same time that people are growing bigger and tray tables have become precious computer stands. The stakes are high for passengers as well. In a pandemic era, each inch of personal space counts.

Ira Goldman, the inventor of the Knee Defender (whose website traffic increased five-hundred-fold after the Denver flight incident), described the problem simply: "What the airlines are doing is, they're selling me space for my legs, and they're selling you the space—if you're sitting in front of me—they're selling you the same space to recline. So they're selling one space to two people."

Can the airlines do that?

The law is silent. In 2018 the Federal Aviation Administration declined to regulate airplane seats, leaving seat design to the airlines. In turn, the airlines use a secret weapon that lets them sell the same space twice on every flight. The weapon is *strategic ambiguity,* one of the tools of sophisticated ownership design. Most airlines do have a rule—the passenger with the button can lean back—but they keep it quiet. Flight attendants don't announce or enforce it except in extreme circumstances.

Ambiguity works to the airlines' advantage. When ownership is unclear—and it's unclear more often than you might imagine—people mostly fall back on politeness and good manners. For decades, airlines have counted on high-altitude etiquette to defuse ambiguous claims to the reclining wedge—that's what Delta CEO Bastian was advocating. Airlines offload the conflicts onto passengers who have to work it out between themselves in millions of small, silent daily negotiations, just as they do when they nudge elbows for shared armrests and jostle for space in overhead bins. Money rarely changes hands. (One study, though, suggests about three-quarters of passengers would agree not to recline if the person behind offered to buy them a drink or snack.)

As airlines continue to shrink the pitch, unspoken rules over the front-to-back squeeze are breaking down. When people don't share an understanding about who owns what, scarcity intensifies their conflicting views, and everyone ends up looking unreasonable. The Knee Defender makes the existing conflicts more visible. Goldman saw ownership ambiguity as a business opportunity and created a technological solution. The problem, though, is that a unilateral move to lock the seat violates customs of politeness. It feels like taking something without asking.

The Knee Defender may seem like a silly novelty item, but it reflects one of the great innovation engines in our society: as valued resources becomes scarcer, people compete more intensely to impose their preferred ownership story, and entrepreneurs find ways to profit.

The same clash profoundly reshaped the American West in the 1800s—but there it was farmers against ranchers. The huge cattle drives we love to watch in westerns existed for only a few decades.

The numberless herds being moved to market were often roaming over private land, but homesteaders had no ability to keep them out. Cows couldn't read NO TRESPASSING signs, and fencing was too expensive. So cowboys drove cattle over unfenced miles to railyards in Abilene and Dodge City.

Then in 1874 Joseph Glidden patented his double-strand barbed wire, hailed as "The Greatest Discovery of the Age." This invention, as simple as the Knee Defender, suddenly provided a cheap, effective tool to exclude cattle, drawing a line where homesteaders could make their stand. The Glidden wire was described as "lighter than air, stronger than whiskey, cheaper than dust." Ranchers fought back, engaging in fence-cutting wars that led to shootings and deaths. As one trail driver said in 1883, "It makes me sick, when I think of onions and Irish potatoes growing where mustang ponies should be exercising and where four-year-old steers should be getting ripe for market." But in time, homesteaders won the war.

Glidden's invention transformed the Great Plains. Arriving homesteaders were able to protect their crops. Small ranchers went out of business as they had no path to get cattle to market. Cowboys became hired hands on large-scale ranches. For many Native Americans, barbed wire—"the Devil's rope"—effectively ended their nomadic way of life. Barbed wire was essential to creating the NO TRESPASSING version of ownership that defines so much of modern life in America.

Changes in the technology of ownership can be painful, embittering the range wars on the Great Plains and the knee wars at thirty-five thousand feet. Just as barbed wire gave farmers a way to fence out cattle, the Knee Defender gives passengers a cheap tool to exclude recliners. Both technologies offer people an effective way to impose their preferred story of ownership on contested resources, thus hastening the decline of old customs and creating disputes over what the new rules should be.

There is a difference, though: while farmers made barbed wire ubiquitous, many airlines have banned Knee Defenders—they prefer to keep selling that wedge of space twice.

The same ownership wars are playing out today on the Internet, a far more consequential and even less visible arena than airplane seats. Our clickstreams reveal much of our private lives—what we buy, who we follow, where we live, and how we vote. Clickstreams seem like they should belong to us, but in most of the world data ownership remains undefined. Facebook, Google, and other Internet behemoths (along with myriad spy agencies) are racing to stake claims. They earn billions in advertising fees as their trackers recline virtual seats into our private space, assembling uncanny profiles based on our likes and looks.

One of the central questions for our time is choosing the ownership story to govern our online lives. A few places, like the European Union and California, have taken tentative steps toward providing people with the digital equivalent of Knee Defenders. Will these protections make a difference? No one knows. There is as yet no dominant principle for data ownership. The answer is up in the air, not just for clickstreams and reclining seats but for a thousand other invisible battlegrounds where people are currently contesting claims to scarce resources.

Conflicts of *mine* versus *mine* go on, mostly out of view, until something like a cheap plastic Knee Defender makes them painfully visible. Then the prize goes to those who know how ownership really works.

"A Guy in New Jersey"

Hanging out in a local Manhattan bar, Jenna Wortham and her friends were talking about evening plans when they realized they all were looking forward to watching the season premiere of HBO's hit show *Game of Thrones*. That should have been a problem. HBO owns the show, and you need to buy a subscription to stream its content. Only one of Wortham's friends subscribed, but everyone wanted to watch in different places. Turns out, this problem was easy to solve because they streamed the show using login credentials that belonged to other people. Wortham used the login from "a guy in New Jersey that I had once met in a Mexican restaurant."

Wortham's story is not unusual. It's become commonplace for people to use others' accounts to stream shows from popular media services. Indeed, the only thing uncommon about Wortham's story is that she is a *New York Times* reporter. She thought so little about the implications of using somebody else's HBO subscription that she published a breezy (some might say, brazen) account of her night out.

What Wortham (and the *Times*) did not seem to realize was that she was likely admitting guilt to a federal crime under the Computer Fraud and Abuse Act, a crime punishable by up to a year in jail. It may be common to stream shows using a stranger's password, but HBO's terms of use expressly forbid it. It's not "legalish," as one *Forbes* writer argued in her defense. Under the law, misguided though it might be, Wortham's act was probably criminal.

But no one seems to care—least of all HBO. Everyone knows someone who's streaming media content using a not-exactly-legit password. Nearly 100 percent of our (law!) students raise their hands when we ask who's illegally streaming media content. About half of these students don't think what they're doing is illegal (really?). The other half realize it's illegal and do it anyway. Why do we tolerate such rampant theft?

For starters, streaming shows doesn't feel like theft. Sharing passwords feels completely different from stealing a DVD of the same *Game of Thrones* show from a store. It's highly unlikely Wortham or her friends would walk out of a store without paying, and they certainly wouldn't boast in print about it.

Maybe the difference between illegal streaming and shoplifting just boils down to the likelihood of being caught. But that cannot be the whole story. HBO can easily figure out who is stealing its content. That's what the Recording Industry Association of America did when it identified music fans who were downloading music via Napster and sued them each for millions of dollars. HBO can find out who you are, but it's choosing to look the other way.

We are taught from an early age to respect others' physical stuff. That respect is consistent with an instinct rooted in the most primitive parts of our brains. Bulldogs, birds, and bears know to stay off others' territories. But our intuition feels different for something intangible, like an idea. As one study found, if you hear "that's mine" coming from a young preschooler, "you can be fairly sure someone stole their toy or their food, and not their joke, story, or song." Perhaps streaming just doesn't activate the same primitive, territorial part of our brains. And maybe this is why sharing passwords doesn't feel wrong, morally or legally.

Content owners understand this. They have been trying, with limited success, to change how we feel about digital stuff and make it seem more like hard, physical stuff. Hence the scary-looking notices at the start of DVDs from Interpol and the stern warnings at the start of every movie that "piracy is not a victimless crime." Even the term *intellectual property* is part of this battle. Copyright, patent, and trademark lawyers made up the phrase to piggyback their clients' concerns onto our intuitions about physical stuff. They know that for our primitive selves, copyright is not property.

In its most basic form, content owners and users are waging a battle over the story of ownership. Should digital goods be free to share, like passing along a catchy tune you heard at a concert? Or should they be ordinary property, like a mug or a bike, which law, custom, and morality prevent us from taking, even if the opportunity arises? Both stories are available.

What drives the content owner's story? It's not the intuitions that animate the Knee Defender conflict—attachment, first-in-time, and possession. Instead, HBO's claims trace back to yet another of our core intuitions, the idea that *labor* justifies ownership—that you and you alone deserve to *reap what you sow.*

Rewarding labor often feels right and just, but it always favors one side of a contested choice. The fashion world provides a powerful counterexample. In fashion, designers build fortunes based on copying each other's creations. The labor that goes into original dress designs is not protected. Knockoffs are not theft. They are perfectly legal. In many pockets of the modern economy—chefs' recipes, coaches' sports plays, stand-up comedians' routines, and numerous other creative arenas—we have decided that vibrant competition and unfettered innovation matter more than rewarding creative labor with ownership. In other words, the rule is often *I reap what you sow.* Every year fashion designers push Congress to change the rules, so they can reap what they "sew," but they lose.

The music recording industry, on the other hand, was more effective than the couture houses at lobbying Congress. It secured legislation so that digital music conforms to the industry's ownership story. Based on that law, the industry has filed, settled, or threatened legal action against at least thirty thousand people. Unfortunately for the big music labels, all that activity hasn't ended illegal downloading— but it did turn popular opinion against them.

HBO watched and learned. It realized that, as *TechCrunch* wrote, "account sharing is generally a gray area in the world of online streaming." HBO decided to embrace strategic ambiguity. Though it may sound crazy, the network encourages theft of its product. HBO executives are well aware of your (and your kids' and our students') unauthorized streaming. But instead of treating potential customers like criminals, HBO is hooking Wortham and her friends on their shows.

HBO's CEO Richard Plepler proudly described the company's pro-piracy strategy as "a terrific marketing vehicle for the next generation of viewers." Password sharing, Plepler continued, "presents the brand to more and more people, and gives them an opportunity hopefully to become addicted to it." In a quote that lit up the Internet, Plepler added, "What we're in the business of doing is building addicts, of building video addicts. The way we do that is by exposing our product, our brand, our shows, to more and more people."

Competitors have noticed HBO's counterintuitive approach to ownership design—and followed suit up to a point. Netflix CEO Reed Hastings said, "We love people sharing Netflix. That's a positive thing, not a negative thing." But Netflix allows only one device to use a basic account at a time.

For HBO and Netflix, the strategy depends on Wortham and other young viewers believing they're stealing, just a little. Plepler and Hastings want lots of viewers to obsess over their shows, whether they currently pay for subscriptions or not. For them, the hope is that when today's pirates start to earn income, more will start paying and will enjoy the feeling of going legit.

The long-term plan is subtler still. Plepler and Hastings aim to recruit viewers to their side of the ownership story: intellectual property is property, and they are being generous in letting you steal content for now.

The Hidden Rules of Ownership

This is a book about fights over airplane seats and sharing HBO passwords. It's about whether immigrants can start food truck businesses and why life-saving drugs do not come to market, along with dozens of other challenges and riddles from all walks of life. What it's really about, though, is how the different ways we own things link all these puzzles—from the rise of America's new aristocracy to solutions for climate change. By the end of this book, you will see the world around you in a new and surprising way, based on a small number of fundamental insights.

Before we take you on this ride, we want to tell you what's driving us. Both of us have been teaching for a long time, more than twenty-five years each. We're not bad at it—our students have voted us both "Professor of the Year." Between us, we've helped train over five thousand lawyers, businesspeople, and environmentalists. What we love most is watching the lightbulbs blink on as students realize that there is nothing preordained about how ownership directs our behavior, and that a few simple principles drive a complex world.

Mine! distills the essence of our work as teachers and scholars so you can get the insights without the big tuition bills. As a taste of what's to come, we want to circle back to the stories we've already told—Beach's Knee Defender and Wortham's password sharing—and highlight the three principles of ownership they embody:

1. Our Core Ownership Stories Are Wrong

Consider, for a moment, how many common maxims there are about what's *mine.* They are the lens through which we learn, from childhood onward, what ownership means. Here are six such maxims that—as it turns out—stand for *all* the ways scarce resources initially come to be owned:

- First come, first served.
- Possession is nine-tenths of the law.
- You reap what you sow.
- My home is my castle.
- Our bodies, our selves.
- The meek shall inherit the earth.

Regardless of whether you fly drones or insist on privacy in your home, support or oppose allowing the sale of kidneys, happily wait your turn in line or push to the front, you may reach for one of these ownership maxims to press your claim.

What is striking about all these maxims is that, despite their ubiquity, none of them are quite true. They go astray because, at root, they share an underlying commitment to a binary view of ownership. Like a light switch that goes on or off, we feel something is either *mine* or *not mine.* This simple conception is as appealing as it is misleading. Today, in an increasing array of ownership conflicts, it is becoming more accurate to say *First come, last served, Possession is one-tenth of the law, I reap what you sow,* and so on down the list.

In early America, the on-off idea described many ownership conflicts reasonably well. In a mostly agrarian economy, people fought over tangible property: farmland, cattle—and, most egregiously, ownership of African American bodies. Slavery was not only the central question of morality and justice in American history, it was also the country's core ownership conflict. You were either free or the property of someone else.

By the twentieth century, the most pressing ownership debates had shifted away from these simple binaries. Instead, we fought over the blurry boundary between private property and public control. Should the owner of a lunch counter be obligated to serve people of another race? Should landowners be subject to limits on what they can build? Should patients own their excised cells that are used for scientific research?

Today the debates are shifting yet again. Many of the pressing conflicts concern the claims of one private owner against another— *mine* versus *mine.* In this new world, the old maxims are more misleading than ever.

If you click "buy now" to get a book on Kindle, you may believe, reasonably, that you own the book. *Possession is nine-tenths,* and so on. But Amazon says otherwise. All you own is a highly limited license. Amazon can, and indeed has, deleted books right off people's devices. One of the company's underappreciated skills is its facility with ownership design. What Amazon realized is that the meaning of ownership is pliable and adjustable. The company could tweak its contours and remove the features it disliked. Amazon knows— and studies have shown—that we still believe our ownership online has remained unchanged, as if owning a virtual book were just like owning a hard copy. It's not the same. The result: we pay Amazon an unearned premium because of our mistake.

Despite the adage, customers are not always right. There is an increasing gap between what we *feel* like we own and what we *actually* own.

2. Ownership Is a Storytelling Battle— Among Just Six Stories

People sold or gave you most of what you own. But where did their ownership come from? It all traces back to a first owner asserting one of the six simple stories—embodied in the maxims we mentioned above—that everyone uses to claim everything.

The battle over those stories is like politicians fighting to win an election. We face dueling claims competing for our loyalty and belief. And these stories work because they rely on strong but conflicting intuitions about what should constitute ownership. The most important thing to realize is that if you know the stories, along with the tools and tricks of ownership design, you will be better equipped to decide for yourself which is the more persuasive story today.

Tall passengers insist on their "right to knee defense," but that story bumps up against tired passengers asserting a "right to recline." The airlines could easily pick one side or the other. They could put a little plaque on the seat back or a note on the boarding pass announcing their preferred rule, then make passengers comply. Or they could "precline" all the seats, setting them at a single fixed angle, as a few budget airlines have started doing.

But for now most airlines prefer ambiguity, packing more seats into the economy section and continuing to sell the same space twice. That's why most have banned the Knee Defender. Angry and anxious passengers turn against each other without realizing the airlines are taking advantage of their conflicting stories about what's *mine*. Even better—for the airlines—the discomfort creates a profitable market for higher-priced seats with more legroom and less hassle. Those skilled in ownership design know that deliberate ambiguity about seat recline can create economic value.

That's the real story behind sky-high seat conflicts.

It's the same with password sharing and clickstreams. At the moment, there's an outpouring of political attention, lawsuits, magazine articles, and books on control of digital content and user data, as though the Internet creates something fundamentally new about ownership. It doesn't. It's the Knee Defender battle all over again. Should we block companies from leaning their data trackers into our virtual laps?

All property conflicts exist as competing stories. Each side picks the story that presents its claims as the moral high ground, and each side wants ownership bent toward its view. But don't be fooled. There are no natural, correct descriptions that frame *mine* versus *mine* conflicts. There are, however, better and worse choices that we can make to solve these dilemmas. And if you are not the one choosing, then someone else is making the choices for you.

3. Ownership Is the Remote Control for Much of Life

Ownership rules pick winners and losers in every imaginable setting. Do you want to zip along in the carpool lane at rush hour? You can if you carry extra passengers—or, in some places, if you drive an electric car. You want to get on the airplane first? Be loyal to that airline or spend more on your ticket. The old first-in-time rule no longer operates at rush hour or the airport.

Owners of valuable resources operate a powerful remote control. They are always trying to design the particular rule that will influence others to do their will—with the most profit and least hassle. Simply by tweaking the meaning of ownership, owners can use their control over valuable resources to steer you invisibly, gently, but powerfully to act how they want. The remote control is effective because ideas about ownership become so incorporated into our everyday behavior that we don't even notice how the rules are being chopped up, fine-tuned, and redefined to push us around.

By changing the fast lane into a reserved lane for carpools or electric cars, governments push people toward behaviors that reduce congestion and air pollution. By tolerating password sharing for the moment, HBO builds its fan base and "addicts" its future subscribers.

Ownership design is best understood as a *social engineering tool* designed to steer your behavior, invisibly and decisively. Ownership is not complicated. It can't be, if we are going to navigate daily life without too much conflict. Once you see how owners can intentionally direct your actions, you may even be able to take hold of the remote control to improve your own life and to promote the common good.

Why Mine!*? Why Now?*

In recent years, engaging guides have helped us understand many of the mysteries of everyday life. If the tools of modern microeconomic analysis interest you, then look at *Freakonomics,* where Steven Levitt and Stephen Dubner provide a fresh perspective on everything from cheating and crime to parenting and sports. If you're more psychologically minded, read *Nudge,* where Cass Sunstein and Richard Thaler show how to make better decisions for health, wealth, and happiness. Economics and psychology are great tools. They explain a lot. But they also miss a lot. Both tend to take ownership for granted, when it is anything but fixed.

In the chapters that follow, we use common sayings and intuitions about what's *mine* as starting points to reveal the ownership design principles that control our lives. Along the way, we will pose some puzzles to consider:

- Why does a chair in the street hold your parking place after a snowstorm in Chicago but not in New York? And, conversely, why does a napkin on your drink hold your seat at some New York bars but not in Chicago dives?
- Why does Disney World charge so much for its VIP cut-the-line pass (a minimum of about $3,000), when it could make even more by charging somewhat less? And why don't the families patiently waiting for Space Mountain protest when the one-percenters pass them by?
- Why can we sell our blood plasma but not our kidneys? And how come it's illegal in Michigan to be paid as a gestational surrogate (carrying another couple's embryo to term) but it's an ordinary business deal in California?
- Why can airplanes fly through the column of air above your house but drones cannot? And why can strangers in half of America come onto your unfenced land without permission and forage wild plants but not pick apples?

How we own things provides the answers to all these questions. And in the pages that follow, you will learn the answers to dozens more puzzles that touch on every aspect of your life as a consumer, entrepreneur, and citizen. What often seems like a natural and immutable limit—*it's mine or it's not*—is actually the result of choices that governments, businesses, and others are making about how to control the scarce resources we all want.

The Rocking Chair

Here's a puzzle to get us started.

Burr McDowell died in 1973 in upstate New York. In his will, he left his rocking chair to his adult children, Arthur and Mildred. The rickety old chair wasn't worth any money, but both kids loved the chair and wanted it anyway. They couldn't agree on how to share, and McDowell's will was silent. So Arthur went to his dad's house and took the chair. Mildred asked for it; Arthur refused. And as so often happens in America, Mildred sued. That's how we know of the dispute. This is a real case.

Imagine you are the judge. New York statutes give no guidance; neither does the existing case law. You just have to make a choice: two kids, one chair. Pause for a moment here, perhaps, and consider what you might do. Here are a few (of the many) options that might come to mind:

- Flip a coin.
- Leave the chair with Arthur, the first possessor.
- Give the chair to Mildred, the first to the courthouse.
- Auction it. One kid wins the chair; the other gets cash.
- Let the judge rock on it until the kids reach a deal.
- Saw the chair in half and give each kid a piece.
- Order them to take turns daily, or maybe annually.
- Just burn the chair.

So what do you decide? Any choice you make opens a window into your core intuitions and impulses regarding ownership.

Flipping a coin may seem fairest. But oddly that's the one solution in the list above judges and juries are explicitly forbidden from using. Coin flips work on the playground and to start football games, but not in the law. As a judge, you need to give a reason for choosing one party—even if you believe both sides have equal merit.

First-in-time is appealing. But how does that apply here? Arthur first took the chair; Mildred was first to court. Neither version of first seems to reward morally attractive behavior. Arthur's actual physical possession is no more appealing as a basis for decision. Auctioning the chair would end the dispute quickly, but it privileges the wealthier child in a context where honoring family sentiment seems more appropriate. Locking the chair away until the kids reach agreement may appeal to our parental impulses, but it favors the stubborn child. Sawing the chair in half has an ironic Solomonic twist but little else going for it.

Making the kids take turns is plausible. That's what the judge decided in the actual case: the kids were ordered to schlep the chair from home to home every six months until one died. That's fine, except it locked these feuding siblings together under ongoing court supervision. Who pays for repairs when one of them rocks too hard and the joints get loose? What if Mildred is a week late delivering to Arthur? Perhaps the hassle and cost of switching back and forth is justified for managing child custody, but this is a chair, not a child. Also, taking turns rewards the sibling who has more time to waste carting furniture around.

How about just burning the chair? That would teach them a lesson—and it might have the useful effect of keeping future squabbling siblings out of court. Work it out yourselves. Don't waste the court's time. But that seems a harsh outcome for Arthur and Mildred.

Here's the punchline: there's no avoiding the hard work of deciding who gets what and why. You can turn to a third party, like a judge or a legislator, to answer on your behalf. But that just means putting someone else's hand on the remote control. Or you can participate in making the choice yourself—as an owner, a consumer, a citizen. Do you favor chance or reason, time or money, speediness or strength, justice or efficiency, reward or punishment?

Unavoidably, you reveal and encode your deepest values in every decision you make about ownership.

Chapter 1

FIRST COME,
LAST SERVED

Line-Standers

The best free show in Washington, D.C. is the Supreme Court. The courtroom is both ornate and intimate. You sit only steps from the justices of the highest court in the land and listen to America's top advocates. This is democracy at its best, open and accessible to all. If you want to witness the fate of abortion, gun control, or religious freedom, you can. But you need to get there early—there are on average fewer than one hundred seats available for the public, and admission is first come, first served.

For high-profile cases, people arrive a day or more ahead of time, armed with camping chairs, sleeping bags, ponchos, and extra batteries for their smartphones. Folks in line tend to look out for one another—Supreme Court police officers refuse to monitor the line. If you have to go to the bathroom, those around you will hold your place. And they will also be on guard for people cutting in or adding friends. If someone does that, they are harangued with cries of "no cutting" and "back of the line."

As the time to enter the Court approaches, though, a strange thing happens. Many of the disheveled people nearest the front of the line exchange their spots with gray-suited men and women. A little later the well-dressed enter the courtroom and take the best seats while those farther back in the line are not even admitted. What is going on?

Welcome to the line-standing business. Companies are paying line-standers, sometimes homeless people, to arrive days ahead, secure a spot at the front, and then wait and wait and wait. At the last minute, by the Court entrance etched with the words EQUAL JUSTICE UNDER LAW, the line-standers give way to paying clients who have the money to get in first but not the time or patience to wait. Small start-ups like Linestanding.com, Skip the Line, and Washington Express charge clients up to $6,000 for a "free" seat, while paying minimum wage to the hired line-standers who wait in the rain and cold.

Line-standing companies have transformed how seats become *mine* not just for Supreme Court arguments but also for open congressional hearings where the nation's laws are debated. Hearing rooms used to be free to anyone willing to wait to see their elected representatives in action. Now those hearings are often packed with lawyers and lobbyists, all of whom paid, none of whom waited. The same transformation is happening in lines for new passports at the local federal building or building permits at City Hall.

Paid line-standers are a booming business in the private sector as well. If you're willing to pay, you can get to the front for new iPhones at Apple stores, hot skatewear apparel at Supreme, rush Broadway show tickets, or even prime spots on New York City streets to watch the Macy's Thanksgiving Day Parade. One line-stander employed by SOLD (Same Ole Line Dudes), a line-standing start-up, waited forty-three hours holding a spot so a client could be sure to get an audition for *Shark Tank*, the hit reality TV show for start-ups. Odds are that Robert Samuel, the entrepreneurial founder of SOLD, would have done better on the show than the guy from Colorado who paid Samuel for his place in line.

The same transition is happening online. The musical *Hamilton* was continuously sold out on Broadway for years after it opened. The producers of the show made most tickets available on a first-in-time basis on their website. The problem was that tech-savvy scalpers created computer programs—bots—that bought up all the tickets the microsecond they became available. As a result, the artists and producers earned only the tickets' face value while fans paid scalpers' premiums, often a multiple of the original price, on sites such as StubHub. Many weeks ticket scalpers earned more from *Hamilton* than did the producers and artists who put on the show. What good is the first-in-time rule if a bot will always jump the line faster than a mortal with a mouse? When *Hamilton* tried to outsmart the scalpers by making some tickets available only at the theater box office, companies like SOLD hired line-standers to snag them.

Bruce Springsteen tried another approach when he played his sold-out run on Broadway. He paired with TicketMaster as it debuted Verified Fan, an online system that aimed to circumvent the bots and line-standers and get at least some tickets directly to prescreened real fans. But even those tickets often ended up on the resale market—you have to be quite committed to the Boss to turn down a $10,000 offer for an $850 ticket.

How should we think about this rapid rise of paying to get to the head of the line?

For many, this transformation seems deeply unfair and undemocratic. One disappointed woman stood for days in line at the Supreme Court and still did not get to hear the 2015 case establishing the right to same-sex marriage. The real system, she said, is "Let's pay the poor Black guys to hold the line for rich white people." On the other hand, maybe line-standing should be viewed as a good thing—capitalism at its best, creating new jobs where none existed before, both for programmers scripting their bots and for the poor and homeless waiting in lines.

We never used to ask these questions. But today we must, because first-in-time is being dismantled from within.

Who's on First?

For most of human history, for most resources, the rule for establishing original ownership followed a maxim expressed in ancient Roman law as "Whoever is earlier in time is stronger in right." In other words, *First come, first served.*

This has long been the practice in families. Think back to your childhood Bible lessons. Why did Jacob put an animal skin on his arm to trick his blind father, Isaac, into thinking he was blessing Esau, Jacob's rough-skinned brother? Esau was born first and by right should have received his father's gifts. Being first got you not only paternal blessings but also earthly treasure. Jacob's trickery let him jump the line.

The practice of *primogeniture,* inheritance by the firstborn son, has long decided the succession of royal families around the world. It still does today, with an egalitarian twist in countries such as Sweden and the Netherlands, which now pass the crown to the monarch's firstborn child rather than just the first son.

First-in-time governed colonial exploration as well. Colonies in the New World were carved up among the European powers based on which nation's explorer was first to plant his sovereign's flag. This may hold some intuitive appeal for uninhabited lands, but what about places with people already living there? If being first is what counts, surely Native Americans had the stronger claim for owning America. Not so, said the international law of the time—as written by the European powers. When Europeans came to America, they defined *first* to mean "the first Christian discoverer."

And here lies a key to understanding this ancient maxim for making things *mine.* Even something as factual-sounding as "who's first" is not self-defining. The right question is "Who decides who's first?" In American law, the answer is "The conqueror prescribes its limits," according to Chief Justice John Marshall in *Johnson v. M'Intosh,* an 1823 Supreme Court decision that most lawyers read during their early days in law school. Being the first Christian European was what justified, as a matter of law, the claims of Spain to the Caribbean, Texas, Mexico, and California; of France to New Orleans, Canada, and much of middle America; and of England to New England and Virginia.

But if that's the case, why did the world not rise in protest when Neil Armstrong planted the American flag on the moon in July 1969? That should have made the moon just as much a U.S. territory as early America was a European one. The answer is that by the 1960s, countries had renounced discovery and conquest as the basis for deciding who was first. In 1967 the United States, along with the Soviet Union and dozens of other countries, signed the U.N. Outer Space Treaty explicitly rejecting first-in-time for extraterrestrial resources.

So when Armstrong became the first human on the moon, he was not asserting American ownership there. Indeed, to make America's intentions clear, in 1969 Congress felt compelled to pass a law stating that when a U.S. astronaut places a flag on the moon, it is "intended as a symbolic gesture of national pride in achievement and is not to be construed as a declaration of national appropriation by claim of sovereignty."

Countries continue to play the "who's on first" game, though, with contested results. In 2007 the Russian Navy tweaked the international community by placing a small titanium Russian flag on the bottom of the Arctic Ocean. Russia was symbolically staking a claim to the mineral-rich seabed beneath the North Pole and the trade shipping routes that cross the pole—all newly accessible because of climate change and melting ice. Though an international furor erupted over the idea that Russia might win these resources simply by flagging them first, the strategy is time-tested. As we shall see in Chapter 4, China is now implementing a version of this strategy by building and claiming islands in the South China Sea.

Territorial claims and family inheritances are not the only venues for first-in-time. Being first is also the default rule for how ordinary people claim all sorts of unowned things. It was how miners staked claims during the 1848 Gold Rush in California. In 1889, Native lands in Oklahoma were opened for pioneer settlement through "land runs" that began with a pistol shot on the state line. (*Sooner* was the derogatory term for those who jumped the gun.) Today well-funded start-ups are aiming to mine the moon and harpoon asteroids for water, platinum, and gold—all in tension with internationally recognized ownership rules. This is also the origin story of Uber, Airbnb, YouTube, and many other Internet businesses that raced ahead of the law to create and then capture markets. Ambiguity about ownership favors the bold, the heedless, the outlaws—those who race ahead first.

But not always.

The law looks not only to who is making the claim but also to what they are doing with it. In the 1800s, homesteaders not only had to arrive first at their 160-acre parcel of earth but also had to show that they cut, burned, fenced, planted, and wrenched sustenance from it continuously for a period of years. This was another reason courts of the day ruled that Native Americans did not own their ancestral lands. Europeans imagined Native peoples treading lightly through the forest while hunting fish and game and did not view that labor as sufficiently productive to sustain an original claim of ownership. They defined *first* to mean first to labor according to the agricultural and commercial ethos of the settlers.

What is first turns out to be a slippery concept—never just an empirical fact, always a legal construct. In the classic children's book *The Little Prince,* we encounter a businessman counting stars. The little prince asks why and hears, "I own the stars, because nobody else before me ever thought of owning them." But being the first to think of owning stars does not necessarily make them owned. By and large, courts and governments define and redefine what's first to guide people invisibly and inexorably toward particular, socially approved forms of interaction with scarce resources.

Almost all the 1.3 million lawyers in America learned this insight by reading *Pierson v. Post,* a case about a fox-hunting dispute from 1805. Lodowick Post was riding horseback with his dogs while hunting down a fox, described by the Court as a "wild and noxious beast," on unclaimed "waste land"—that is, a beach. In the last moments of the chase, after the fox had been exhausted, a man named Pierson appeared on the scene, easily killed the fox, and carried it away. Post sued, claiming Pierson had taken his property—the fox was Post's because he had hunted it first and was on the verge of making the kill. (Note: it's always worth asking who is suing. Who goes to court over one fox pelt or a rocking chair? Litigants are often deviants. Life is short. Work it out.)

So who wins? The law was silent. The judges all agreed that the first-in-time rule should convert the wild animal into something owned. But what counted as first? Here the judges split on one of the big divides of ownership design: whether to apply a *bright-line rule* or a *standard.* Bright-line rules define precise terms that tend to be predictable and easy to apply across a range of cases. Standards offer general guides that allow for fine-grained judgments and can lead to fairer outcomes in particular cases. Think of the difference between highway signs that say SPEED LIMIT 55 and DRIVE SAFELY UNDER THE CIRCUMSTANCES.

The majority of the judges wanted a bright-line rule. They did not want disappointed hunters in court arguing the fine points of the chase. So they created what became known as the *rule of capture* and decided for Pierson, the "saucy intruder." The fox belongs to whoever "mortally wounds the wild animal and brings it under certain control." Being first means finishing the job—not thinking about the fox or even chasing it around.

In dissent, one judge asserted that *first* should be defined to mean whatever maximizes the destruction of the "wily quadrupeds." For him, the way to achieve that goal would be to ask if Post had a "reasonable prospect" of capture—an open-ended standard. Because he thought Post had such a prospect, Post was first and owned the fox. This makes a sort of intuitive sense: what was the point of investing in horses and hounds if, at the last minute, a random passerby could scoop up the fox exhausted by your chase?

So what happened after Pierson won? Did fox hunting grind to a halt? No—just the opposite. It turned out that in a first-to-capture world, hunters stepped up their game. Time has shown that the majority's bright-line rule turbocharges innovations in capture technology, and not just for fox hunting. If you want to be first to own any wild animal, you had better adopt the most lethal methods. And this hunting rule was extended by analogy to many other natural resources. In many parts of America, if you want to own flowing underground resources—water, oil, gas—you have to innovate to ensure that you actually pump them out first.

Today the same is true for ownership of inventions. For two centuries, America used a version of a reasonable prospect rule, giving patent monopolies to those *first to invent*—an open-ended standard that led to much litigation. Then in 2011 America switched to a bright-line *first to file* rule: regardless of how much progress competing inventors made, the patent went to whoever won the race to the Patent Office. America was the last country in the world to adopt the rule of capture for patents, following a debate in Congress that substantially tracked the majority and dissenting views in *Pierson* two centuries earlier.

The rule of capture has substantial benefits. It motivates everyone to race harder and faster. But choosing this sharp definition of *first* also imposes costs. In the natural-resource context, it has led to species extinction and crashing fisheries—environmental tragedies whose solutions we will explore in Chapters 4 and 7.

None of the judges in *Pierson* understood the real-world consequences of their opinions. And that's often the case when courts—and legislatures, businesses, and parents—aim to achieve any policy goal. We fix ownership based on guesses about how the world works.

But we often have no real clue. We call this decision-making strategy *casual empiricism,* and it's everywhere in law and life. Be alert when someone deploys it against you. If you hear, "We need rule X to get outcome Y," ask: How do you know we will get Y instead of Z?

Over time even the most intense battles to define what counts as first fade into the background. After the relevant community—hunters, inventors, nations, movie ticket buyers—agrees on what counts as first, people are off to the races, not just in old-timey cases but all around us today. This is how countries claim orbital parking spaces for geosynchronous satellites and also how you order a sandwich at the deli: "First in line, step up."

In short, first-in-time is a powerful tool of social engineering, and it's the default rule for getting along in a crowded world. But why? What are its essential advantages?

For starters, as the *Pierson* majority recognized, it's simple to understand and easy to apply. Even kids are adept at using the rule. The first to sit in the playground swing gets it for recess. Solving disputes over who is first is usually cheap and fast. There is no need for a lot of information or for long discussion, no need for parents or teachers to intervene. Lines are often completely self-policing.

First-in-time also appeals to a primitive, intuitive sense of fairness. Temporal priority seems to generate a moral claim: if you make the effort to get in line first, if you play by the rules, you should go in ahead of everyone else. For many of us, this result also dovetails with our democratic and egalitarian impulses—we all have the same chance to get in line early, whether we are prince or pauper. Time is the great equalizer in the battle to own scarce resources. First is fair.

For reasons of history and tradition, of efficiency and productivity, ease of administration and coordination, justice and fairness, societies have converged repeatedly on a core rule for ownership: *First in time means first in right.*

So far, so good.

But today first-in-time is under attack from all sides. We have seen how line-standing businesses and bots are undermining the rule. Savvy entrepreneurs, like SOLD, have figured out how to convert time into money. Getting to the head of the line provides a great business opportunity.

Despite its virtues, first-in-time suffers from a crucial defect—it leaves a lot of value on the table, available to be captured by anyone who knows how to game the rules of ownership. Governments, businesses, and ordinary owners are realizing they can create more value for themselves if they ignore those who got there first.

We are increasingly living in a world where *First come, last served* is the more accurate rule. To understand why, let's move from linestanders at the Supreme Court to another type of court—the crazed world of university basketball.

Cameron Crazies

When Jim Salzman joined the Duke Law School faculty, the dean said, "Salary is negotiable, but basketball tickets are off the table. I can't help you with that."

Duke's basketball team is famous throughout the country—five national championships; a coach, Mike Krzyzewski, with the most wins in history; a cramped, old-fashioned arena known as Cameron Indoor Stadium; and student fans known as Cameron Crazies who are among the most enthusiastic in the land. Duke basketball tickets aren't easy to come by. And if it is hard for faculty to get tickets to games, it can be even harder for students.

Every year during the third weekend in September, Duke graduate students participate in what has become known as Campout. From Friday night through Sunday morning, students camp outside the stadium. At random intervals, day and night, a horn blows, and students have ten minutes to check in at a central table to prove they are on site. Students from the business school often rent RVs and

U-Haul trucks with mattresses in the back; English and history grad students rough it in sleeping bags and hope it doesn't rain.

The event is festive, and the energy level is high, though, truth be told, the waiting can get pretty wearing by the end. On Sunday morning, those students who have endured win the chance to enter a lottery. All that camping doesn't even assure them tickets. The lucky lottery winners get the right to purchase season tickets so that they can stand on bleachers in a special student section right next to the court. They pay a bargain price, well below what most students would happily give to attend a Duke home game. It's hard to resell these tickets because students must show their ID cards to enter the stadium. Most students wouldn't want to sell anyway, even at a multiple of the tickets' face value.

Campout has become something special. Many students say it was their favorite experience at Duke. But it's a bizarre way to distribute basketball tickets. Why force grad students to camp out for thirty-six hours, when Duke could simply do what many other schools with top teams do—offer seats first come, first served at a ticket line or website?

Understanding the power that comes from control over ownership design points to the answer. Duke faces a dilemma. It holds a scarce resource—basketball tickets at courtside—that a lot of people want. The key is to ask: What does Duke want from its ownership?

Duke doesn't just want to fill its stands. It doesn't just want enthusiastic students. Duke wants the Cameron Crazies—students standing a few feet from the players the entire game, stomping and cheering until their throats get hoarse. It wants students who will paint their faces the school color, blue, who, as Duke's slogan proclaims, will "bleed blue." It wants to enhance its brand as the premier basketball school in the country to millions of television viewers. To the outside observer, Campout may seem nonsensical, but it serves Duke's interests brilliantly.

First-in-time would be an easier way to distribute tickets, for sure, but it would provide the wrong fans. Campout represents a powerful way for Duke to leverage its ownership to ensure that those who get tickets will be special fans. The Campout ordeal transforms a Duke basketball ticket into something distinct—evidence of belonging to a very exclusive club. Only Cameron Crazies would camp out for thirty-six hours straight, through rain and shine, for just a chance in a basketball ticket lottery. And their experience of shared hardship bonds them into a community (not to mention creating loyal alumni who may be tapped for generous donations later in life).

Campout may seem just a trivial or weird story, but its implications run deep. Duke has figured out something important and subtle about ownership. First-in-time may feel pervasive and right, but it is not inevitable. Ownership rules can be, and indeed typically are, designed to channel and change people's behavior in highly targeted ways that serve owners' interests. Duke's concern is how best to allocate a valuable scarce resource—basketball tickets—to achieve its distinctive goals. And this means having different rules for different fans.

Rich alumni have another system that also deviates from a strict first-in-time rule. Just to get into the alumni line requires that potential ticket buyers pay an annual fee of $8,000 to join the Iron Dukes club. They then wait for their name to rise to the top of the list to purchase season tickets when they become available. It may take years.

And Duke has a third rule for undergraduates: old-fashioned first-in-time. These students get in for free and can usually just wait in line for a few hours before a game starts. Except for big games. For Duke versus the nearby University of North Carolina—the rivalry of the season—undergrads set up tents two months ahead, waiting on the grass lawn in front of the stadium (an area known as Krzyzewskiville). The first tents to set up, and then maintain the required number of students present at all times, are front of the line on game day—a two-month wait for a two-hour game. Undergrads seem to enjoy the camaraderie of tenting in K-Ville or waiting in shorter lines for ordinary games.

Duke's athletic program saw that it could extract three kinds of value by deploying an elaborate ticketing system: crazed fans, a packed house, and lots of money. Rather than rewarding the person at the front of the line, it treats ticket allocation as a social engineering tool, a sophisticated remote control that it uses to redirect behavior. It's remarkable, if you stop and think about it, that Duke can get graduate students to camp out for days, and undergrads for months, with enthusiasm rather than protest, to maximize the value Duke gets from its basketball program.

Duke is not alone in reengineering first-in-time to serve its purposes. All kinds of owners of valuable resources are realizing they can create even more value (for themselves) if they don't simply reward those who patiently wait in line. And everyone bows before Disney, the true master of pushing people around and getting thanked for it.

Disney Private VIP Tours

Disney may be amazing at creating rides, but even more, it is the expert at managing lines. After the terrorist attacks of 9/11, airports brought in Disney employees to consult on how to ease the horrendously long lines that were forming because of heightened security screening. Disney's expertise comes from its careful management of how people wait at its theme parks around the globe.

For decades, kids have lined up to ride Space Mountain, the Jungle Cruise, and other popular rides at Disney World. When the park is busy, which is most of the time, the waits can be very long, even hours. Most kids are not known for their patience, but that's the way it used to work—first-in-time. People waiting in the lines, with time on their hands, policed strenuously against ordinary line-cutters. There are Disney fan boards devoted to the topic, and many news reports of fistfights breaking out as enraged line-waiters confront cutters.

In the 1990s, Disney realized that the long lines were making the park experience unpleasant for too many of its visitors. But it faced a basic challenge—Space Mountain can only accommodate a limited number of riders per hour. Was there a way to adjust who got to ride that would ease the line frustration and maybe yield more profit along the way?

Disney World found an answer by introducing what's now called the FastPass+. Families can reserve three of them for specific, coveted rides ahead of their visit, valid during a timed entry window. This allows the most impatient visitors and those who plan ahead to skip some of the endless lines. Instead they walk around, perhaps go on a less exciting ride with a small line, then arrive at a short FastPass+ line and enjoy their special ride. After they use their three passes for that day, the family can send a parent to get another one, valid an hour or two later, while the kids wander. And then another pass . . . till they run out or the family collapses from exhaustion. The FastPass+ (with slight variations across Disney resorts) proved effective at spacing out crowds and improving visitors' experiences.

But the real magic of the FastPass+ was that it kept people in the park longer—and kept them spending money rather than idling in line. Over the course of the day, a family might get to enjoy a few rides with minimal line time and an hour or two between each ride. What do folks do in the meantime? The rides are far apart, and pathways between are lined with highly engineered ways to spark kids' desires. There is an endless array of Mickey merchandise to buy and Dole Whip pineapple slushies to drink.

Disney faced a challenge similar to Duke's. It had a scarce resource—access to popular rides—that it historically allocated first-in-time. This seemed a fair system that treated everyone the same. Today thousands still wait in lines for hours, but everyone knows that a

FastPass+ is equally available to them—not super-convenient, but an alternative to standing around.

With the FastPass+, Disney gets three benefits: first, it comforts those who hate waiting in long lines; second, it gets line-standers back in circulation and buying merchandise. The third and last effect of the FastPass+ is subtler but perhaps even more valuable for Disney: it gets park visitors accustomed to the idea that first-in-time is not the only rule governing who rides Space Mountain. FastPass+ taught people that limited, visible, and sanctioned line-cutting exists and that they too can choose to be part of it.

Then Disney took the next step—the genius step in ownership design.

Some wealthy people have a lot more money than time, like the families of the lawyers and lobbyists who pay line-standers to wait for seats at the Supreme Court and for first-day purchase of the newest iPhone. Some will pay whatever it takes never to stand in line for It's a Small World. Disney created the Private VIP Tour for just these customers. It's like a SuperDuperFastPass++, and it lets you skip every line on every ride all day long. If you want to ride Splash Mountain five times in a row, knock yourself out. For some people, this benefit is worth paying Disney a lot of money.

This seems an easy way for Disney to increase profits. But there's a catch: if Disney visibly moves too many groups of wealthy visitors to the front, it risks angering the many families patiently waiting in line.

Disney has solved this problem by raising the price of the Private VIP Tour just high enough to extract more profits without alerting the line-waiters that anything is amiss. It's a tricky calculus. It turns out that in practice, the precise point for optimal line-cutting is between $3,000 and $5,000, depending on the season. That's what Disney charges per group (on top of admission fees) for a minimum of seven hours of nonstop line-cutting, which is the most time even the wealthiest families want to spend on Splash Mountain. For the fee, Disney assigns a guide to each group so they can navigate the line-cutting adroitly and discreetly. Usually the group enters through the FastPass+ lane, so the families waiting in line can't tell anything unusual is going on. But for some rides, the Private VIP Tour guides will even take their charges in through a side door or the exit.

Until recently, Disney had even more channels for line-skipping. The most notorious was the line it had created as an accommodation for disabled visitors. Upon requesting a disabled pass at the entry to the park, a party of up to six people with one disabled customer enjoyed quick access to the rides. To its dismay, Disney learned that disabled people were renting themselves out at $130 an hour or more to act as line-skipping chaperones for able-bodied families—quite a bargain compared with the Private VIP Tour.

Worse, some people were faking disabilities to get the pass by showing up in rented wheelchairs. As a savvy Disney visitor commented, "Who wants a speed pass when you can use a black-market handicapped guide to circumvent the lines altogether?" A New York mum who hired a disabled guide said matter-of-factly, with no apparent guilt or shame, "This is how the one percent does Disney."

In response, Disney ended the priority access program, stating, "We find it deplorable that people would hire the disabled to abuse [our] accommodations." If one-percenters want to skip the lines, Disney wants to be the one getting paid.

Once you start to look around, you can see cracks in first-in-time. But should we be worried? After all, Campout is cherished as a special Duke experience. A FastPass+ reduces frustration for ordinary families. Even Private VIP Tours perhaps have redeeming social value, at least to Disney stockholders.

Dynamic Tolling and Korean Taco Trucks

We necessarily choose winners and losers every time we shift to a new rule for ownership. How you evaluate the change depends on where you sit. Or perhaps where you drive, if you are in the carpool lane.

Dedicating a lane to carpoolers or electric cars, as many cities do, seems like a good thing. It means fewer cars on the road and better air quality. But does it change how you feel about carpool lanes if you learn that they may be available to solo drivers in gas-powered cars who agree to pay extra, in the form of *dynamic tolling*? With dynamic tolls, drivers are charged amounts that vary from moment to moment as necessary to keep cars in the lane moving speedily.

In December 2016 commuters on Interstate 66, driving from Virginia into Washington, D.C., began facing dynamic tolls during rush hour. Interviews with drivers ahead of time suggested they were fine with the idea. In theory, they'd pay a few dollars more in exchange for a faster ride. But then one crowded morning, tolls rose to almost thirty-five dollars for a ten-mile stretch. "Obscene," one woman told *Washington Post* reporters.

But the dynamic toll did exactly what it was designed to do: as prices rose, many solo drivers got off Interstate 66, thus clearing up traffic. Traffic speed increased from an average of 37 to 57 miles per hour. It was smooth driving for those willing to pay for a quicker commute—perhaps the same one-percenters who buy their seats at congressional hearings and go on Private VIP Tours at Disney World. But perhaps it's just ordinary working people who really need to get into town quickly.

Virginia took hold of ownership design, just like Duke and Disney. The old rule of first-in-time imposed costs in the form of congestion and air pollution. Dynamic tolling forces people to choose between time and money. On balance, maybe carpool lanes with dynamic tolling make the world a cleaner, healthier place. Perhaps the state funnels the new cash to subsidize bus routes, thus getting even more cars off the road. Or maybe it's just another venue for the wealthy to displace everyone else.

For a final insight into how the principle of first-in-time works as a tool for social engineering, consider ongoing battles over where food trucks and carts can park. Hipster food trucks have been one of the most innovative sectors of the national food economy, often introducing new dishes that have gone mainstream. In 2008 Roy Choi's Kogi BBQ truck in Los Angeles fused Korean barbecue with Mexican tacos. The resulting standout tacos, and many variations, have since appeared on menus in upscale restaurants.

Even more important than their contribution to foodie culture, food trucks and carts have been a vital pathway for immigrant entrepreneurs seeking to establish themselves in America. Traditional brick-and-mortar restaurants view the rapid rise of mobile food vendors with alarm. Restaurants have to pay rent and utility bills while complying with tougher health and safety regulations. Not surprisingly, because of these higher operating costs, restaurants see the growing number of food trucks and carts parked outside their dining rooms as an unfair form of competition. But what does this have to do with ownership?

It turns out, everything. Restaurants frame the parking debate around first-in-time. They have been lobbying local officials to prevent competitors from parking near already-existing restaurants. Restaurants were there first, they argue, so trucks and carts can't be. Nearby parking should remain allocated by first-in-time, but *first* should be defined to exclude food service competitors.

Baltimore County was persuaded, banning food trucks from parking within two hundred feet of a restaurant—effectively driving competition out of busy downtown areas. Chicago adopted the same rule and enforces it by requiring food trucks to carry city-monitored GPS systems. It is no coincidence that Chicago has only seventy food trucks while Portland, Oregon, a city one-quarter its size with no parking restrictions, has more than five hundred trucks. Not surprisingly, their local food scenes are very different. At first glance, where you come down on parking restrictions may well turn on whether you prefer the old-school diner or the fusion taco truck.

More is at stake. Restrictive rules may shield incumbent restaurants and protect the city's tax base. But they stifle culinary innovation and limit new employment. And they cut off a pathway for immigrant entrepreneurs. This is an important part of what people are fighting about in the debate over who and what counts as first for parking spaces. It's *Johnson v. M'Intosh* all over again ("the conqueror prescribes its limits"), with newcomers versus natives. Except this time, the newcomers lose.

The key to keep in mind is that every definition of first-in-time is a form of social engineering that advances some other—often undisclosed—goal. Whoever controls ownership design can change people's behavior in finely tailored ways that serve owners' interests, such as selecting for a very specific group of blue-painted fans (Duke), or maximizing profits (Disney), or promoting environmentally beneficial, toll-paying behavior (Virginia). For all these owners, rewarding those patiently waiting in line left too much value on the table. First-in-time was old school and bad business.

What's at Stake?

A hundred times a day, without giving it any thought at all, we have to figure out accurately which ownership scheme controls the resources we want. Whether getting space at the bar to buy a drink or choosing a place to lay our towel at the beach, we unconsciously ask ourselves, *How do I make this mine?* Part of becoming a well-socialized adult is developing a fine-grained understanding of which ownership rules apply in which context.

More often than not, first-in-time is still our go-to rule. It's the default rule when we drive to the supermarket parking lot—we can pick whichever open space we want. To implement any other scheme, parking lot owners need to make the alternative rule crystal clear. Sometimes they'll stencil names in the pavement or post signs that say BY PERMIT ONLY or HANDICAPPED SPACE. It's the same on the beach, in the cinema, at the deli, or waiting to enter the Supreme Court.

Next time you are standing in line, apart from passing the time by wondering whether the people in front are being paid to wait, think about the choices that went into the line's design. Owners with valuable resources had to decide to allocate that access by line-standing rather than by one of their other available options. They had to decide whether to design a hybrid system that would engineer a particular experience. The bottom line is that first-in-time is a technological and moral choice that owners make to achieve their often-unstated goals, whether it's to extract your money, increase carpooling, keep out competition, or get you to paint your face blue.

Knowing this, you may ask yourself, *How do I use ownership design to get others to behave as I want?* Don't assume old-fashioned first-in-time will advance your interests best. As a parent or teacher, do you reward the kid who speaks up first, or who lines up first, or do you choose to reward some other behavior? As an Airbnb host, should you rent to the first asker, limit yourself to highly ranked guests, or do your own due diligence?

First-in-time has many advantages—it's easy to manage and appeals to our intuitive notions of fairness and equality. There's a reason it has been around since biblical times. But it's a crude tool, vulnerable to being captured and transformed. It can leave money on the table. It can bring the wrong customers in the door. And that's leading owners to shift their default for how their things become owned.

Sometimes intermediaries like line-standers extract value by cornering resources and reselling them to impatient wealthy bidders.

Other times owners themselves initiate the shift. Rather than sell to everyone at the same price, they create a premium experience for the few. By deploying a hybrid system, owners can extract more value from a limited pool of scarce resources.

This ownership alchemy goes far deeper than just transferring money from ticket buyers to ticket scalpers. Line-standing start-ups like SOLD are leading us into a social revolution, a quiet one but a revolution nonetheless, as entrepreneurs realize they can profit by replacing time with money.

Though it is rarely understood this way, the fate of first-in-time is part of an ongoing debate about our society's core values. Is line-standing the problem or the solution? Should ordinary citizens be able to get in and listen to Supreme Court cases without competing against paid line-standers, or is it more valuable for society that those seats go to lawyers and lobbyists motivated to pay thousands of dollars? Maybe the Supreme Court should reserve seats for student groups. Or auction the seats and use the revenue for guided high school tours of its awe-inspiring building. Or—and this is our view—the Court should implement a different path to access altogether, such as video livestreaming arguments so they are freely available to everyone online. During the COVID-19 shutdown, the Court moved partway there with audio livestream, and the administration of justice did not noticeably falter.

Put another way, every rule for making things *mine* rewards a different idea about what to value, like the options for the rocking chair we discussed in the Introduction. Old-style first-in-time rewards those who have the time needed to get there first and patiently wait—a currency that everyone holds in equal measure. You have twenty-four hours in your day, just like the rest of us. *First come, last served*, by contrast, often rewards wealth. It favors those who may have less free time but can pay—or can pay for the time of others.

With this understanding, we can begin to decode the customer service practices of the world's most successful businesses, like Starbucks with its line-cutting app; United Airlines, where loyal frequent flyers board early; and Walmart, with its "twenty items or less" lines. Enduring businesses are masters at tweaking the conventional understanding of first-in-time so that customers are willing, even glad, to part with their time, their money, or both.

Designing ownership is not like deciding between chocolate and vanilla ice cream. Our most important values are at stake. Quietly, across the economy, owners are shifting the background rules from *first* to *last*, from *time* to *money*, and from *equality* to *privilege*, all to advance their own interests, not necessarily yours. These choices are neither timeless nor inevitable. They do, however, come to define who we are as consumers and citizens in our interactions with each other over the essential goods of modern life.

Chapter 2

POSSESSION IS
ONE-TENTH OF THE LAW

The Parking Chair

If you grow up in a snowy part of urban America, you know the drill. Following a blizzard, you trudge outside, identify your car beneath suggestive lumps of snow, and start shoveling. After some heavy labor, you free your car and drive to work. But there's a problem: the next driver who comes along will gratefully take the spot. Where are you going to park when you return home later? Much of the street is still buried in snow. Enter the parking chair.

Bostonians have long used these space-savers to hold spots they've cleared after a heavy snowfall. In Chicago, the system is called "dibs"; in Philadelphia, its "savesies"; elsewhere in Pennsylvania it's the "Pittsburgh parking chair." In all these places, a chair holds the spot until the snow is off the streets and normal rules resume. For at least a few days, residents claim control over public parking spots, and city officials defer. Locals are often proud of this informal practice. They all know the unwritten rules, and they aren't picky: most will respect an orange cone, a vacuum cleaner, a broken ironing board, even a box of Froot Loops—the key is to communicate effectively to other drivers that "this spot is mine."

Older residents trace the rise of parking chairs in their city back to a moment when cars began to outnumber street parking spaces. According to Brian Mahoney, a lifelong South Boston resident, when he was growing up, "People didn't have to put things out, because

everyone would know whose parking spot it was. We were all generational. We knew everybody on the street." Southie—a colloqualism
for South Boston—neighbors helped each other dig out, watched
over the street, warned away interlopers, and didn't need chairs to
signal which spot was whose.

Starting in the late 1970s, however, condos began replacing the
old triple-deckers, bringing an influx of newcomers. More cars were
circling around a fixed number of parking spaces. Some say the Blizzard of 1978 was the turning point. That's when residents adopted
space-savers as a simple way to communicate their possession, and
for the most part, neighbors understood the signal. Those who disre-
spected it faced vandalism or assault.

Even as the parking shortage grew more acute, official Boston
looked the other way. Businesses objected because customers had
nowhere they would dare to park. Service people stayed away, and
houseguests circled. Spaces with parking chairs sat empty, wasted
all day, waiting for their "owners" to return. Amid increasing complaints, in 2005, Boston introduced a rule limiting parking chairs to
forty-eight hours after a major storm. The reaction was swift. South
Boston city councilmember James Kelly vowed to defy the mayor,
saying, "The issue speaks to the basic principle of what it means to be
an American. . . . Like the gold miner and pioneers, residents have a
right to stake their claims." Southies initially ignored the forty-eight-
hour limit, but over the past decade, it slowly gained some traction.

The South End, a wealthier neighborhood across I-93 from South
Boston, has taken a different approach. In 2015, responding to pressure from a united front of local neighborhood associations, the city
council declared the South End a "space-saver-free pilot neighborhood." The pilot program lets South End residents call the city to
have trash crews come and remove "abandoned furniture" right
away—no forty-eight-hour possession. Mayor Marty Walsh supported the change: "The space isn't your space. You did the work to
get your car out . . . but it's a city street." The mayor has a point. After

all, most people shovel out their cars because they have to get somewhere. Why should your effort earn you the extra reward of holding the public space empty for you alone?

Reflecting on the conflict, one Boston native, Adam Leskow, diagnosed the rise of parking chairs as part of a struggle against neighborhood change. "In a bigger-picture type of view, I think that this is also a way for the 'old guard' to hold onto some sort of neighborhood feel," he says. "It's one more thing that the citizens of the city—[who] have seen their longtime neighbors get priced out of their neighborhoods—just want to hold onto."

Brooke Gliden got caught between the new rules and neighborhood custom. In 2015 she moved to South Boston from New York City. There, if you shovel a space and put out a chair, you lose both your space and your chair. So when she dug out her car, she followed New York practice, leaving the space available for the next driver. Generally, when parking, she tried to be a good neighbor and looked for open spots with no chair. But arriving home late one night, she parked in a space marked by a cone, left after a storm many days earlier. The next morning, written on her windshield in permanent red marker, was the message, "Where is my cone? Did you take it as well?"

Gliden filed a police report but learned that Boston police don't intervene around parking-chair kerfuffles. She did not back down and, days later, removed another cone from the same space. "There's no excuse for defacing someone else's property," she says. Gliden got off easy. Parking disputes can escalate quickly. Folks who disrespect a cone or a chair have returned to find their doors keyed, windows shattered, or tires slashed. Only when space-savers assault parkers, or shoot at them, as sometimes happens, do police intervene.

The choice over what to do with parking chairs is caught among respect for local customs, the demands of newcomers and merchants, and decreasing public tolerance for violence. For old Southie neighbors, the chair communicates a possession claim. Others, like Gliden, hold to first-in-time. Chairs have never saved anything in Rochester or Buffalo—upstate New York cities that get more snow than Boston. Farther south, Philadelphia launched a #nosavesies campaign, trying a move like the South End's "space-saver-free" zone. In many cities, the ownership rule remains unsettled. You remove a parking chair at your peril. So what *should* a chair in the street mean?

There is no right answer.

Possession forms a secret language, one we pick up as children and that marks us as well-socialized grown-ups. Like any language, possession is in constant flux, with people, businesses, and governments all jostling to reshape its terms—far beyond parking chairs. Hundreds of times each day we unconsciously evaluate possession claims in parking lots, cafeterias, elevators, playgrounds, everywhere. These claims occur mostly through silent signals, deference, and custom. Our understanding of them determines where we sit, stand, and move, and how we interact with valuable resources in our daily lives. This chapter helps decode the signals.

On a small scale, neighbors, entrepreneurs, and governments deploy the symbols of possession to push us around in ways we don't even notice. On a larger scale, political leaders leverage our instinct for possession to justify wars and conquest. In the end, possession is a powerful tool to shape reality as owners would like it to be. These rules of possession are often not the law—they are more compelling than law.

Sandboxes and Shopping Carts

Why do Southies feel justified slashing tires? Their reactions reflect more than just casual disagreements with outsiders. The claims may be based partly on being first in time (Chapter 1), or on productive labor (Chapter 3), but possession establishes their ownership. As Carol Rose, a leading property scholar, writes, "The useful act of shoveling snow does not speak as unambiguously as the presence of an object that blocks entry."

Think for a moment about times when someone took "your" regular spot in the church pew or at an exercise class. You likely did not respond violently, but recall how you felt.

Claims based on physical possession of a thing—*This is mine because I am holding on to it*—activate our most primitive understanding of ownership. And yes, we intend the adjective *primitive* literally here. Possession is a primal instinct rooted in animal behavior and hardwired in our brains. It justifies much of what we claim as ours in everyday life.

The drive for physical possession is a core part of human psychology and emerges in the earliest stages of child development. Near the end of their first year, infants in every culture begin showing a strong sense of possession for specific objects, such as blankets. These "transitional objects" provide security as infants start separating physically from their mothers and begin crawling. For babies, the objects are extensions of themselves. By eighteen months, *mine* is an important part of a child's vocabulary. Many of the tantrums we associate with the terrible twos are fights over possessing things.

Signaling physical control over an object is crucial to the emerging sense of self and independence. If a doll or truck is *mine,* then it is not yours or anybody else's. Toddlers are relentless in their struggle to get ahold of what they want. These childhood battles are where humans start learning how to assert and defend our stuff, while we begin to understand and defer to others.

The urge to possess goes beyond early childhood development. It's core to adult behavior, too. Nobel Prize–winning economists Daniel Kahneman and Richard Thaler showed how the power of "I'm holding on to it" affects the value people place on ordinary items. In a now-classic experiment, they gave some students nondescript coffee mugs, then asked how much cash they wanted in exchange for giving them up; they gave others cash and asked how much they would pay to acquire an identical mug. The prices should have been similar. After all, the mug was nothing special. In this experiment, it shouldn't really matter whether you start out holding the mug or holding the cash.

But that's not what happened. Time and again, sellers thought the mug was worth more than double what buyers would pay, $5.78 versus $2.21. Hundreds of clever experiments have shown this discrepancy using chocolate bars, basketball seats, lottery tickets, music albums, and more. Chimpanzees and capuchin monkeys also demonstrate this behavior.

All show the same basic psychology: as soon as you physically possess something, it becomes more valuable than it was the moment before. Your attachment transforms its value, and you demand more to give it up than you would have paid in the first place. It's no longer a case of just selling a coffee mug. You're now selling *your* mug, giving up a part of yourself. And that comes at a premium. Thaler called this the "endowment effect."

The endowment effect shapes many everyday behaviors. Think about the last time you were in the checkout line at the supermarket with your shopping cart. Imagine a stranger had come up, peered into your cart, taken out the cereal box, then looked again and grabbed the carton of milk. This seems insane. It never happens (although we did come across one example during the panicky early days of COVID-19: toilet paper filching). You would probably shout at the person, "What the—what are you doing? That's mine!" But why are the cereal box and milk carton yours? You haven't bought them yet. What makes you so confident, even though your physical possession is not legal ownership?

Retailers have always understood, and taken advantage of, this possession instinct by creating conditions where customers can get attached to products for sale. The open floor plan and managed chaos at Apple stores is no accident. Staff are instructed to make customers feel welcome, letting them stay and play with the iPhones, iPads, and other cool products for as long as they want. As customers develop a sense of possession, as their physical connection deepens, their estimation of the iPad's value goes up. "That iPad" becomes "*my* iPad," and the asking price no longer feels so steep.

The psychology of possession is also part of why clothing stores encourage customers to use fitting rooms and car dealers encourage test drives. After you start wearing new clothes or driving a new car, it's easier to imagine them as yours. It's why Zappos makes it so easy for you to try on a variety of shoes and mattress-sellers give you a six-month free return period. This is also why some companies ask you to pay only after delivery. If it feels like it's yours, then parting becomes more difficult. First you get physically attached, then you value the item more.

When it can, the law generally piggybacks on our gut instinct for physical possession. Consider the things you carry around every day: your wallet, phone, or backpack; your clothes or comb; this book when you put it down on the coffee shop table. How could you prove that any of it was yours if someone started to carry it away? The answer, perhaps surprisingly, usually comes back to physical possession. Nothing more. If I take your book, the law presumes your ownership, based simply on your possession prior to mine. And that's true even if you are a thief who stole the book from someone else. Your prior possession beats mine.

This rule also drives another vital set of economic relationships. Think about when you give your clothes to the dry cleaner or your car keys to the parking valet. What gives you confidence you'll get your suit or car back? The answer is grounded in your prior physical possession. You don't have to rely on contracts, deeds, or court records to prove that you are actually the legal owner. All you need is a claim check, which shows only that you were holding on to the thing before you handed it over. Lawyers call this *bailment*—when you keep ownership of something but transfer physical possession of it for a particular purpose and a limited time. We hand valuable stuff to strangers without a moment's thought, entrusting them with our goods, then they give them back, no questions asked.

Confidence in the meaning of physical possession enables a tremendous amount of useful economic activity. It means we don't have to carry around a pocketful of receipts for our books, sunglasses, and other stuff. It's why a pickpocket doesn't own your wallet when it's lifted from your pants; a trespasser doesn't own your land as soon as they set foot on it; and a finder doesn't own your watch the moment you drop it. "Finders keepers, losers weepers" sounds catchy, but law and practice say the opposite. The real rule is "Finders give it back," an experience all of us have had many times in our lives. Most people try to give things back to the prior possessor, most of the time.

Physical possession provides a super-simple, time-tested, low-cost, easy-to-verify method for resolving conflicts: all else equal, the person who was holding the thing earlier usually wins over whoever holds it later. But not always.

Backyard Bandits

Back in the 1980s, Don and Susie Kirlin bought several adjoining lots on Hardscrabble Drive in Boulder, Colorado, with stunning views of the nearby Front Range of the Rockies. They were careful planners who left the lots undeveloped with the intention of selling them later to support their retirement. After growing in value to a million dollars, the land seemed a shrewd investment. Or so the Kirlins thought.

Richard McLean, a former mayor of Boulder and a county judge, and his wife, Edie Stevens, lived next door to the vacant lots. For two decades, they had openly used one-third of the Kirlins' land, treating it like their backyard. They regularly held parties there, stored firewood, and maintained "Edie's Path" across the lot. To the outside world, McLean's physical possession of the land looked like ordinary ownership. Anyone who didn't know the actual lot lines would have assumed the land belonged to McLean and Stevens.

In 2007 they tried to remove all doubt, suing for title to "their backyard." The Kirlins were shocked. McLean and Stevens were trespassers on their land, and they had the audacity to assert a claim? They were even more shocked when the judge sided with McLean and Stevens. The Kirlins weren't alone in their outrage. Soon after the decision, McLean and Stevens received an anonymous package with a bullet and a threat, "Back in the Old West we had a way to deal with your kind."

But the threat was misdirected. In the Old West, physical possession claims were even stronger and more frequent than they are today. Back then the settlers who lived on and worked the land sometimes aimed bullets at absentee owners asserting claims based on distant, unreliable official records. Surprisingly, a lot of landownership in America traces back to illegal squatters in the 1800s who banded together in "claims clubs" and successfully pushed territorial and early state legislatures to ratify their land seizures. In much of the world today, this is still standard practice.

McLean and Stevens were relying on the law of *adverse possession.* This is an ancient rule, appearing four thousand years ago in the Code of Hammurabi and likely in existence earlier still. The ownership maxim that anchors this book chapter—*Possession is nine-tenths of the law*—traces back to this old law.

The rule from back then is the same rule today, more or less. If people actually enter your land without permission, then openly and continuously possess it for long enough (eighteen years in Colorado), they can claim it as their own. Before eighteen years, they are trespassers, and you can repel them—your home is your castle, after all. States with stand-your-ground laws may even permit you to use lethal force when a stranger wrongly enters your land, even if you face no mortal threat and retreat is possible. But if a trespasser succeeds in entering your land and gets established there, then the rules shift; you can no longer use force but must go to court to evict the possessor, a potentially lengthy and costly process. If you fail to act, and enough time passes, the trespasser automatically becomes the new owner. A lawsuit like the one against the Kirlins simply confirms the facts on the ground: physical possession has ripened into legal ownership.

This rule explains the small bronze plaques in plazas and wide sidewalks all over American cities bearing opaque messages like PRIVATE PROPERTY, PERMISSION TO PASS REVOCABLE AT ANY TIME. By giving explicit permission, owners ensure that pedestrians' sidewalk use is not "adverse." In the future, the owners may be able to reclaim that land and change its use.

Columbia University, where Heller teaches, goes a step further. It physically closes the gates to College Walk on a single quiet Sunday morning during the summer, not for maintenance purposes but to demonstrate that it can keep you out and is granting permission for you to enter. Rockefeller Center closes its plaza the same way, along with many other institutions trying to protect private ownership of seemingly public spaces. Even more than the plaques, whoever has the power to close the gates shows the world, *This really is mine.* Asserting physical control helps defeat claims based on adverse use by the public.

Every year our students are shocked when they learn about adverse possession. It seems unfair, looks like theft, and sounds so primitive. The Kirlins certainly felt abused. But then about a dozen students out of every hundred slowly realize that their families are unwittingly directly involved in real-life adverse possession dramas. Are neighborhood kids cutting a path across your yard? Who's taking care of the rosebushes alongside your house? What does the deed say about that shared driveway? Does your fence really track the property line? Though few disputes escalate into court battles—most neighbors are not deviants—this is not an esoteric problem.

Adverse possession reflects the power of physical connection, an urge rooted deep in human psychology. As Oliver Wendell Holmes, Jr., an esteemed Supreme Court justice, wrote back in 1897:

> A thing which you have enjoyed and used as your own for a long time, whether property or an opinion, takes root in your being and cannot be torn away without your resenting the fact and trying to defend yourself, however you came by it. The law can ask no better justification than the deepest instincts of man.

In essence, this is the core of the argument for McLean and Stevens. They had grown attached to their extended backyard. They acted like owners, and to the outside world, they looked like owners. By contrast, the Kirlins' ownership seemed relatively remote and abstract.

While we value ownership, as a society we have often rewarded active physical possession even more. And for good reason. In general, compared with absentee owners, adverse possessors defend their claims more vigorously, are easier to identify, and put land to developmental uses that our culture esteems. Environmentalists can't win adverse possession claims—keeping land in its natural state does not qualify. In America and the UK, transforming the land through actual physical possession can win over paper deeds, court records, and the retirement plans of patient investors.

Physical possession matters, but it's not the only thing that matters. Today we have much more accurate and cheaper-to-access official ownership records than people did at the time of Hammurabi or the Old West. And today, as a society, Americans do value passive uses of land—for environmental conservation or investment purposes—on par with active uses like McLean and Stevens's backyard garden. Indeed, public outrage at the Kirlins' loss prompted the Colorado legislature to make adverse possession cases harder to win.

The state now gives the judge discretion to order adverse possessors to pay market value for the land they acquire, a shift that reduces possessors' motivation to make a claim in the first instance.

Even McLean and Stevens backpedaled after winning at trial. While the case was on appeal, they settled with the Kirlins, keeping just Edie's Path alongside their house, about a third of the lot the judge had awarded them. Why did they give up the rest? Don Kirlin speculates, "Their friends abandoned them. They want to try and attempt to regain some of their stature in the community." Recall that it was McLean and Stevens, not the Kirlins, who received the bullet in the mail.

Physical possession may have instinctive roots, but if you push its boundaries too far, the community pushes back, with neighbors gossiping "How rude!" Law matters, but reputation often matters more. So today, even when adverse possessors have good claims, they rarely press them in court and win even more rarely, not just in Colorado but across the country, as well as in the UK. As a result, in current practice, adverse possession has been dialed far down from nine-tenths of the law.

Trails of Tears

The Hardscrabble Drive dispute is one small instance of a larger struggle. It's no exaggeration to say that human history is a series of adverse possession conflicts writ large. Conquests, genocides, historical injustices, and dispossessions create new land claims. Over time these brutal, profoundly destructive events become the basis of ownership. It's not pretty. Nor is it fair. But it's everywhere you look.

When you buy a home, your ownership is traced through the *chain of title*—the record of sellers and buyers of that parcel going all the way back to the origin of ownership. Often that chain starts in a grant from the American government or a state following the conquest of Native peoples. Native ownership is erased from the records. To give just one example, following the Indian Removal Act of 1830, federal soldiers forced Native Americans from the Cherokee, Seminole, and other tribes in the Southeast to leave their ancestral lands for resettlement in Oklahoma. This brutal march, which left many dead along the way, became known as the Trail of Tears. Why don't descendants of Native survivors still have a claim to the North Carolina lands that their families were forced to leave?

The unsatisfying answer is that current ownership of that land is based on more than 170 years of occupancy, dating back to white settlers who were given control after soldiers forcibly removed the Native Americans. Ultimately this claim is rooted in a version of adverse possession and justified by the long passage of time. This is true not just in North Carolina but for virtually every plot of land in the world.

The significance of physical possession was one of the most contested issues after the fall of the Berlin Wall, when Communist countries reintroduced market economies. Working in the region in the early 1990s, Heller advised many postsocialist governments on how to create the legal framework for private property. Government leaders had to decide between pre-Communist owners (and their heirs) demanding return of confiscated property and current occupants trying to stay in their homes. How to respond to a Hungarian living abroad who says, "The Communists killed my family and put their loyalists in our Budapest home"? How to answer an elderly Jewish claimant, faded deed in hand, who says, "The Nazis took this Warsaw apartment from me and my family in 1942"? Aren't we compelled to right the wrongs of Communism and Nazism?

This is a heartfelt argument. But as we've seen, ownership is always a choice among competing narratives backed up by the state's coercive power. In the decades after the expropriations, generations of Hungarians, Poles, Czechs, and Russians raised their families in these apartments—not fundamentally different from North Carolinians today. Most of these occupants were just ordinary families who did not personally dispossess the previous owners. They were generally renters, told by Communist governments where to live. Surely their decades of actual physical possession, along with their own suffering under the Communists, their family ties to these homes, and the reality that they had nowhere else to go should carry weight against faded deeds held by faraway heirs.

Faced with this dilemma, postsocialist governments mostly left current occupants in place, favoring their claims over those of prior owners. Why? In part, their decision aligned with Justice Holmes's caution: long occupancy "takes root in your being and cannot be torn away without your resenting the fact and trying to defend yourself." By converting mere physical possession into outright ownership, emerging governments transformed hundreds of millions of apartment dwellers into instant advocates for market transition. Even Communist Party functionaries (apparatchiks), who had often seized the best apartments for themselves, suddenly had a material stake in capitalism's success.

Leaving current occupants in place did not mean freezing out prior owners entirely. Ownership design rarely requires an all-or-nothing choice. In Central and Eastern Europe, governments offered a range of compensation for expropriated property—cash, vouchers, corporate shares, sometimes just a public apology. Each government chose its own distinct path, responding to local capacities and values. The point was to jump-start markets rather than tying up courts to seek a precise measure of justice for each prior possessor's heirs. Kicking out existing occupants would have frozen nascent real estate markets and ensured mass opposition.

The list of conflicts over land possession is as long as the Earth is large and as old as time. Consider conflicting claims today in Jerusalem between Israelis and Palestinians, in Havana between current residents and Miami exiles, in Kashmir between Indians and Pakistanis, in Crimea between Russians and Ukrainians. Physical possession is powerful and not always aligned with abstract notions of historical justice and morality.

The shadow of adverse possession falls over cultural objects, too. Can Iraq reasonably demand return of Babylonian sculptures from the Metropolitan Museum of Art in New York? Should Egypt be able to claim the return of mummies and statues from far-flung collectors? The same can be asked of claims by China, Cambodia, Greece, Peru, and Benin for treasures looted from their ancient civilizations. Is art seized from Holocaust victims different merely because it was taken from identifiable victims?

The story of modern international law—including the founding of the League of Nations and then the United Nations—has revolved substantially around efforts to stop countries and people from grabbing physical possession in the first place. Conquest and expropriation are now unambiguously illegal under international law. But armies and looters don't always listen, and time works to their advantage.

We have no neat or simple answer to *Might makes right.* All we can do is note that one blunt equation often governs the fight to control scarce resources: *Possession + time = ownership.*

Sorry, This Seat Is Taken

Most claims of possession don't actually turn on physical control. They can't, for the simple reason that it is impossible to hold on to everything you want to own, all at once—though little kids will try. We need ways to communicate *Hands off, that's my stuff.* This requires adding symbolic claims of possession to physical ones, a challenge that takes us back to the parking chair and before that to the basics of animal territoriality. In this realm, possession drops even further from nine-tenths. As Rose argues, it "amounts to something like yelling loudly enough to all who may understand. The first to say, 'This is mine,' in a way that the public understands, gets the prize."

And this is true not just for humans. The chirp, warble, and whistle of birdsong that delights many a spring hiker communicates something quite different to its intended bird audience. Sometimes birds call to mark food sources, as in the 2003 film *Finding Nemo*. The threatening flock of seagulls caw "Mine! Mine! Mine! Mine! Mine! Mine! Mine!" as they try to eat Marlin and Dory while encircling Nigel the helpful pelican. More often, though, scientists have found that birds sing to mark territory and attract mates (and they do so with regional accents). The calls of a red-breasted robin may sound sweet, but to his fellow robins he's shouting—imagine a Southie accent here—"Hey, Mister, back off! This is my wicked awesome territory. Stay away or else!" Birds want to control more resources than they can physically occupy. So they sing.

When dogs on a walk seem to take forever choosing just which tree or post to pee on, they're symbolically claiming their territories and decoding those of others. Hyenas also pee to mark their territories, rhinos mark theirs with poop, bees use their scent glands, and bears rub against trees to make visual marks. But over time these symbols decay and become uncertain. In the law of the jungle, accurately placing and decoding the signals of possession is a life-or-death matter. Is the scent or mark fresh? Does it come from a higher-status animal? If you guess wrong, will you be eaten?

Back in the human world, this unspoken language has a simple three-part grammar. Imagine you're in a crowded cinema, the film is about to start, and you see a napkin on the back of one of the few remaining seats. The conversation inside your head may go something like this: (1) Identification: *I know a jacket saves the seat, but a napkin?* (2) Evaluation: *Even if the napkin is a signal, nah, it doesn't hold the last few seats.* (3) Action: *No one will mind if I sit here* or maybe *Whoa, you're scary big, sorry, take the seat.* In South Boston, Brooke Gliden engaged in this possession dialogue: she saw the cone and understood its intended meaning, but chose to ignore it and had her windshield defaced.

A challenge for understanding symbolic possession is that the language has dialects, and they vary at all three stages. In some New York City bars, a napkin on the glass signals to fellow bargoers that you are coming back to your seat and tells the bartender to save your drink. In Wisconsin and parts of Pennsylvania, that same napkin means you are finished with both seat and drink. In parts of Europe, it means "Don't bring me another beer unless I ask." If you speak the wrong dialect of possession, the sanction may be a padded bill, a lost seat, or a bar fight.

The bar is only one of dozens of venues for seat-saving. Everyone saves seats—at the movies, in church, at Alcoholics Anonymous meetings, on the train, for the Disneyland evening parade, or in the bleachers at the baseball game. Every year at the State of the Union address, some members of Congress arrive hours early to save high-visibility aisle seats so they can be seen on television high-fiving the president.

People tailor their signal to the context. To say "This seat is taken," they may use a full popcorn carton at the movies or an embroidered pillow at church. At Phish concerts, people use colorful tarps to stake out spots. Usually seat-savers meet no resistance. But sometimes, as the resource becomes scarcer, conflicts erupt—even among otherwise mellow Phish fans, when the tarps get too big.

You have certainly been on both sides of seat-saving disputes. When do you respect the jacket, pillow, or tarp? A fiercely passionate debate today revolves around Southwest Airlines and its open seating policy. Under the policy, people board in groups A, B, or C (generally determined either by how quickly you check in the day before your flight or whether you paid an extra fee to assure entry into group A).

Once people enter the plane, they can take any open seat. Group A boarders have more choice than those in group C, who board last and generally face only middle-seat or far-back options.

But sometimes early boarders try to save seats for friends and family in groups B or C farther back in the queue. So intense are the resulting conflicts that *Psychology Today* ran a story headlined "What Would Buddha Do on Southwest Airlines?" You may not be surprised to learn that, according to Allison Carmen, the story's author, the Buddha would neither save seats nor judge those who do: "I doubt he would worry much about the location of his seat. He would probably even bless the passengers who saved the seats for their friends."

In any event, Stu Weinshanker is not the Buddha. He is six-foot-two, a sales rep, a frequent flyer, and an apostle of physical possession. He pays Southwest a fifteen-to-twenty-five-dollar early bird fee, which lets him board toward the front of the queue, in group A. On a flight to Las Vegas, he and his wife found their perfect spots—exit row, aisle seats across from each other—with no one sitting there. Perfect, except for an iPad on one of the seats. A passenger sitting in a middle seat had placed it there and told Weinshanker she was saving the seat for her boyfriend, who was boarding about one hundred passengers later with group C riffraff.

Explaining that Southwest has an open seating policy, Weinshanker politely handed the iPad to the woman, suggested she try saving the window seat instead, and sat down. When her boyfriend boarded a few minutes later, the woman with the iPad burst into tears, saying her neighbor had intimidated her, according to a *USA Today* story on the encounter. By placing the iPad on the seat, the woman had symbolically signaled her possession. Weinshanker had understood her signal perfectly well and, by moving the iPad and sitting down, rejected it.

So who's the jerk? The seat-saver or seat-sitter? Is symbolic possession (iPad) or physical possession (butt in seat) the rule for seating on Southwest?

The debate about this conflict is shockingly robust. Siding with seat-sitters, roughly half of online commenters criticize "seat cheats," "seat-hoarders," and "cheapskates." The most vitriol is directed at group A boarders who try to save whole rows, especially prime exit rows, for group C travel companions. The other half of the commenters admonish Weinshanker-sympathizers to "chill," "find another seat," "fly another airline if this stuff bothers you," and "#firstworldproblem." In other words, be the Buddha.

Where you stand on possession may depend on where you sit.

Oddly, few passengers direct their anger at Southwest, which cultivates a reputation as a friendly airline, yet designs its open seating policy to pit passengers against each other. Southwest is hypervigilant about not admitting that it allows seat-saving and equally careful not to say it forbids the practice. The airline is a master at playing all sides of the possession game. Southwest could resolve the conflicts in a minute: it could announce a "no seat-saving" rule. Or "no seat-saving in exit rows." Or "no seat-saving in the front half of the plane." Or saving one seat is fine. Or saving a row is okay. Or it could reject both symbolic and physical possession and instead assign seats like every other airline. Southwest could adopt just about any seating rule it wanted to. It chooses not to do so. Why?

In part, Southwest profits from open seating because passengers board more quickly than they do with assigned seats, so the planes spend more time in the air. And it profits from early-bird boarders like Weinshanker who are willing to pay for boarding in group A. In addition, and this is key, strategic ambiguity about saving open seats lets Southwest simultaneously achieve a trifecta of corporate goals: telegraphing a distinctive, easygoing brand reputation ("choose your seat"), keeping repeat customers reasonably satisfied ("save a seat"), and maximizing revenue ("less time on the ground"). Seat-savers feel they are getting something for nothing—an extra bonus value for their "bargain" seat. It's as if Southwest studied the coffee mug experiments and then designed the boarding process so many passengers would feel they have gained a special endowment, with its associated higher value, once they have reached their seat and saved another—like a world with all sellers, no buyers.

Southwest's strategy is reminiscent as well of the Knee Defender story from the Introduction. There we saw that airlines sell the wedge of seat-reclining space twice, leaving passengers in front and back to sort out the resulting conflicts. Southwest creates a similar type of *mine* versus *mine* battle, pitting iPads versus butts in seats. It's symbolic possession against physical possession.

In practice, the iPad usually holds the seat. Later-boarding flyers understand the unspoken language of possession and mostly show respect. But boarding a Southwest flight can have unsavory subtexts as well: Are men more often saving seats and hoarding armrests and women giving way? Is seat-saving a tool for seatmate shopping—and a cover for discrimination? In an environment where almost no one knows the actual rules, passengers experience anxiety about seating as a personal failing. Most people want to be good sports, so the "nicer," or less privileged, party continues toward the worse seats farther back—except perhaps in the coveted exit rows, where passengers' silent negotiations may break down.

Open seating is Southwest's airborne version of the law of the jungle, with iPads and jackets instead of scent marks and scratches on trees. As one flyer succinctly put it on an online Southwest community board, "If you want to save a seat on Southwest, you say 'This seat is saved.' If someone wants to sit there, then there is nothing you can do to stop them, and your saved seat is now not saved any longer." But whatever the outcome, it's the result of an ownership strategy Southwest has put in place for its own benefit. Intentional ambiguity works to Southwest's advantage; millions of micronegotiations between passengers resolve most tussles.

But not all of them. In practice, Southwest pushes resolution of the sharpest conflicts onto flight crews. "It's something that at times has put our flight attendants in a difficult position," says Audrey

Stone, president of Southwest's flight attendants union. Seat-saving conflicts arise on every flight, and when they do, Southwest flight attendants often respond by being friendly to all and helpful to none. They won't intervene to assist a passenger claiming that a jacket saves the seat, and they won't rebuke a passenger who moves the jacket and sits in a "saved" seat. Flight attendants limit their role to policing the punishment step of the possession dialogue, ensuring only that irritation and sharp words do not escalate into open violence.

Keep in mind that Southwest, not Weinshanker nor other group A passengers, owns the seats. The airline will continue to rely on deliberately ambiguous ownership design until and unless it becomes too costly—if, say, too many fed-up customers switch airlines or flight attendants stage a work slowdown. Then Southwest may ratchet down symbolic possession ("early boarders can hold just one extra seat").

If the number of fistfights rises and Southwest still chooses not to act, then federal regulators could step in and order Southwest to remedy the problem, perhaps by assigning seats. The FAA, and not just the airline, can always choose to ignore symbolic possession or replace it altogether if another rule suits its needs. As with parking chairs in Boston, we can often find layers of ownership rules. People create symbolic possession languages among themselves, with businesses and governments imposing increasingly formal legal rules from above—like a series of Russian dolls.

Secret Savers

Usually you know who is trying to communicate *Back off, it's mine,* like the Southwest passenger saving the aisle seat. But possession signals are often deployed anonymously—and the person claiming possession may not be whom you expect.

Think about your last vacation by the pool or beach. When you sought out a reclining chair, many were probably taken, with magazines and towels strewn on them but no one in sight. Perhaps you passed by, frustrated, but were not prepared to risk a confrontation by moving the towel and taking a chair for yourself. Might it change your mind if you knew this scene of symbolic possession was highly deceptive?

Now and then the resort's chair attendants are running a covert side business for in-the-know guests. Pay the attendants, say, twenty dollars per recliner, and they quietly reserve you chairs early the next morning, creating a realistic tableau of beat-up magazines, plausible summer novels, and pool toys. The objects signal to vacationers *Another guest claims this recliner* and—crucially—reassure hotel management *Nothing amiss here, just our valued guests sorting it out among themselves.*

Profit opportunities for self-appointed intermediary "owners" arise when the ultimate owner isn't paying close attention. Look around, and you will start noticing microentrepreneurs—like the pool attendants—creating businesses based solely on their close attention to the cues for symbolic possession, not on any actual ownership. Pool attendants monetize the maxim that *Possession is nine-tenths of the law,* deploying its signals for a fee.

The people who run resorts are well aware of chair hoarding, both by poolside entrepreneurs and by guests—either way, their customers complain there's nowhere to sit. The issue crosses national borders: if you credit the international tabloids, British vacationers in Spain think that German tourists are the recliner-hoarders, and Germans assert the opposite. According to Carolyn Spencer Brown, editor-in-chief of CruiseCritic.com, chair-hogging on cruises is "the hottest issue next to bringing alcohol on board. People get really unhinged. They're paying for vacation, others are abusing the system and it's not fair to anyone."

With scarce vacation time, people at resorts and on ships take their waterside recliners seriously. Data back this up: 84 percent of respondents to TripAdvisor's Beach and Pool Etiquette Survey said they get agitated when others save beach or pool chairs by leaving belongings on them. And 86 percent think chair-hogging for any longer than an hour is unacceptable. But only 37 percent think there should be a thirty-minute limit on saving seats. Vacationers' patience runs out a little after one half hour.

With data in hand and empty chairs in view, what did Carnival Cruises do? It dialed down the duration of symbolic possession claims by having pool attendants place time-stamped notices on unoccupied, saved recliners. After forty minutes, employees scoop up people's towels, magazines, and other detritus of symbolic possession. They free the chair. The response from paying customers has been "overwhelmingly positive," according to Carnival. Norwegian Cruises implemented a dot system, limiting away time from a dotted chair to forty-five minutes. The Water Club at the Borgata in Atlantic City has taken it up yet another notch: having attendants create a wait list for saved recliners, remove possessions after thirty minutes, and text the next guest in line that a recliner has become available.

This redesign of symbolic possession is big news in resort management, but it is terrible from the enterprising attendants' point of view. The least empowered, lowest-paid employees face an increased workload, and some lose their under-the-table side business altogether. They have fewer friendly chats with guests and more complaints from displaced chair-hoarders. Instead of engaging in tip-generating interactions, they walk around with clipboards, logging times and storing belongings.

Every ownership system has trade-offs. For owners of crowded resorts with complaining guests, dialing down symbolic possession is likely a win. They shift chairs from passive to active users and capture more value through happier, repeat guests—but only if they calibrate the new ownership scheme just right. Time limits focus customer frustration on the resort's rules and the staff who implement them. For business owners, the "it's out of our hands" quality of symbolic possession cuts in its favor, so it can take quite a high level of customer dissatisfaction to catalyze change. Unlike Southwest, Carnival decided it could no longer afford to offload resolution of many small contentious interactions onto guests.

Even if the ultimate owner does not step in, the language of possession continues to evolve. Why? Because all symbolic possession claims have some physical component—a jacket, magazine, or blanket. Some *thing*. But things do not speak directly. They need to be interpreted, and their meaning is always up for revision. Boston parking chairs hold the spot, but do they hold it for a day after a snowstorm or a week? On Southwest, can a single passenger save an entire exit row? People, like birds and lions, often push the boundaries of possession, and others push back.

On crowded New York subways, riders have long used backpacks to hog multiple seats. Polite strap-hangers may ask, "Are you holding that seat for someone?" More determined ones just move the backpack and sit, with a cursory "Okay?" One version of this is man-spreading, in which passengers, usually men, claim two or more seats by widely spreading their legs while they sit. The subway responded by posting pictographs of man-spreaders and followed up with rules threatening fines and arrests. But you'll rarely see subway police enforcing the rules. When possessors push boundaries, the real punishment usually operates at the layer of scoffs and sighs.

Recently, a sandy version of man-spreading appeared on New Jersey beaches—beach-spreading. Beachgoers are staking out ever-larger footprints, arming themselves with a wide range of beach products, from tents and coolers to towels and grills. One party member comes early, claims a prime spot, spreads out the stuff, and leaves. Eventually others show up to enjoy the encampment. So closely spaced are these islands of gear that casual beachgoers may not be able to sit anywhere near the shoreline. Can they squeeze in between the cooler and the beach chair? Hard to say. The conflicts are growing more acute: as beach-spreaders are pushing the boundaries of possession, rising sea levels are shrinking New Jersey beaches. Local residents pay for lifeguards and beach upkeep and get mad when beach-spreaders keep them away from the water.

Regional variations in beach possession symbols matter even more in the COVID-19 era. That's why White House coronavirus adviser Deborah Birx urged beachgoers to defend circles of sand around their umbrellas: "Remember that is your space, and that is the space you need to protect." She was arguing for uniform beach spacing nationwide. Bad ownership design can have deadly consequences in New Jersey, Florida, and elsewhere.

As we saw with Carnival Cruises, owners can try to dial down possession by changing the meaning of the symbols. One approach is imposing time limits. But that takes sustained enforcement. When Boston tried to limit parking chairs to two days after a storm, Southies mostly ignored the new rule. Chairs do not fold up by themselves after forty-eight hours. For people to associate the signal (parking chair) with the limit (expires forty-eight hours after a storm), the city would have to deploy teams of sanitation workers to time-tag chairs and then engage in relentless chair-collecting.

A second approach is to limit allowable categories of possession symbols. That's what some New Jersey towns have been trying in the face of beach-spreading. Seaside Heights imposed limits on large tents. But checking tent sizes is costly. So some towns have adopted easier-to-enforce approaches like prohibiting certain possession symbols altogether. Belmar introduced legislation simply banning beach tents. "It's to the point that it looks like tailgating at MetLife stadium," Matt Doherty, the Belmar mayor, said. "And I love tailgating at MetLife stadium, I really do. It's just not what we're looking for on the beach." Manasquan took it a step further, adding a ban on grills. Seaside Heights banned "serving trays, warming trays, pots, pans," and other food preparation "devices."

Every time owners undercut existing symbols of possession, though, they increase the role of some other ownership rule, sometimes with surprising consequences.

Surf and Turf

The systems of possession that endure are often those that are most fiercely defended. If you are reading this book on a beach vacation, you may see families agreeably jockeying for sand around you. But look out at where the waves are breaking. There, struggles for possession are often not so polite.

Along the California coast, surfers have a reputation as mellow dudes, but the reality can be far different. Certain surfers claim the best beaches for the community of locals. Everyone else is a "troll" (outsider) or "kook" (amateur). At Lunada Bay Beach, just south of Los Angeles, the Bay Boys—all middle-aged men, "spoiled trust fund babies" to critics—have physically monopolized the beach for decades. The big waves are powerful, uncrowded, and tempting. But if you, as an outsider, enter the water, you will be surrounded, harassed, and maybe assaulted. The surfers' friends may roll clods of dirt down the cliff as you try to climb up from the beach. Your car may be vandalized with surf wax and sand. To coordinate their attacks, the Bay Boys built their own stone fort on the bluffs above the beach, with an ice cooler and a sign etched in the table, RESPECT THIS PLACE.

As far back as 1991, the *Los Angeles Times* reported, "The area is known as a war zone of sorts." Local surfers have been unashamed about defending their possession: "Too many damn surfers, not enough waves. If we let every nice guy surf, there'd be a hundred guys out here. You have to nip it in the bud. The reason it's not crowded is that people protect it." Another says, "We'll burn you every single wave."

Jordan Wright tried to surf Lunada Bay, protected by his L.A. County sheriff father, but was driven away. "It's run like an organized crime or racketeering outfit," Wright said. Surfer Cory Spencer said, "I worked South Central for the LAPD, but it took time to gain the courage to go down" to Lunada Bay. On his second wave, a Bay Boy attacked him: "He was 75 yards away on the wave behind me. We had plenty of space, but he tried to spear me with his board . . . and he left a nice little slice in my hand," Spencer said. Malibu can be just as rough, according to surfer Johnny Lockwood, who notes, "I had dreams I'd come to California and everything would be groovy. There's this sort of under-the-wire terrorism. It's like dealing with warlords."

Outsider surfers staged a protest, renaming Lunada Bay as Aloha Beach and protecting each other by surfing en masse. They were asserting an alternate claim to be the rule-making surfer community, able to enforce their own possession rules. That worked for a day. But the Bay Boys regained iron control. According to a local police officer, "It is like a game on the schoolyard to them and they don't want you playing on their swing set." Expanding the community to include trolls and kooks is hard when existing possessors play rough.

Over the years, the police and local governments have tried to open Lunada Bay, Malibu, and other surf beaches via an escalating series of strategies: webcams, lawsuits, fines, and arrests. More recently momentum seems to be picking up to assert public control and create a new, more inclusive community of surfers. The new police chief at Lunada Bay sent patrols to the bluffs four hundred times in a single year. The California Coastal Commission, a no-nonsense statewide regulator, forced the Bay Boys to dismantle their stone fort.

But apparently the Bay Boys later rebuilt it. Lawsuits against them are continuing. It makes sense that possessors fight hard to keep self-serving rules in place. But why has the government tolerated the existing rules for so long? That's not quite the right framing. The crucial ownership design question always is, compared to what? If governments crush local rules, they have to commit resources to craft, impose, and enforce a more public-regarding ownership scheme. Otherwise we may end up with a free-for-all. The net result may be trolls and kooks crowding the waves, crashing into each other, no one able to get a clean ride. Possession may be a violent and wasteful strategy, but it can help manage a scarce resource.

To illustrate this last point, consider Maine lobsters. Year after year, the state supplies restaurants with a steady supply of lobster rolls. It might seem that anyone can set a lobster trap off the coast, but if everyone did so, there would be overfishing and Maine would be a lobster desert. Instead, the offshore waters are considered to be among the best-managed fisheries in America. Why?

Like California surf beaches, many Maine ports have local "lobster gangs"—in this case, a set of interrelated multigenerational families and allies who aggressively defend their self-identified territory, marked by lobster traps with distinctive buoys. Lobster gangs coordinate on everything: when to start the fishing season, catch limits, port facilities and sales, and mutual aid when boats break down on the water. When internal and intergang disputes arise, they resolve them at the local bar, church, or family home. And they all work together to warn away outsiders. If an outsider sets a trap, he gets a verbal warning. If he persists, his traps and lines may be tampered with and cut—an anonymous, relatively gentle warning message like a note on a Southie car windshield. If newcomers don't get the message, the lobstermen—and they're almost all men—may escalate their response, even sinking boats and shooting at rivals.

These lobster gangs operate outside the law, but the sanctions they impose have an upside: they have long ensured a robust supply of lobsters because they limit strangers' catch. Their rules work wonderfully—if you are an insider or if you care primarily about consuming lobsters. The gangs support the local fishing economy and have ensured jobs for multiple generations, as sons take over for their fathers. Shouldn't that count for something? On the other hand, outsiders and newcomers can't get access. And the catch limits that the lobster gangs set are solely for their own benefit—they do not consider how lobsters interact with other marine species and affect the larger ecosystem. By driving off groundfish that compete with the more lucrative lobsters, the lobstermen may have created a fragile aquatic monoculture.

For decades, Maine has largely left lobster gangs alone—state regulations have not touched their territorial control. Trying to dial down their claims to possession would have many costs. It would take an enormous policing effort to break up the gangs and defend outsiders' traps out on the open sea. Perhaps with enough effort, Maine could eventually dial gang possession down to one-tenth. But then what?

Replacing gang possession may be a worthy goal—fairer (to outsiders) and perhaps more efficient (for maximizing overall ecosystem health). But there's no guarantee the cure will be better than the problem. If regulators were to succeed in breaking up the gangs but then couldn't enforce limits on the number of traps, newcomers could rush in and overfish. Perhaps no more violence, but no more lobsters, either.

It's a similar challenge at Lunada Bay, but with different stakes. The Bay Boys have a strong vision for the bay's best use: few surfers, epic rides, lovely photo ops. If the California authorities were to succeed in opening the waves to all, the result could be fairer to newcomers. But it might well mean hundreds of kooks bumping around: many surfers, crummy rides. If you want a different outcome from these extremes, that's fine. But what ownership path gets you there?

Negative Truthful Gossip

Resource owners tolerate privately created signals of possession as long as they serve their goals, and they undercut them when they do not. These stories share a similar trajectory.

On the upswing, the possessors' mantra is "this is how it's done around here." People close to a resource evolve finely tailored cues that reliably signal control and resolve conflicts. Locals understand the language and are often highly motivated to respect each other's claims, even without law's coercion. Negative truthful gossip at the sports game, church, or bar—"how rude!"—turns out to be one of the most powerful disciplinary forces humans have devised, often more binding than law itself.

But as the audience grows larger and more diverse, negative truthful gossip and shaming lose their bite. All is not lost, however. Signals may become simpler—like placing a jacket over a cinema chair, an iPad on a Southwest Airlines seat, a threatening note on a car windshield, or emptying a lobster trap. Often when disputes arise, strangers can continue to sort things out using a reduced set of possession signals, rarely escalating to violence or lawyers. In sum, over a wide range of settings, mere symbolic possession can provide an adaptable, low-cost, bottom-up, effective tool for resolving resource conflicts.

In time, though, possession systems often fray around the edges. We have already accounted for internal causes of collapse—overreaching intermediaries like pool attendants, boundary-pushers like beach-spreaders, overly insular communities like Bay Boy surfers, and escalating violence as with lobster gangs.

In addition, three external trends put pressure on possession signals: ever more people, scarcer resources, and new technology. Populations move and grow. As a New York transplant, Gliden understood the Southie signal, but she didn't see why she should care. Negative truthful gossip may not constrain newcomers—they don't play, pray, or drink together. Eventually, governments may step in and displace localized possession dialects altogether. Growing cities are not terribly respectful of local custom.

Second, economic growth often makes existing resources more valuable. Increased scarcity, in turn, makes fighting possession rules more worthwhile. Looking for parking for ten minutes is annoying, but after circling for an hour, you just move the damn cone and take the risk. In Boston, businesses and service providers joined newcomers in the antichair alliance. Eventually, public debate shifted away from celebrating neighborhood control to promoting citywide economic growth. City officials came to see parking chairs as a violent anachronism deployed as an exclusionary tool, not as a charming feature worth preserving—like, say, historic Back Bay row houses.

Finally, a claim of possession is a form of legal technology. This means better technology can come along to displace it. Entrepreneurs have been trying to introduce parking apps to monetize physical possession—just as line-standing companies charge for being first in line. With a parking app, as you prepare to pull out of a space, the app sells possession to a nearby circler, giving you a cut. Cities don't like this type of innovation. Some, like Boston, Los Angeles, and San Francisco, have banned the apps. If there's money to be made from parking, the cities want the cash. Cities have also responded by raising the price of parking—reducing competition for spaces and capturing part of the profits directly. San Francisco has been experimenting with variable parking meter pricing—a technological innovation like the dynamic tolling on highways we discussed in Chapter 1. With dynamic parking meters, prices rise during busy periods and drop in off-hours so some parking is always available for those able to pay.

Auctions to the highest bidder can replace possession battles—cities gain revenue; local businesses gain customers; well-off car owners can drive right up to empty spots. Even the environment can win if people spend less time circling the block looking for parking. There's money to be made in technology that replaces simple possession as a basis for ownership. But local residents and the less-wealthy lose out. Where do they park?

It won't be long before the experience of saving seats at a cinema becomes a historical curiosity. The ArcLight Cinema in Los Angeles has long had all-assigned ticketing; the megachain AMC Theatres is moving in that direction too. As assigned seating gets cheaper for owners to administer, why impose the irritation of open seating on customers? Cinemas have to compete hard to draw people away from Netflix and other streaming services. So seats in theaters are becoming bigger and more comfy as the industry shifts to selling a premium experience, complete with upscale food and drinks. It's the opposite of flying, where the plane itself is never the destination and seats keep shrinking.

Ownership technology evolves to provide more low-cost, fine-grained control over resources. As it does, the new rules can replicate many of the virtues of possession, but with less violence and more flexibility for owners trying to capture value. Symbolic possession can come to seem like a blunt tool by comparison, deployed where ultimate owners are not paying attention or don't have the capacity to impose their preferred ownership design. In time, a jacket on the chair may become as obsolete a technology as shelves of *Encyclopaedia Britannica* (in print 1768–2012) and the yellow pages (1883–2019).

Possession is a deep-rooted and powerful basis for ownership. It's not going away anytime soon. But the claim *It's mine because I am holding on to it* is also easily misunderstood, unjust to newcomers and outsiders, and prone to conflict in changing times.

The Million-Dollar Ball

In late 2001, San Francisco Giants slugger Barry Bonds's pursuit of the home run season record became a national news story. The final home run ball of the season would be worth a lot.

Alex Popov wanted to catch that ball. He studied the paths of Bonds's past home runs, bought a ticket where the home run ball was most likely to land, and sat waiting with a softball mitt. He guessed right. Bonds blasted his seventy-third home run straight into Popov's section of seats. The ball came down, down, right into his glove—for a split second. A mob immediately swarmed him and knocked the ball free. It caromed around until it was plucked from the ground by the lucky Patrick Hayashi, a fan who had come simply to enjoy the game. Hayashi left with the record-setting ball—estimated to be worth $1 million.

That should have ended the matter. The ball was in Hayashi's physical possession. But should he own the ball? Wasting little time, Popov sued, claiming *he* did. He had taken possession when the ball momentarily entered his glove, and he had lost control only because the crowd mugged him. In Popov's view, Hayashi was a thief, and a thief's possession should count for zero tenths of the law. (Actually, it's more like one-tenth: as we've seen, thieves lose only to true owners and win against everyone else.)

Hayashi countered that generations of baseball fans have followed a simple possession rule: the owner is the fan who holds the ball at the end of the scramble, not those who make hopeful touches along the way. Hayashi's final possession should count for all—more like Pierson's capture of the fox than Post's chase.

The law, it turned out, was silent on the issue. No existing statute or case determined the outcome. There are many rules that could have applied. Some options—like flipping a coin, tossing possession back and forth, cutting the ball in half, or destroying it—we discussed in relation to the rocking chair in the Introduction. Those options were available here as well. And there were others:

- Giants win, as the prior possessor
- Bonds wins, since his labor created the value
- Hayashi wins, as the final possessor

- Popov wins, as the mugged first possessor
- Auction the ball, split the proceeds

How you decide gives some insight into where you stand on competing core views of ownership—or maybe it just reveals that you spend a lot of time in baseball bleachers. To jump to the bottom line: fans usually prefer Hayashi. The judge ordered the ball auctioned and proceeds divided. We would go with Popov.

Let's start with the top two options in our list above. How about them Giants, the prior possessors? The Giants bought the Rawlings ball and brought it to the game. (Major league baseball teams use about one hundred balls per game, over two hundred thousand game balls per season.) The team unequivocally owned the ball a moment before Bonds's hit. Why not the moment after?

Soccer, football, and basketball teams demand balls back when they fly into the stands, and they make sure fans comply. But not baseball teams. Since the 1920s, they have chosen to abandon ownership of balls that leave the field of play. The law says abandoned property is free to the next possessor. The Giants could change their position and choose not to abandon their ownership if, say, fan violence gets out of hand. But there are good business reasons to continue the current ownership scheme. Baseballs are cheap. Abandoning them to fans' possession makes fans happy. As every American kid knows, when you buy a baseball ticket, you also get the thrilling possibility of coming home with a game ball.

Bonds is our next potential owner, based on his prodigious labor—a core justification for ownership that we explore in the next chapter. Bonds's (likely) steroid-enhanced slugging substantially created the ball's value. The ball is contested precisely because it was the seventy-third one he hit out of the park. Indeed, in many ballparks, fans routinely understand sluggers' labor to be the basis for ownership, not possession. They freely hand over balls worth thousands of dollars (or even hundreds of thousands) to the ballplayers who hit them—in exchange for no more than a photo op or a signed jersey. When Los Angeles Angels slugger Albert Pujols hit his six-hundredth home run, the fan who caught it, Scott Steffel, handed it back, saying, "It's not my ball, it's his. He deserves it." But in our case, Bonds made no claim, and neither Hayashi nor Popov offered up the ball.

How about the fans' view? Serious baseball fans we've queried say this is an easy case. In most stadiums, the law of the bleachers sides with Hayashi. What happens in the scrum stays in the scrum, and whoever emerges with final possession owns the ball. The universal signal is to hold the ball up with one hand, smile for the giant TV screen, then turn left and right to acknowledge nearby fans. This rule has the benefit of simplicity and ease of administration. There is no need to debate values or appeal to judges. Fans follow the rule in the fox case described in Chapter 1. And this rule respects the role physical possession has played for most of human history. It may be primitive—the law of the jungle—but it is time-tested.

Judge Kevin McCarthy thought he could do better. For him, the dispute boiled down to the meaning of possession. When the ball landed for a split second in Popov's outstretched glove, it was not yet caught and not yet dropped. At that instant, said the judge, Popov "was set upon by a gang of bandits, who dislodged the ball from his grasp." Hayashi was an innocent victim, too, of this same "band of wrongdoers," banged around before emerging with the ball in hand. In the judge's view, "both men have a superior claim to the ball as against all the world. Each man has a claim of equal dignity as to the other." Rather than ordering the ball rotated back and forth, as with Arthur and Mildred's rocking chair, Judge McCarthy decided it should be auctioned and the proceeds equally split.

The ball sold for $450,000 to comic book creator Todd McFarlane. Hayashi paid his contingency-fee lawyer (owed a percentage of any money recovered) and cleared some cash from his brush with fame. Popov, however, ended up insolvent, owing hundreds of thousands to his hourly-rate lawyer. One life lesson here: if you hire a lawyer, think hard in advance about how the fee will be paid—your lawyer certainly does. And never forget: ownership disputes are rarely worth litigating.

On balance, we are skeptical of Judge McCarthy's division rule, but we also reject the fans' rough-and-ready endorsement of final possession.

Step back a moment from the specifics of this case and consider the game as a whole. About 1,750 fans are injured annually in baseball stands, many by hard-hit foul balls or sharp elbows in ensuing melees. Some fans (not coincidentally, perhaps, those paying the highest ticket prices) are screened by safety nets. For the rest of us, our best protection is an alert fan nearby with good glove skills.

The fans' solution—ownership tracks final possession—does little to encourage mitt-wielding protectors to keep us safe. Why bring your mitt to the stadium if the law endorses mob rule and Hayashi wins the day? Judge McCarthy's rule does not do much better. Getting your mitt on the ball becomes a ticket in an uncertain litigation lottery.

In our view, the law should define baseball possession to address the everyday fan experience, not the one-in-a-million case where auctioning the ball is even possible. Therefore let's decide what we want fans to do, then point the remote control of ownership to drive fans there.

Consider this rule: "If you get your glove on the ball, and the mob tackles you, the ball is yours." It sends a positive message to future Popovs, the superfans who keep the rest of us safe as an unintended consequence of their eager fielding. It tells them, *Bring your glove and stay alert. If you protect the rest of us, the law will protect you. The mob won't win.* And it tells the mob, *Stay back.* Convincing fans to abide by this interference rule may be tricky, but high-profile cases, like the Bonds home run ball, are important precisely because they are so rare and can reach a wide audience. In our view, Popov should have won outright.

You may note our solution shows zero concern for the real-life Popov or Hayashi. That's intentional. We view their ownership dispute primarily as an opportunity to improve safety for future baseball fans. In this case, we are asking, what ball possession rule will have the best safety consequence going forward? This is an *ex ante* approach to ownership design, one that forecasts the future "before the event." Such reasoning relies on casual empirical (that is, often unfounded) predictions about what will happen. And it applies a moral framework that cares about a rule's consequences for individual fans and for society as a whole. Would our rule actually make fans safer? We don't know. But safety for future fans is our goal here—maybe because we're far more likely to be hit by fly balls than to catch them.

By contrast, note Judge McCarthy's quite different approach. He is primarily trying to do justice between these two particular claimants. While he appreciates that judicial rulings affect how people behave, he focuses more on an *ex post* inquiry (looking back, "after the fact"). The judge is asking fine-grained questions like Who acted badly? Who well? On balance, what is the fairest outcome I can craft for these two people here in court?

Every ownership choice boils down to a version of these two strategies. According to one legal commentator, "If I had to choose only one theoretical tool for a first-year law student to master, it would be the *ex ante/ex post* distinction." We agree, but we would extend the point: everyone should have access to this, the most powerful of ownership tools.

The key takeaway of the Bonds ball story is that possession is not a fact waiting for a judge to uncover; nor is it something the law compels. Instead, the meaning of possession reflects a choice—a better or worse choice, depending on your animating values—among competing ownership stories.

Chapter 3

I REAP
WHAT YOU SOW

I Have a Dream, Pay Me Now

What's your strongest image of Dr. Martin Luther King, Jr.? For many of us, it is his "I Have a Dream" speech. Standing on the steps of the Lincoln Memorial before 250,000 people, King proclaimed, "I have a dream that my four little children will one day live in a nation where they will not be judged by the color of their skin but by the content of their character." The speech remains one of the most celebrated in American history.

Soon after King spoke in August 1963, several companies began selling printed copies of "I Have a Dream." A month later Clarence Jones, King's personal lawyer, registered a copyright for the speech and sued to prevent its reproduction without permission and payment. When King was murdered in 1968, he was not wealthy, but his estate did include everything he had copyrighted.

King's legacy became a brand. All of his written words, videos, letters, and artifacts became the property of a for-profit company, known as King Inc. If you listen carefully to *Selma,* Ava DuVernay's inspiring movie about King's role in the 1965 civil rights marches, you may notice that the speeches sound like King but do not use his actual words. Says DuVernay, "We never even asked" for permission to use the speeches. King Inc. had already sold the rights to Steven Spielberg.

Without payment to King Inc., most of King's words cannot be used. When CBS included part of its own original broadcast of King's speech in a documentary, King Inc. sued. Before the King Memorial could be built on the National Mall in Washington, D.C., King Inc. collected $800,000 for the use of King's likeness and words. Then after the memorial was finished, King Inc. prevented the foundation that had raised the construction funds from continuing to use King's name. It became simply "The Memorial Foundation." King Inc. even demanded $20,000 from Clarence Jones to use the "I Have a Dream" speech—which Jones helped draft—in his book about the civil rights movement.

King Inc. has licensed the speech to hawk cell phones, computers, and cars. In 2018, Dodge aired a Super Bowl commercial using excerpts from another King speech that originally had condemned car advertisers—"You know, those gentlemen of massive verbal persuasion," who teach people that "in order to make your neighbor envious, you must drive this type of car." King Inc. let Dodge edit those inconvenient sentiments out of the ad voice-over.

King Inc. has long been controlled by King's younger son, Dexter. He has engaged in bitter disputes and repeated litigation with the other King children, civil rights movement leaders, everyone. Says Jones, "It is so painful. . . . They might be fighting for the disposition of the King legacy, but most of it is really driven by money, money, money." As a *Newsweek* magazine account described these disputes, "Friends of the family tried to convince Dexter that there was a difference between profiting and profiteering." King likely had a different vision for how to honor his legacy.

Let's step back to a more basic question. Why does King Inc. own King's speeches in the first place? On the one hand, those speeches are the fruits of King's labor for a racially just America. He should be able to "reap where he has sown," just like other writers and artists. On the other, King died more than fifty years ago. Why should King Inc. still be able to keep his words out of documentaries yet market them to sell cars? More generally, who should own intellectual labor?

Zero ownership is, perhaps surprisingly, the baseline rule in American law. The law encourages copying because people don't necessarily need ownership to be creative. King did not write the iconic speech because he expected monetary profit. His goal was to transform civil rights in America; copyright was, quite literally, a lawyer's afterthought.

Most creators, though, are not like King. They expect to be paid for their creative labor. Why would drug companies invest billions, and employ thousands, if competitors could just copy the breakthrough drugs and ignore the duds? To encourage productive innovation, the argument goes, we must reward labor with ownership. Maybe King Inc. should be free to monetize King's legacy as it pleases—consistent with the approach that also brings us life-saving drugs, cool tech, and hot culture.

Rewarding labor with ownership is not, however, a single on-off choice. King died in 1968, yet King Inc. still controls access to his legacy today. We have to decide whom to reward, with what ownership rights, and for how long. And we must choose who should be making these decisions. Should it be Congress or the states, the legislatures or courts? These questions may seem narrow, but their answers determine every aspect of our well-being—the speeches we hear, the fashion we wear, the entertainment we enjoy, and the drugs our lives depend upon.

Sweat of the Brow

The labor claim—*It's mine because I worked for it*—is the third basic justification for ownership. Quite simply, after a hard day's work, I feel I've earned the right to the fruits of my labor. And this feeling of deserved reward underpins many of our other ownership intuitions. If I hustle to get in line first, I should be served before you. If I shovel my car out of the snow, my parking chair should hold the space.

This intimate connection between labor and reward is ancient. Variants on *You reap what you sow* appear throughout the Bible. For the agricultural peoples of ancient Israel, the idea made literal sense: most survived by planting and harvesting. The great English philosopher John Locke, writing more than three hundred years ago, put this connection at the center of his theory of ownership. He started from a commitment to self-ownership, the idea that "every Man has a *Property* in his own *Person*." And building from that (gendered) touchstone, Locke continued, "the *Labour* of his Body, and the *Work* of his Hands, we may say, are properly his." Ownership of the world's previously unowned resources arises (with important caveats and provisos) once we mix in our labor.

For Locke, America was the prime example of an unowned resource, waiting to be transformed through labor into private property. He wrote, "In the beginning, all the world was America." But America was not an empty continent when European colonists first arrived. Native Americans lived there in the millions, working the land. So why didn't they own America, where they had, after all, long been laboring?

Soon after America's founding, courts had to decide whose labor mattered and what type of labor counted. As we saw in Chapter 1, in the 1823 case *Johnson v. M'Intosh,* the Supreme Court asserted, "The tribes of Indians inhabiting this country were fierce savages. . . . To leave them in possession of their country, was to leave the country a wilderness." The Court was not just expressing prejudice against Native Americans, though that was certainly a major part. It went deeper.

For the Court, ownership in America was founded on a specific vision of productive labor. The ways some Native Americans hunted and gathered—moving in a seasonal pattern to follow wild game, fish runs, and ripening berries—simply didn't count. Neither did the ways Native peoples farmed land—which many did. Ownership, to the Court, required improving the wilderness in particular ways, such as by cutting trees, clearing fields, and building stone walls. In other words, labor led to ownership only if you made New England look like the England the colonists had left behind. If this reasoning seems shaky, well, yes, it is. But it was enough for the Court to justify dispossessing the Native peoples of America.

Labor—like *first-in-time* and *possession*—is not self-defining. There is no value-neutral way to decide whose labor counts. These are not empirical facts but contestable conclusions—shorthand labels that colonists and courts clumsily wrapped around their choices about who should control scarce resources.

This point represents the biggest gap between lay and legal views of property, and it is a hard lesson for new law students to grasp: ownership is a social engineering choice, a conclusion we come to, not a fact we find. First, we decide the goals we want ownership to achieve. Next, we decide what means will most likely get us there. Finally, we affix the legal term *owner* to the sum of those oft-hidden value judgments and casual empirical guesses. Ownership is the endpoint, not the start, of analysis.

The Supreme Court's decision in *Johnson* chose a definition of ownership that reflected and reinforced the worldview of European farmers and merchants. That choice may seem cruel and arbitrary today, but it was one that even a child could understand—that is, a child raised with Anglo-American values of those times.

We have evidence from one particular child, Laura Ingalls Wilder, who wrote down her story in the classic *Little House* series. Laura's third book, *Little House on the Prairie,* was set on land her family had seized from Native Americans in 1869. During that summer and fall, a large group of white squatters moved on to what was then known as the Osage Diminished Reserve. Laura's dad, Pa—the character most sympathetic to the Osage—had this to say about settler landownership: "When white settlers come into a country, the Indians have to move on. . . . That's why we're here, Laura. White people are going to settle all this country, and we get the best land because we get here first and take our pick. Now do you understand?"

The Ingalls family did not labor long enough in Kansas to complete their claim. The land was poor, the winters rough, and the Native Americans strong enough to resist. So the Ingallses pressed onward. In the Dakotas, they found Native land that was more fertile and less well defended. After years of hard toil, planting trees and watching them fail and trying again, the Ingallses' labor was finally rewarded. They claimed title under the Homestead Act—one of a series of laws that translated settler labor into "original" ownership. After establishing his claim, Pa rode around singing a ditty that captures the spirit of settler ownership:

> Oh, come to this country
> And don't you feel alarm
> For Uncle Sam is rich enough
> To give us all a farm!

During the 1800s, the United States more than doubled in size. The federal government desperately wanted to secure these newly added public lands against competing European and Native claims. The challenge was to settle the area west of the Mississippi quickly, visibly, and at low cost. To achieve this goal, the government chose to reward labor like Pa's. If he went west and worked the land, he could become a landowner. The initial Homestead Act formalized this deal by granting 160 acres of public land to any adult citizen who lived on and—this is crucial—improved it by clearing fields, building a dwelling, and cultivating the land for five years. Roughly 270 million acres, or 10 percent of the vast American landmass, were transferred from the public domain into private ownership through homesteading.

The General Mining Act of 1872 worked in a similar way. It

allowed citizens and companies to stake claims on public land. Prospectors needed to search for valuable minerals, prove a discovery, and put in at least $100 worth of labor or improvements annually. So long as they met these minimal requirements (and a few others) and paid $2.50 to $5.00 per claimed acre, they owned the minerals below and sometimes the surface land above. The claim fee has never been updated since 1872. Mining companies still extract $2 billion to $3 billion each year from public lands and pay close to nothing for the privilege. In addition, mining claims have created pockets of private property—"inholdings"—pockmarked throughout western public lands that today threaten access to backcountry recreation trails and unbroken wilderness.

Similar laws transferred public water to private use—often worth more than land or minerals in the arid western landscape. Divert the river and visibly put the flow to beneficial use, then it's yours. It's no exaggeration to say that the shape of the American West today arises directly from choices the country made well over a century ago regarding whose labor and what labor counted for ownership of land, minerals, and water.

To establish ownership, purchase was not enough. Being first in time was not enough. Possession was not enough. Settlers had to transform the land through specific forms of labor. Only then did they become the legal owners. Throughout history, law has reinforced this close relationship between sowing and reaping—at least for certain people engaged in certain acts.

But each generation decides ownership anew. Today there is no more homesteading on federal lands. The law was repealed in 1976 (though it continued in Alaska until 1986). Laura's world is gone. How should labor matter today?

Very Important Babies Daycare

Consider the case of Very Important Babies Daycare in Hallandale, Florida. Toddlers there long enjoyed playing beneath a mural, painted on their wall, of five-foot-high images of Mickey Mouse, Minnie Mouse, Donald Duck, and Goofy. The day care was a happy place.

But lawyers at the Disney Company were not happy when they learned of the unauthorized Mickeys. They sent investigators to document the offending murals and then threatened to sue the day care center. While they were at it, Disney also sent threatening letters to Good Godmother's and Temple Messianique—two other Hallandale day care centers harboring pirate Mickey murals.

The kids were upset. "If they took them off the wall, I'd be sad," said Christopher, age five. "It's not fair at all," said Amanda, age seven. Erika Scotti, the day care director, expressed it in grown-up terms: "I think it's totally ludicrous." Nevertheless, she spent her time negotiating with Disney lawyers, seeking a compromise.

The City of Hallandale joined the fray, passing a resolution supporting the day care centers. Mayor Gil Stein said, "It is such a shame and a loss to the children of Hallandale that of all the illustrious names in our corporate spectrum, the Disney Company, built to mammoth size by its own genius and the nickels, dimes and quarters of America's children, cannot be kinder in spirit and more generous of heart." But the Disney Company, owner of "the Happiest Place on Earth," was implacable. A spokesperson announced, "This is our final reply. We have nothing further to say to the city." Mickey had to go.

The company's aggressive stance traces straight back to Walt Disney himself. In 1923 Disney created his first hit character, Oswald the Lucky Rabbit, but then lost control of Oswald to his film distributor. Disney went bankrupt and had to start over from scratch. His new character, Mortimer Mouse, launched in 1928. Quickly renamed

Mickey, the mouse became the basis of the cartoon empire. Disney was not about to be burned again, and ever since then the Disney Company has zealously protected against what it views as unauthorized uses of its Mouse.

Luckily for the Very Important Babies, their plight received national media coverage. Universal Studios Florida, a theme park competitor, arrived to save the day. With cameras rolling, Universal staff painted over the murals at the Hallandale day cares and replaced them with their own Flintstones, Scooby-Doo, and Yogi Bear characters—all for free. Yabba dabba doo!

Many other innocent Mickey users have not fared so well. Disney is relentless. Its in-house legal department, known as the Disnoids, files hundreds of lawsuits a year and threatens more. As one story put it, "As rabbits love to propagate, the Mouse loves to litigate." How is it possible that more than fifty years after Disney's death, nearly a century after he first drew Mickey, the Disnoids can still go around threatening little children's happiness?

The answer arises from a basic distinction in ownership design. Ownership rewards two types of labor: physical and intellectual. Tending an apple orchard is physical; creating an apple pie recipe is intellectual.

Granting ownership for physical labor is time-tested—that's the origin of the intuition behind *You reap what you sow.* For producers, ownership motivates them to grow more apples because they can charge for what they grow. Consumers benefit, too. Ownership provides a quick and easy way to decide who gets the apples: whoever pays the market price gets a bite. If one person eats an apple, another can't.

But this trade-off does not hold for consumers of intellectual labor. If I use your recipe, you can still use it, too, and so can the next hundred apple pie–lovers. All intellectual property law grapples with this single insight: with intellectual labor, everyone can reap if just one person has sown.

President Thomas Jefferson explained the point in a much-cited 1813 letter using the example of a candle: "He who receives an idea from me, receives instruction himself without lessening mine; as he who lites his taper at mine, receives light without darkening me." In other words, we don't need ownership, prices, or markets to decide who should use the recipe. Everyone can use it with no harm to any future users. In the same letter, Jefferson—also America's first patent examiner and author of the first Patent Act—expressed skepticism about granting patent "monopolies [that may] produce more embarrassment than advantage to society." From the standpoint of consumer well-being, intellectual labor should not be owned.

Concern for consumers is why the default level of protection for intellectual labor has always been zero—free copying is the rule, unless there's a legislative exception that says otherwise. After Disney has created Mickey, society is better off if we can all use the Mouse freely, even if the Disney Company objects. After King gave his speech, we can all benefit if we can hear it for free, even if that puts King Inc. out of business. And once a life-saving drug exists—and can be reproduced for, say, a penny a pill—why should even a single person die from lack of access?

Zero protection for products of intellectual labor may seem to be the best rule for consumers. But here's the rub: we also have to take producers into account. If Disney and Pfizer know they get zero, maybe we end up with zero Mickeys, zero life-saving drugs. If labor does not earn a monetary reward, why bother? And that would indeed be a loss—for consumers, too.

So we're left with a trade-off. This is the trillion-dollar conundrum driving intellectual property law: What is the least reward we can give creators so they provide enough benefit to consumers? And who decides?

When the Framers crafted America's government in the 1780s, they already recognized the challenge. Their solution was to take some of these decisions away from state legislatures—no states' rights here. The Constitution instructs Congress to create a national scheme for copyright (for creative expressions) and patent (for useful inventions)—the main legislative exceptions to the free copying rule. And the Constitution further commands that ownership be given only to the extent it will "promote the progress of science and useful arts." Finally, these rights must last only for "limited times"—so the public at large is sure to benefit.

"The primary objective of copyright is not to reward the labor of authors," said the Supreme Court. "Originality, not 'sweat of the brow,' is the touchstone of copyright protection." In America, creators get limited rights, and only for the "progress" they contribute. In the 1790 Copyright Act, one of America's first laws, authors were given up to twenty-eight years of exclusive control (fourteen years initially, and an option to renew for fourteen more). After that period, the public got to enjoy the entire creation for free.

Patent works much the same way: the inventor gets monopoly ownership for a limited time, now twenty years. In exchange, inventors immediately disclose how to make the invention, thus adding to our store of common knowledge. And after the patent period expires, the invention itself enters the public domain, free for anyone to use. For centuries this has been the basic deal legislatures have struck with authors and inventors.

But creators often demand more. Whenever the Mickey copyright has come close to expiring, the Disney Company has flooded Congress with money and lobbyists. The company does not focus on its market position. Instead, it tells a story of its founder's struggles, Oswald, Mickey, and just rewards to creativity. Disney indeed loved Mickey—he personally voiced the Mouse in cartoons for a decade. Wouldn't it disrespect his creative labor if others could use Mickey for unsavory ends? The shocked makers of *Sesame Street* certainly realized this when a movie trailer appeared with depraved, drug-snorting Muppets.

Nor was the Disney Company alone in its lobbying strategy.

Owners of rights to works by Irving Berlin, George and Ira Gershwin, Richard Rodgers and Oscar Hammerstein, and other icons of the Great American Songbook joined its push to extend copyrights. The lobbying labor paid off. Mickey was poised to enter the public domain in 1984 under the rules in force when Disney created him. As the date approached, Congress extended all copyright terms, pushing ownership of Mickey to 2003 (and Pluto to 2005, Goofy to 2007, Donald Duck to 2009). In 1998, as Mickey again neared expiration, the Disney Company and allies went back to work, persuading Congress to pass what came to be known derisively as the "Mickey Mouse Protection Act." With this newest act, the Disney Company can threaten and sue Mickey-lovers like Very Important Babies Daycare through 2023.

What began in 1790 as a twenty-eight-year maximum term now extends to nearly a century.

In all, the Disney Company has spent millions lobbying for Mickey, including making direct campaign contributions to nineteen of the twenty-five congressional sponsors of the 1998 act. The payments were a fabulous bargain for Disney and its allies. Mickey generated an estimated $5.8 billion in 2004 alone, according to *Forbes*, making the Mouse the world's "richest fictional billionaire," earning more than any actual celebrity, dead or alive.

That was great for Disney Company stockholders (and for the Berlin and Hammerstein estates), but what did the twenty-year extension do for the public? Zilch. The fifty-six-year copyright term existing in 1928 had been enough to motivate Disney to create Mickey. He reaped what he sowed until his death in 1966. Extending his old copyright into the future will not spark him to create more characters or George and Ira Gershwin to write more songs. Nor will it push young animators today to work any harder—the extension kicks in only after they've been dead for decades. The Mickey Mouse Protection Act is unlikely to produce any public benefit whatsoever, not a single cartoon character or song. It's pure corporate welfare.

The act provides a stark example of how the Disney Company and allied copyright owners use the story of reward for labor to steer ownership rules for their own benefit, while depleting the public domain and harming the rest of us. It's not just the Very Important Babies Amanda and Christopher who lost out. When ownership of intellectual labor is extended time and again, culture is held hostage.

Thousands of works from 1923 were set to enter the public domain in 1999 but were then locked away for twenty more years. Finally, starting in 2019, we gained free use of Virginia Woolf's *Jacob's Room* and Robert Frost's "Stopping by Woods on a Snowy Evening"; 2020 bought us George Gershwin's *Rhapsody in Blue* and Thomas Mann's *The Magic Mountain;* 2021 freed F. Scott Fitzgerald's *The Great Gatsby* and Charlie Chaplin's film *The Gold Rush*. As one observer noted. "Most of twentieth-century culture is still under copyright—copyrighted but unavailable. Much of this, in other words, is lost culture. No one is reprinting the books, screening the films, or playing the songs."

When ownership of intellectual labor expands, consumers lose out from delay and also in more surprising ways. After copyright holders die, their ownership is often split among heirs who do not even know they have become owners. Then ownership splits again among the heirs' heirs, creating the family ownership dilemma that we explore in Chapter 6. For copyright, the proliferation of unknown rights holders results in what are called "orphan works," still owned but out of print. No one dares reproduce these artistic creations—which constitute perhaps 70 percent of all works still potentially in copyright—because remote heirs might appear and sue.

Paradoxically, the orphan works problem means fewer books from the mid-1900s are available to us today than from the late 1800s. Why? Google, working with libraries, was able to scan and post online more than 100 million out-of-copyright works—everything from before the 1920s—and make them available to all for free. Google tried for later copyrighted works as well and eventually reached a comprehensive agreement with publishers and the Authors Guild. That settlement would have allowed Google to make orphan works available for paid download, reserving 63 percent of the revenues in a pool for rights holders to claim. But then Justice Department antitrust enforcers stepped in, worried that Google would corner the dormant orphan works market, and a judge shut down the effort. The net result: Mickey and his pals are still blocking free access to the great flowering of American culture in the 1920s, '30s, and '40s—works that would already be in the public domain but for the Mickey Mouse Protection Act.

Lengthening Mickey's term of copyright not only diminishes the public domain and strands orphan works, but it also harms the very authors whose creative labor copyright is meant to protect. For short-story writers, especially, fame can depend on coming out of copyright. It can mean the difference between being included in an anthology and being taught in English 101—or being forgotten. By locking works away for a century, copyright term extensions have all but erased many authors' posthumous reputations. One researcher sums it up: the overlong copyright term "makes books disappear," while its expiration "brings them back to life."

Hank Brown (R-Colorado)—the sole U.S. senator to vote against Mickey—nicely captured the danger of long copyright terms: "The real incentive [was] for corporate owners that bought copyrights to lobby Congress for another 20 years of revenue. I thought it was a moral outrage. There wasn't anyone speaking for the public interest." Senator Brown was right. Because the Constitution expressly puts Congress in charge of copyright law, lobbyists need to sway only a small group of politicians. No one else stands in their way. Not even the Supreme Court, which deferred to Congress's assertion that the most recent lengthening of the copyright term is still limited enough to satisfy the Constitution's minimal requirements.

Ownership design is only as good as the designers.

Dead Celebrities Walking

State legislators and judges are also free to create intellectual property—other than copyright and patent—and they have not been shy about doing so.

In the early 1950s, the Bowman Gum Company signed exclusive deals with baseball players to put their faces on trading cards. But Topps Chewing Gum printed competing cards. Topps argued that baseball players did not own their images, so they could not control their use. In the ensuing battle, a court interpreted a New York statute to create something new: a *right of publicity*. This novel form of ownership gives celebrities the exclusive right to control and profit from the commercial value of their personas—their names, their likenesses, even the sound of their voices. Based on this new right, Bowman won its case against Topps, but Topps prevailed in the end when it acquired Bowman. The merged company used its ownership of players' personas to monopolize baseball trading cards for the next three decades.

By 1970 the right of publicity had spread to seven states; now it's recognized in more than half. Sports publicity rights, in particular, have evolved from trading cards to video games and then to fantasy sports leagues for professional players. Even the NCAA, after decades of opposition, is now allowing university players to cash in by licensing their names and likenesses (for reasons we explore in Chapter 5).

Among the states that recognize publicity rights, there's wide variation on whether they survive death and for how long. In Tennessee, rights last ten years after death; in Virginia, twenty years; in California, seventy; and in Indiana, one hundred. New York terminates them when the owner dies. So when Marilyn Monroe died as a New York resident, her heirs could not cash in.

Why such variation? California has many notable dead celebrities whose heirs succeeded in pushing the state for lengthy ownership. No surprise there. New York is a bit of a puzzle—lots of dead celebrities but no rights. How about Indiana? Why does posthumous ownership there last for a century? Follow the money.

Few celebrities are from Indiana, but CMG Worldwide is headquartered there—and the company licenses the commercial use of many famous dead people, including James Dean, Ingrid Bergman, Jack Kerouac, Duke Ellington, Amelia Earhart, and even Malcolm X. CMG Worldwide went to the Indiana legislature asking for a handout—as the Disney Company went to Congress—and who was going to argue against them?

Dead celebrities now rake in billions per year for the owners of their personas. *Forbes* publishes an annual list of top dead earners: Michael Jackson brings in $60 million; Elvis Presley, $40 million. Even Marilyn Monroe brings in over $10 million—CMG Worldwide and others license some of her images and writings.

What's the rule in Georgia, where King resided at his death? The Georgia legislature never created a publicity right, posthumous or otherwise. But King Inc. sued anyway. It wanted to force payment from the makers of plastic King busts. In 1982 the Georgia Supreme Court ruled for King Inc., judicially creating a posthumous right of publicity for dead Georgia celebrities, very much including King.

Emergence of the right of publicity reveals an important feature of how ownership operates: in each sphere of life, there exists a menu containing a small number of preset ownership forms—a limitation the ancient Romans called the *numerus clausus* ("the number is closed"). This closed number is a feature of every legal system. Historically, for intellectual labor, Congress was in charge of two available forms: copyright and patent. Early on, states developed a third area: trademark law. Starting in the late 1800s, Congress began enacting federal legislation, taking trademark away from the states. The right of publicity is one of the newest entries in our limited menu of ownership choices.

Why allow this new item on the ownership menu? Ownership—

like all technology—evolves in response to new resource scarcity, market opportunities, and changing values. Each ownership form reflects a delicate bundle of value choices regarding freedom, community, efficiency, and justice. Marriage, condominiums, co-ops, partnerships, trusts, corporations, and such—these ownership forms are the building blocks of social life. They are like words in a language that let us quickly communicate complex messages, sometimes to a few people, sometimes to the world. And that's the key: to communicate with each other we need to understand, more or less, what each ownership form conveys.

The challenge is that sometimes there are good reasons to create new ownership forms—just like new words in a language. And they do not invent themselves. Legislatures, courts, businesses, and even individuals try to create them, but all have flaws. Legislators are too easily influenced by lobbyists wielding campaign contributions, as with the Mickey term extension. Judges are also blinkered: for the most part, they listen to lawyers arguing individual controversies that have already occurred and lack the tools to craft comprehensive ownership forms. (This is the *ex post–ex ante* distinction again.) Businesses and individuals aim to advance their private interests. The net result is that in America, the creation of new ownership forms depends critically on who is taking the initiative.

Law students want to debate what the law should be; experienced lawyers know the real question more often is: Who decides?

In the plastic King bust case, the Georgia Supreme Court neglected to specify an end date for the posthumous right of publicity it created. Nor did it craft a "fair use" exception, as in copyright law, that allows for educational uses, criticism, or parody without payment to, or permission from, the copyright owner. The court created a flawed, overly expansive ownership form—with national consequences. King Inc. keeps suing everyone who uses King's likeness, though he's been dead more than fifty years.

To change the state judges' rule and fix an end date—freeing people to share King's legacy—the Georgia state legislature would need to take over ownership design from its courts, or Congress would have to take over from the states. Some legislature would have to decide the difficult moral and economic trade-offs that the Georgia Supreme Court dodged. But who is going to lobby for that?

Eyes Off the Prize

Excessive reward for intellectual labor has another, even more insidious, effect. Too much existing ownership can make it impossible for people to create new, more valuable things. How can that be?

Private ownership usually creates wealth. But too much ownership has the opposite effect—it creates a phenomenon Heller has called *ownership gridlock.* Ownership gridlock is a paradox he discovered some years back. When too many people own a piece of one thing, cooperation breaks down, wealth disappears, and everybody loses.

Think back to King and his legacy, where we started the chapter. Few of us marched with him in Selma or attended his speeches; most know him solely through his writings, interviews, and videos. For millions of Americans, King came alive through the 1987 Emmy Award–winning public television documentary *Eyes on the Prize.* To make the documentary, the filmmakers talked with hundreds of people who knew King and used video footage from 82 archives, 275 still photographs, and 120 songs. Each item had to be separately licensed from its copyright owner, and many of those permissions expired after the film was first shown in 1987. So the film sat unwatched in a vault for two decades.

Why? Gridlock. To rerelease the film, the producers had to make hundreds of licensing agreements, a process called "clearing rights" in the trade. Clearing rights is neither cheap nor fast. It's like driving down a highway chockablock with separate tollbooths, each charging whatever fee it chooses. Gridlock arises when any one of the multitudes of tollbooth operators can veto the project as a whole.

If it's too easy to create ownership tollbooths, then we pay a price on the other end, when people want to assemble those rights into some useful new resource—like a documentary film. It took the filmmakers until 2006—along with a million dollars in donations—to clear the rights to (or replace) elements in the film and finally rerelease *Eyes on the Prize,* which you can now watch online for free.

James Surowiecki, writing in *The New Yorker,* is right when he charges, "The open fields of culture are increasingly fenced in with concertina wire." The *Eyes* film is just one example. To give another, gridlock radically changed the sound of hip-hop. Consider the classic 1988 album by Public Enemy, *It Takes a Nation of Millions to Hold Us Back.* The album helped transform hip-hop by assembling a musical collage sound from small samples of hundreds of borrowed works. Over this wall of sound, Chuck D rapped:

Caught, now in court 'cause I stole a beat
This is a sampling sport
. . .
I found this mineral that I call a beat
I paid zero.

After the Public Enemy sound took off, the major record companies responded by demanding license fees for even the briefest samples. Chuck D said, "Public Enemy's music was affected more than anybody's because we were taking thousands of sounds. If you separated the sounds, they wouldn't have been anything—they were unrecognizable. The sounds were all collaged together to make a sonic wall."

If you are one of the millions of fans of the early Public Enemy sound and wonder why hip-hop artists today often rap over just one primary sample, that's the reason. It's not necessarily that musical tastes changed. It's that song owners used their copyrights like toll-booths. One music critic notes, "If you take the hip-hop tradition seriously, then you have to acknowledge that the current situation has killed off part of that art form."

Gridlock is also why we don't have cool pictures illustrating the stories in this book—it would involve too much cost and complexity clearing rights, too much delay getting the book to production. (But we've managed to link to lots of our intended pictures at MineTheBook.com, if you are wondering, for example, what a Knee Defender looks like.)

Drug Development Gridlock

Now, you may not care about the health of the hip-hop industry, film documentaries, or illustrations for *Mine!* But here's a life-or-death example of too much ownership that hits closer to home. The head of research at a Big Pharma drug company told Heller how gridlock affects drug development. His researchers, he recounted, had developed a potential treatment for Alzheimer's disease (call it compound X). But biotech research partners—not drug-selling competitors—blocked its development. How could that be?

Before 1980, ownership gridlock was not a major problem for drug developers. Scientists published their research findings more or less freely and were rewarded for their labor with academic tenure, peer recognition, lecture invitations, awards, and maybe even a Nobel Prize. Recognition (and not ownership) was enough to spur the great twentieth-century biomedical innovations—humanity-transforming discoveries from penicillin to the polio vaccine. Many scientists believed that owning their research, financed by universities, foundations, and government, would be immoral. By freely sharing discoveries, scientists rapidly built on each other's creative labors. There were no ownership tollbooths to negotiate.

Then in 1980, the United States changed its patent law. With patents, Big Pharma plays a role similar to the Disney Company's role with copyright—they're the heavies that push Congress around. Big Pharma persuaded Congress that the way to turbocharge drug research was to transform the culture of science: motivate scientists to labor harder by giving them ownership. So in 1980, Congress started allowing patents for scientists who developed basic medical research tools and tests. The idea was to use ownership to encourage industry to invest more in basic research, previously the realm of public and nonprofit financing.

Pressing this new button on the ownership remote control worked, in a sense. Suddenly scientists could seek patents, not just grants, tenure, prizes, and reputation. Lured by potential profits and protected by new patent monopolies, private investment money poured into basic medical research—and sparked the biotech revolution. But as drug research patents began to accumulate, they started to have exactly the opposite effect from what Congress expected. One patent may spur innovation. But a thousand of them, held by separate start-ups, can function like multiple tollbooths on the highway to medical discovery.

Compound X affected the brain through numerous pathways. Biotech firms mapped those pathways and were, after 1980, able to secure patents for their discoveries. Each start-up viewed its own narrow patent as the crucial one—it's easy to overvalue our own labor. (Recall the endowment effect from Chapter 2.) Each firm demanded a corresponding fee, until the sum of the demands exceeded the drug's likely profit. And ignoring even one patent tollbooth would invite an expensive lawsuit if the drug succeeded.

The result? This story does not have a happy ending. No one came along to bundle the patents and license them to the compound X developers. The executive who spoke to Heller could not figure out a safe path through the patent thicket. Instead, he (and many other drug executives) shifted their research priorities to less ambitious options, like spin-offs of existing drugs for which the firm already controlled a portfolio of relevant patents. During the 1980s and '90s, research and development spending by pharmaceutical companies went up, but many of the new drugs that would actually save lives never came to market, as Heller and Rebecca Eisenberg wrote in *Science*.

Biotech start-ups are not evil. They are run by innovators who are laboring exactly the way the patent system directs them. This is how ownership works—reward people for particular forms of labor, and they will respond. Individually, biotech scientists were behaving rationally. But together, they created gridlock: too much reward to basic medical research labor meant too few life-saving drugs. And we all bear those costs, as people are now dying from diseases that could have been cured long ago. No one protests, however. Where do you go to complain about life-saving drugs that could exist—*should exist*—but don't because of bad ownership design?

In the years since Heller discovered ownership gridlock, thousands of scholarly articles have explored the phenomenon. A subfield of economics now documents and debates its effects. Recently, in the journal *Science,* one commentator suggests that the most prominent danger of gridlock today may involve certain gene-editing technologies (CRISPR, for those in the know). Innovations using these tools could save your life—indeed, the first emergency-use test approved to detect COVID-19 relies on CRISPR. But multiple companies control aspects of the technology, and all have incentives to set up competing tollbooths on the path to drug development.

There has been an unnoticed shift in how inventive labor creates wealth. When the patent system was first set up, each patent more or less led to a single product: Joseph Glidden's patent covered barbed wire. But the old *one patent, one product* rule now seems quaint. Today wealth creation requires assembling separate ownership fragments, and not just with basic biomedical discoveries. Bringing a cell phone to market or operating an ATM network requires having access to thousands of patents all at once. Licensing the full bundle of patents can prove impossible. The way we innovate has changed, but we are still stuck with an old-style story about ownership.

For centuries, we thought that the paramount value of ownership was to give clear rewards to labor. The idea was that so long as ownership was secure, people could easily trade among themselves. From this perspective, increasing rewards to labor had no cost. If we want more inventiveness and creativity, simply expand patent scope for Big Pharma and give longer copyright terms to Disney.

The gridlock problem shows the flaw in this logic. Sometimes we should reward labor *less,* so there are fewer tollbooths along the path to creativity and innovation. With fewer owners who can block agreement, the remaining parties may find it easier to reach a deal.

What to do? Think of ownership design like organizing dinner for a group of friends. The task gets exponentially harder as the crowd grows. He's vegan; she's gluten free; they eat only sushi; this one's on a juice cleanse; and the other is only free on Tuesdays. If everyone gets a dinner veto, no one dines together. The Senate works this way, with every senator able to filibuster the chamber into gridlock on most issues; similarly, the United Nations is often paralyzed, with the five permanent members of the Security Council—China, France, Russia, the United Kingdom, and the United States—each able by design to veto the others' agendas.

If you've already invited too many guests and given each a veto over the details, all is not lost, however. For dinner parties, there are technological fixes: you can use a scheduling app like Doodle to find workable dates; Postmates to deliver food from multiple restaurants (vegan, sushi, steak); and Venmo to collect everyone's share of the bill. Governments can do the same with ownership design for intellectual property, for example, by enabling "patent pools" and "standard setting organizations." Pools and SSOs bundle together crucial patents needed for a new technology, license them as a group, and share the proceeds pro rata among the owners. (We'll see compulsory versions of this solution with oil unitization in Chapter 4 and music licensing in Chapter 5.)

A second approach, if you've already sent the dinner invites and gotten too many yeses, is to listen to each friend's needs, give none a veto, but still offer them something. It's your party and you decide. Choosing how to compensate those who feel harmed is key to ownership design. For lawyers, this choice is often between what are called *injunctions* and *damages*. An injunction is like a veto; it blocks any further action by the harming party—if I don't get vegan, no one meets for dinner. Historically, when patents were infringed, courts would order offending products off the market, and no one got them. There was no way around a patent tollbooth if a certain patent was essential to your product. You paid the price the owner demanded or you left the market.

But vetoes are not the only way patents can motivate innovation and protect ownership. Smart design can avoid gridlock by switching protection from injunctions to damages, from vetoes to cash. If you decide to serve sushi, you can take your aggrieved vegan friend out for tofu scramble next time or give her a gift certificate to order out. Indeed, the Supreme Court decided that, in some circumstances, courts can order patent infringers to pay money damages to patent owners rather than having to remove the infringing product from the market altogether.

The best dinner party solution, though, may be to invite fewer friends initially—you'll likely have a better conversation anyway. The smaller the group of initial owners, the more likely they are to be able to reach agreement, whether it's about a dinner destination, a documentary film, or a blockbuster drug.

Perhaps Congress and the states should be cutting intellectual property rights, not expanding them. Not every innovation deserves a patent or copyright—despite what Big Pharma or Disney might argue. Less ownership up front would mean less gridlock to fix later on.

In practice, though, that's hard to achieve.

Politically, there's not much lobbying for legislation in the public interest; psychologically, no one wants to give up something they already own; and constitutionally, the Fifth Amendment protects owners from having their property taken "without just compensation." Once created, ownership is hard to roll back. It is a one-way ratchet—a reality that counsels for caution before we create even more rights. It's painful to disinvite friends from the party.

I Stole It Fair and Square

After a fashion designer strikes gold with a new look, knockoffs quickly appear on store shelves. For example, Carrie Anne Roberts, founder of the brand Mère Soeur, learned that Old Navy was copying her best-selling T-shirt "Raising the Future." Says Roberts, "I was a single mom, and the idea behind this T-shirt inspired my whole business. Now it's been stripped of all meaning, and it feels really violating."

Magazines such as *Marie Claire* and *Cosmopolitan* highlight these copies in regular "Splurge vs. Steal" features. Balenciaga comes out with a $795 sneaker; Zara immediately offers a nearly identical-looking shoe for $35.90. Taylor Swift wears a $2,675 Rick Owens biker jacket; H&M sells the knockoff for $37.80. High-end designers pay homage to each other as well. Gucci's 2018 cruise collection included a jacket copied from Harlem couturier Dapper Dan's work in the 1980s.

This is all perfectly legal. To the designers whose work is copied, copying may feel like a rip-off or theft. But it's not. Theft, like ownership itself, is a legal conclusion, not an empirical fact. In America, there's no protection for the labor that goes into fashion design. The business model of fast fashion—including global retailers like Zara and H&M—is to copy speedily what's hot and sell it for less. As a rule, in fashion, everyone copies everyone. Copying design ideas is not theft.

Every few years the Council of Fashion Designers of America lobbies politicians for its own Mickey Mouse Protection Act to provide ownership for its members' fashion design labor, thereby turning copying into theft. The council points to small, independent fashion designers like Carrie Anne Roberts to make the case, just as Disney refers back to Walt. But fashion doesn't have Disney's clout on Capitol Hill. Ariele Elia, at New York's Fashion Institute of Technology, says Congress doesn't "see ramifications, that copying hurts the industry and makes it difficult for designers to emerge."

Elia's frustration is understandable but overstated. As the line-standing and parking chair examples in Chapters 1 and 2 suggest, legal ownership can be a much less important tool than people assume—and than creators assert. Sure, designers want more reward for their labor. Producers always do. But for intellectual labor, the dominant thrust of American law, in contrast with UK and European Union law, is to reward producers only to the extent it ultimately serves consumers' interests. Would more ownership in fashion design help consumers? Probably not.

Tweeting can be more powerful than the courts. Being first to market can be decisive. Politeness and manners steer behavior. Legal ownership is just one tool for social control—a visible and salient battleground, to be sure—but it is often not the most effective way to motivate and reward creation. Nonlawyers and lawyers alike make this mistake, overvaluing law and missing effective alternatives. After all, the goal of shaping intellectual property is not to create more law, but to spur more innovation.

Kal Raustiala and Chris Sprigman have identified powerful alternatives to legal ownership that sustain creativity in the fashion world. Raustiala remarks, "Copyright has an intent behind it, and the intent is to protect creators so that they continue creating. When we looked at fashion, we saw an industry that was very, very creative and puts out tons of new ideas every season and has done that continuously for decades." All without copyright. They call this the "piracy paradox" and show that copycats actually help the fashion industry innovate.

Fashion is not a strange outlier. We explained earlier that giving zero ownership for intellectual labor may remove a producer's incentive to create. No Mickeys. No "I Have a Dream." But that's not quite right. Many economic arenas thrive with no ownership rights for producers. As Raustiala and Sprigman show, comedians do not copyright their routines; chefs do not own their recipes; sports coaches' innovative plays are all freely copied. And yet new comedy routines, recipes, and sports plays are created all the time. The piracy paradox describes many creative industries and endeavors.

Even old-school companies are increasingly recognizing the value of no ownership for intellectual labor. Take IBM, said to be the world's largest patent holder. IBM now earns less from licensing its patent portfolio than from revenues related to Linux, a so-called open-source software language that no one owns. It's created and maintained by volunteers. The intellectual labor behind Linux is free for anyone to use—including IBM, which sells hardware and services that work atop a Linux platform.

Wikipedia is perhaps the most familiar no-owner online resource, relying on donor time and money. It's such a successful piece of free intellectual labor that it displaced an entire industry. Do students today even know what an encyclopedia is? Wikipedia has become so reliable that Apple uses it to answer your random Siri questions, as does Amazon with Alexa. Indeed, much of the crucial software enabling modern life has been created with no intellectual property ownership. If you use Firefox as your browser, you are reaping where others have sown. Same with Apache, which is open-source software that may be powering your airplane or ATM.

Reaping where others have sown is a much more integral part of everyday life than people realize. How is this possible?

Lawyers and laypeople alike have a bias—an unjustified faith, really—that legal ownership matters. Often it doesn't. Creators rely on at least four strategies to make a living off their labor, even without legal protection.

The so-called *first mover advantage* is a powerful reward to creative labor and one that comes without many of the downsides of formal ownership. Coaches, for example, find it worthwhile to develop new tactics each season. Why? Because the first use of, say, tiki-taka soccer helped win games—few knew how to counter it—advancing the innovators before competing teams had time to adapt. Or the innovator gets hired by another team at a higher salary, or is paid more to stay put. Being first is often enough reward without any additional reward to labor. Michael Bloomberg built a multibillion-dollar business licensing terminals that give a fraction of a second lead time advantage on news and information relevant for trading.

Shame can also protect innovation. Comedians face the same dilemma as do fashion designers and coaches: they have no copyright protection. And as Stan Laurel once said, "All comedians steal from all comedians." So how do comedians protect themselves, if telling the joke first is not enough? They use snarky asides during stand-up routines at comedy clubs to shame joke-stealers. For example, in 2007 during a Carlos Mencia performance at the LA Comedy Store, comedian Joe Rogan ran onstage and accused him of being "Men-Steal-ia." In the close-knit community of comedians, money matters, but the real reward is the laugh, and shame makes the room go quiet (like negative truthful gossip, as discussed in Chapter 2). Shame can be a more powerful tool to reward labor than a lawsuit. It doesn't always work—Milton Berle made his career as "the thief of bad gags"—but comedians think twice before lifting material, wary of potential harm to their reputations.

In fashion today, *social media* creates a third powerful, if imperfect, reward mechanism for creators. After Carrie Anne Roberts noticed the rip-offs, her fans swung into action, panning the copied "Raising the Future" T-shirt on Old Navy's website. After days of Instagram shaming, Old Navy stopped selling the shirt and canceled further orders. Roberts was mad that her work was copied, but the David versus Goliath social media kerfuffle raised her profile higher than it had ever been. She came out far ahead.

Finally, it can make commercial sense to give away knowledge for free because it *grows the pie.* IBM gets so much value from Linux that the company willingly donates millions of dollars of its engineers' time to maintain and improve the software. The better Linux performs, the more IBM can make by selling its services layered on top. So it contributes even though Linux benefits IBM's competitors as well. Linux continues to improve, but no one owns it.

Entire industries thrive in a no-ownership world through these strategies—first mover advantages, shaming, social media, and growing the pie. None of these tools is perfect. Shaming can lead to violence; social media can become mob rule. Each tool for rewarding labor has advantages and limits. But that's true for law as well.

And when creators do rely on law to counter copying, enforcement is often counterproductive. For years, the recording industry went around suing students so they wouldn't download music without paying. But much of this litigation backfired. Suing your customers is not a great marketing strategy. The exception was when the band Metallica sued Napster, the music-sharing website, because, as the band's drummer aptly put it, "They f—ked with us. We'll f—k with them." Metallica's fans reacted well to their band's in-your-face approach.

Even industries heavily fortified with intellectual property often decide they benefit from tolerating theft. As we described earlier, HBO knows that people are sharing its passwords illegally—and sees it as a good thing. The company doesn't mind having its pockets picked because sharing creates a new generation of HBO "video addicts," as the company's president described its illicit viewers. When these viewers are older and wealthier, HBO believes they will pay for their own accounts. Tolerating theft is a long-term investment. In the meantime, theft creates valuable buzz for the network's shows.

Surprisingly, tolerating theft can also benefit makers of luxury goods. Yves Saint Laurent prints its trademarked logo all over its handbags, and Rolex emblazons its watches. But zealously enforcing trademark protection may not always be a good strategy. The tourists buying fake YSL bags and Rolexes from shady vendors in Times Square are not taking sales away from legit stores—but they are teaching young consumers what they should aspire to. Fakes can be the best free advertising. Buyers of counterfeit luxury goods can form a pipeline of future customers for the real deal. One study found that 40 percent of people who bought counterfeit luxury goods ended up buying the high-end version after their trial run with the cheap fake. Other research has shown that for many luxury brands, tolerating a market in fakes increases the value of the original.

Even the Disney Company, the most incorrigible copyright-hoarder, may be coming around. The Very Important Babies Daycare spat was pivotal. The terrible press Disney received—compared with the publicity bonanza for Universal Studios—perhaps moved Disney to rethink its ownership strategy.

The original Mickey Mouse copyright expires in 2024, and Disney has not geared up to buy itself another extension from Congress. How could that be? Isn't it always cheaper just to pay lobbyists and make a few targeted campaign contributions? The roughly $100 million the company spent on prior extensions has paid off many times over. But Disney has found an even better ownership design strategy, one that lets it profit more by relying less on copyright: it adopted HBO's pro-theft stance.

Disney now unofficially tolerates hundreds of small online shops run by die-hard fans selling T-shirts, buttons, pins, patches, jewelry, and thousands more items that leverage Disney characters. These stores don't pay Disney a dime in licensing fees. Why the pivot to tolerating knockoffs? Because Disney learned that fan-made, unlicensed twenty-five-dollar T-shirts drive their wearers to Disney parks, where they buy expensive entrance tickets and pass the day spending even more money.

Another reason for Disney's newfound tolerance: it has discovered the marketing research value from the hundreds of small knockoff shops. These shops turn out to be a vibrant source of ideas for new official Disney merchandise. In 2016 the online vendor Bibbidi Bobbidi Brooke came out with a hugely popular line of rose-gold sequined Mickey ears, something that had not occurred to the Disney licensors. So Disney copied the design, which sold out immediately in its official stores. Bibbidi Bobbidi Brooke was gracious, posting "always excited to see new merch offerings." Her fans replied, "Yours will always be the original!!!" Everyone wins.

"I still don't think they're interested in letting anyone build a multimillion-dollar business, but they are much more understanding of the role that fan engagement plays," one intellectual property professor said of Disney's new approach. "As the record industry found out, it looks bad to sue your fans if they're doing it because they are your fans."

In many places in our economy, the real rule is *I reap what you sow,* yet innovation proceeds apace. Even when no one can claim ownership, people find ways to make creative labor worthwhile. Copying, sharing, and tolerated theft are key engines of growth. The question is not Should we increase copyright protections for fashion? With fashion as our guide, the question should be Where else can we eliminate legal ownership for intellectual labor?

The Wild West of Genetic Data

We wrap up with a puzzle. How should we own our genetic data? Kristen Brown, a Bloomberg reporter, mailed out a dozen saliva samples as part of her story-writing research. For an article on her ethnic heritage, she mailed spit to Ancestry.com and 23andMe; for insight into her athletic ability, diet, and sleep patterns, she sent a sample to Helix; for a genetically tailored beauty regime, she uploaded her DNA data to a cosmetics start-up.

Then she had second thoughts.

Brown realized she had given away unlimited commercial access to her genetic secrets. And she had indirectly exposed her relatives without their permission. Today roughly two of every three Americans of northern European heritage can be individually identified because a different family member has sent in a sample. Soon genetic data companies may well be able to identify just about everyone's most intimate traits—not only your predisposition to diseases, but also perhaps your longevity, athletic prowess, and many other variables—whether you've mailed in spit or not.

Control over genetic data raises questions beyond personal privacy and dignity, though those matter, too. As people submit more DNA, the commercial value of gene databases grows exponentially. Medical data licensing has become a multibillion-dollar business. GlaxoSmithKline paid 23andMe $300 million to access data for targeted drug development. 23andMe went one step further, developing an anti-inflammatory drug based on its data. The company already has over 9 million individual profiles; the industry as a whole has over 25 million. There are ever-growing fortunes at stake.

Brown decided to retrieve her genetic data. But could she take it back? Alternatively, could she get a share of the money earned by database companies licensing her data? Ownership of genetic data is contested, ambiguous, and does not define itself—just like every other valuable new resource. As Brown reported, trying to disentangle her individual data from gene databases was "brutally difficult." Ultimately, she failed.

How about you? Are you one of the millions who has swabbed

your cheek and sent off a sample? Any second thoughts? Has a family member sold you out? Here are some options for who owns your genetic data after you send the sample:

- No legal ownership, keep data free.
- Database assemblers own the data.
- Individuals keep ownership of their genetic data.
- Assemblers and individuals share ownership.

Today genetic data is the Wild West of ownership design, with innovation racing ahead of the rules. We could decide to leave data free—as with fashion, jokes, and sports plays. Perhaps a no-ownership world creates more value than the rules that lawmakers would likely impose. But who benefits from this value?

For 23andMe and its industry cohort, no-ownership would be fine: the companies do not need law to reward their labor. Nor do they rely on shaming and first mover advantages as in fast fashion conflicts. Instead, they can use *secrecy* and *scale* to control genetic resources without ownership.

Secrecy is straightforward: the industry doesn't publish its gene databases; it licenses access instead. Here secrecy substitutes for copyright; it can replace patents, too. For example, Elon Musk, founder of SpaceX, says, "We have essentially no patents. Our primary long-term competition is China. If we published patents, it would be farcical, because the Chinese would just use them as a recipe book." Savvy entrepreneurs often rely on discretion, not law.

Scale also matters, wholly apart from ownership. In the past, identifying new drug targets was cumbersome and costly, requiring scientists to observe actual patients. Now they can get better results faster by combining large private gene databases with people's confidential insurance and medical records—and potentially other records, like those generated by fitness trackers, cell phones, and browsing histories. Myriad Genetics learned the value of scale a few years back

when the Supreme Court invalidated the company's gene test patents for breast cancer. If you thought Myriad's market would disappear as soon as the patent was invalidated, you would be wrong. Myriad discovered it didn't need patents to fend off competition because the company already controlled access to the largest breast cancer mutation database. With its head start in collecting samples, the database now lets the company detect a wider range of mutations than competitors are able to find—and charge for the information.

As databases scale up, they can become exponentially more valuable. The key is to grow the database fast. This is why 23andMe decodes your heritage for just $99: your genetic information is raw material for the real product, its database.

To preserve the Wild West regime, the industry has been working to fend off ownership regulation. In a savvy move, companies like 23andMe decided not to fight Brown and others like her. Gene companies have learned the lessons of Napster and music streaming, of HBO and password sharing. Don't hassle your customers; find less irritating ways to extract value from scarce human resources. In the genetic data market, existing companies already have all the advantage they need. Their scale deters new competitors; their secrecy is hard to pierce; and social media tweets don't inflict much shame.

One industry strategy is to foster the illusion of individual ownership. 23andMe realized it was better off disclaiming ownership in Brown's data. The company did not want to provoke Brown to feel her self-ownership was violated—*It's mine because it came from my body* (see Chapter 5). Provocation can lead to activism, and activism can catalyze legislation. Better, instead, to keep your raw material suppliers happy while they swab and swipe.

When Brown tried to retrieve the spit samples she had mailed in, the companies readily agreed . . . in principle. In practice, though, 23andMe told Brown the procedures needed to delete physical samples were "not currently available." And Ancestry.com told her no one had ever asked to have their spit returned. Turns out, the gene companies are warehousing the spit. Perhaps one day new sequencing techniques will let them unlock even more data from those stored samples.

How about retrieving the already-existing DNA data? Many genetic data companies readily concede the data is yours, perhaps to avoid triggering your attachment intuition, the idea that *It's mine because it's attached to something mine* (see Chapter 4). If you want data deleted, fine—in principle. In practice, though, Brown reports, "23andMe may tell you that you can delete your data, but in reality, the law says you can't." Scrubbing data is impossible in part because of record-keeping obligations on health care testing labs. "The 'minimal amount' of information the company was required to keep on hand," Brown found, "was, essentially, all of my raw genetic information." And after your DNA profile has been assembled into the database and licensed out to third parties, you have no real way to retrieve your data. "When you delete your DNA information, you are mainly hiding your information from yourself," Brown concluded.

Instead of asserting ownership of DNA profiles, the data industry has focused on securing binding permission to use your information—that is, it shifted from *ownership* to *contract,* another realm where industry exercises masterful design control. When you submit spit, gene companies ask you to check an "I consent" box. Nobody ever reads the underlying agreement. But that one simple click gives the genetic data industry all the rights it needs, even without ownership. You may own the data or the company may own it. No one knows. With a binding contract, it doesn't matter.

On the Ancestry.com form, your click grants the company "a sublicensable, worldwide, royalty-free license to host, store, copy, publish, distribute, provide access to, create derivative works of, and otherwise use" your genetic data. That's a lot. More than 80 percent of Ancestry.com customers check the box, letting the company sell or share their data. According to 23andMe, "The average customer who chooses to let 23andMe share their data for research contributes to more than 230 studies on topics including asthma, lupus, and Parkinson's disease."

And what happens if the gene database leads to a cure? You have no stake. As one commentator notes, "You can't go to them later and say, 'Hey you need to compensate me for this blockbuster drug that you developed using my data.'" When you click "I consent," contract takes over—without ever clarifying the underlying data ownership. We contribute our seeds of data, those seeds grow, and someone else reaps.

At present, Americans have few protections for how their data are used. The 2008 Genetic Information Nondiscrimination Act (GINA) restricts how health insurers and big employers can use DNA data. But other types of insurers—such as long-term care, disability, and life insurance—are not covered. They may be able to discriminate against individuals based on genetic information gleaned from another family member's spit. And companies with fewer than fifteen employees, along with the entire U.S. military, are altogether exempt from GINA's genetic discrimination protections in the employment sphere. The rules for DNA ownership and use reflect a complex and rapidly changing patchwork of federal and state laws. Some states are increasing levels of individual protection, while industry is pushing to cut already-limited rights—as they find ever more uses for personal data, from solving cold case murders to marketing toothpaste.

European regulators take a different approach, focusing on protecting *privacy* rather than divvying up *ownership*. With its 2018 General Data Protection Regulation, the European Union gives its citizens the "right to be forgotten": more concretely, in the DNA context, the right to have one's gene sample destroyed and data deleted—what Brown was seeking. In the United States, states like California are at the forefront of protecting individual privacy rights in sensitive data. These rights work somewhat like the Knee Defender we discussed in the Introduction—they are meant to keep industry from leaning its DNA databases into your virtual lap.

The industry is delighted to frame the debate around either this emerging privacy approach or its existing contract permission strategy. Both let you say no and be (more or less) forgotten. With forethought and effort, you may be able to cut yourself out from the databases. But excluding one DNA profile, or even ten thousand, is largely costless to the industry so long as it controls the real prize, the millions-strong databases of people who did not realize the stakes in deciding whether to check "I agree."

Reframing control of genetic data in ownership terms, though, has an important virtue that the privacy and contract stories lack. Ownership design can help highlight the "yes, if you pay me" option, not just the "no, leave me alone" default. Having the yes option treats us with dignity, respecting our status as free individuals empowered to make important choices regarding our most intimate resources. And not incidentally, industry itself may even benefit from having an aboveboard, transparent self-ownership regime (as we'll explore in Chapter 5). As *New York Times* columnist Eduardo Porter notes, "If people were paid for their data, its quality and value would increase."

Today people of northern European heritage are heavily overrepresented in gene databases. They are the ones who buy DNA-based cosmetics, fitness, and ancestry profiles. Historically excluded communities of color are substantially absent from these databases—and by extension, from medical research and discoveries that might benefit them. If the baseline ownership rule were that 23andMe paid people for data, instead of the reverse, perhaps we would see more diverse contributors and more inclusive drug development.

But if our goal is to advance a "yes, if you pay me" story, watch out: industry pros are often better than ordinary citizens at the ownership design game. As we've seen, Disney and its allies dominate Congress on copyright; companies like King Inc. and CMG Worldwide rule the states on the right of publicity. The data industry stands ready to write federal database copyright rules and state-by-state trade secret laws (these are additional emerging entrants in the limited list of allowable ownership forms). You can predict the industry story: we should reap where we have sown; our productive labor should be the root of ownership; genetic databases save lives; individual ownership will create gridlock; and so on. And the industry's story has a point. But it's not the only story.

The design challenge is to balance the competing claims of individual genetic self-ownership and attachment with industry labor. That's not an easy feat for Congress to achieve, but neither is it an impossible one.

In the meantime, alternatives are bubbling up. On the public side, there are efforts to create a *genetic commons*—freely available genetic databases that are large and diverse enough to turbocharge medical research and help diagnose rare diseases. On the market side, start-ups have begun offering contributors a stake in the aggregated value of their genetic data. "You can't say data is valuable and then take that data away from everybody," says Dawn Barry, a co-founder of one of these start-ups. Twenty days of data from a fitness tracker is worth two of Barry's shares, valued at 14 cents; a 23andMe–style test earns you $3.50 in shares; your whole genome nets you $21. People cash in if the start-up shares do well—thus reversing the cash flow from the 23andMe model.

But the stock ownership model has downsides, too. It's meaningfully available only to the handful of sophisticated consumers who search it out, prefer stock to cheap testing, and deliberately *opt in* to this ownership relationship. Most people keep on mailing in 23andMe and Ancestry.com kits, clicking "I consent," and getting no direct compensation (though there may be some indirect compensation if it costs companies more to test than consumers pay). True, consumers can *opt out* of inclusion in genetic databases, but few do. And—more important—we have no simple way to link our individual contributions with valuable medical discoveries that come from aggregating our samples.

Designing *opt-in* and *opt-out* rules is a notable part of ownership design, and it works in tandem with strategic choices about *ownership baselines*—the automatic defaults that people come to see as the ordinary, natural, and correct use of scarce resources. It is hard to overstate how important it is to capture the baseline: it means your ownership story wins, and competing stories soon seem deviant.

One hundred years ago, standing pools of water were mosquito-breeding *swamps*. Landowners would naturally fill them in. Today, those same pools are ecologically sensitive *wetlands*. Owners can be required to protect them in their natural state. Swamp or wetland is solely a matter of where we set the ownership baseline.

What if we switched the ownership baseline for our DNA? We could set an automatic default rule such that everyone who contributes genetic data—not just the savviest—owns a small share in medical discoveries derived from their genetic data. Companies like 23andMe could still offer cash today in exchange for a future ownership share, but the opt-out transaction would have to be deliberate and transparent, not buried in "I agree" licensing gibberish.

We have been able to change the baseline in other ownership contexts. Employees save more for retirement if employers are required to set the baseline at automatic deductions. People must affirmatively opt out if they want cash now. Few do, so tax-favored retirement savings grow. If the baseline is no automatic deductions, fewer opt in and savings lag. Similarly, organ donations go up when the baseline is that drivers are donors. If they don't like that choice, drivers may opt out when they renew their licenses. With a no-donation baseline, relatively few opt in. (In Chapter 5, we explore additional solutions for organ shortages based in self-ownership.) These behavioral asymmetries around ownership baselines and opt-in versus opt-out rules are the engine that drive what Cass Sunstein and Richard Thaler have called the "nudge" lever in policy making.

The conflict between individual self-ownership and industry labor arises every day—it's not just genes. Our phones help marketers (and law enforcement) compile databases of our every location; omnipresent cameras feed facial recognition databases; most valuable of all, our every online move creates a clickstream of trackable data.

Think about how much personal information you provide Google with as a by-product of your searches. Or what you reveal by clicking "like" on Facebook. Collecting, analyzing, and selling this data is truly what drives the Internet economy. In 2018, insights into American's desires, attitudes, and activities online were worth an estimated $76 billion—if just half of that revenue were shared with individuals, each would receive a check for $122. Shoshana Zuboff has named this business model "surveillance capitalism." As one economist puts it bluntly: "Imagine if General Motors did not pay for its steel, rubber or glass—its inputs. That's what it's like for the big internet companies. It's a sweet deal." This is why so many apps are free. But as tech articles repeat: when the app is free, you are the product.

The Wild West of no-ownership works for fashion, jokes, and sports plays, but not so well for genes, locations, faces, and clickstreams. What's the difference? Perhaps it's that all these types of data share a common thread, one central to ownership design today: individually they count for little, but collectively they are worth everything. Online industries prefer to stick with the Wild West. If you disagree, then it's time to speak up.

Chapter 4

MY HOME IS
NOT MY CASTLE

Three Blasts of Number 8 Birdshot

William Merideth was in his Kentucky home on a summer day in 2015 when his daughters came in from the backyard. The girls said, "Dad, there's a drone out here, flying over everybody's yard." This did not sit well with Dad.

"I came out and it was down by the neighbor's house, about 10 feet off the ground, looking under their canopy that they've got in their backyard," Merideth described. "I went and got my shotgun and I said, 'I'm not going to do anything unless it's directly over my property.'"

It didn't take long for the drone to cross his property line. "Within a minute or so, here it came," he said. "It was hovering over top of my property, and I shot it out of the sky." He downed the $1,800 drone with three blasts of number 8 birdshot. A few minutes later John David Boggs, the drone's owner, appeared and asked, "Are you the son of a bitch that shot my drone?" Merideth, wearing a 10mm Glock holstered on his hip, replied, "If you cross that sidewalk onto my property, there's going to be another shooting." Boggs had the presence of mind to call the police, and Merideth was arrested for wanton endangerment.

The arrest perplexed the #droneslayer, as Merideth soon began calling himself. "It was hovering; I would never have shot it if it was flying." As he put it, "It would have been no different had he been standing in my backyard. As Americans, we have a right to defend our rights and property." Merideth was also puzzled that firing a shotgun in a residential area might be any kind of problem: "Now, if I'd have had a .22 rifle, I should have gone to jail for that. The diameter of those things are going to come down with enough force to hurt somebody. Number 8 birdshot is not. Number 8 is the size of a pinhead. The bottom line is that it's a . . . defending my property issue."

At trial, Boggs produced video evidence proving the craft had been flying above two hundred feet when it was shot down. Despite the video, Merideth testified that the drone was hovering below the tree line. The Bullitt County judge sided with Merideth and dismissed all charges. The decision made national news because it suggested suburban homeowners could fire away at drones—a surprising possibility. In the United States, as a general matter, landowners are entitled to sue trespassers, not shoot them.

But was Merideth correct even in saying the drone was trespassing?

The answer turns on the principle of attachment, a primitive, powerful, and often-overlooked basis for ownership. As we use the term, *attachment* describes the intuition that *It's mine because it's attached to something mine.* Drones raise the same conflict we saw with the Knee Defender in the Introduction. Your boarding pass describes a seat number—like 10C—the two-dimensional plane of fake leather where you plant your bottom. The seat number does not resolve conflicts over the wedge of space where the seat reclines, nor the contested terrain around armrests. For that you need an additional principle, one that makes ownership three-dimensional. Attachment is that principle.

When you buy land, it's a lot like getting a boarding pass. Your deed outlines the boundaries of a flat plane you can locate on a map, like "Lot 10 in the Aspen Hills Subdivision." But when you stand on your parcel, the deed does not tell you whether your ownership extends to the "droneways" above, the groundwater below, or the deer bounding by. These plausibly connected new and existing resources are the terrain where the intuition of attachment operates. For most of history, few people paid precise attention to just how much they owned far above or deep beneath, because it didn't much matter. Ownership conflicts mostly took place close to the surface, where people lived and worked.

Old-fashioned intuitions of ownership don't work well for drones. Unlike airplanes, drones roam unpredictably. They can hover near the ground, peep into windows, or listen from outside; they may even be armed. Merideth had an expansive view of attachment, arguing that Boggs's drone had crossed over an invisible fence that extended high above his two-dimensional property. "You know, when you're in your own property, within a six-foot privacy fence, you have the expectation of privacy," he said. "To me, it was the same as trespassing."

Merideth's claim has deep roots. As far back as the thirteenth century, landownership was said to extend in a column "up to the heavens and down to hell." That expansive notion becomes even more robust around our homes. In 1628 Sir Edward Coke, the great codifier of Anglo-American common law, wrote, "A man's house is his castle." When you combine the column "up to the heavens" with "home as castle," you may arrive at Merideth's view.

But old maxims are just that. Maxims. They were never the law. Our invisible castle walls never expanded in a lighthouse beam up into outer space; nor did they converge down to a point deep below. The rhetorical power of ownership maxims always exceeds their legal force. One hundred years ago, at the dawn of commercial aviation, airplane overflights were a lively debate. Some landowners asserted "column" and "castle" to say airplanes were trespassing high over their homes, and they demanded payment for permission to cross.

Courts quickly rejected unlimited attachment: it would have grounded a transformative industry. The reason you can't shoot down airplanes above your property is not that you lack the appropriate surface-to-air missile. It's that when countries needed unimpeded highways in the sky, courts and legislators examined our competing ownership intuitions and decided ownership of land should not extend thousands of feet up.

The boundaries of claims based on attachment are constantly shifting as new technologies, population growth, and increased scarcity force us to rethink ownership. Amazon, UPS, and Domino's see a future where drones efficiently deliver packages and pizza. Whether drone delivery becomes a viable industry is partly a technological problem, but at this point, it is primarily a question of ownership design. Drone delivery works most easily if drones can cross above people's land. So should attachment or some other ownership principle decide control of droneways? Where do we draw the boundary between private land and public access? As far up as you can shoot an arrow, fire a gun, or launch a missile?

When Merideth says, "The bottom line is that it's a defending my property issue," he is making an aspirational claim. Drone-crossing airspace two hundred feet up is Merideth's property only if we decide it should be so, otherwise not.

It's the same debate with sunlight and wind, which are increasingly contested and valuable renewable energy commodities. When your neighbors' trees shade your solar panels, or their windmills disturb your air flow, are they taking property from you? Everything you own above your land is a distinct choice—perhaps implied and shaped by medieval maxims, British traditions, and American practice, but not commanded by them. It's all up in the air, as it were.

And the same is true going down into the earth. Your deed does not tell you which belowground resources are yours alone, are shared with neighbors, or belong to the public. Water flows in great aquifers, oil pools in large fields, and hard rock minerals meander in veins. With the rise of fracking and other extraction technologies, conflicts for belowground resources are becoming ever sharper. Resolving these conflicts turns on the varying choices we make about the attachment principle. These choices are always in flux.

With one exception. So far as we know, every legal system for all recorded history follows a *rule of increase* regarding farm animals, in which the owner of the mother owns the offspring. According to the ancient Laws of Manu, "Should a bull beget a hundred calves on cows not owned by his master, those calves belong solely to the owners of the cows; and the strength of the bull was wasted." This rule has remained constant from four thousand years ago in India to everywhere in the world today.

Why? Newborns quickly reveal their mothers, while paternity is uncertain. Moreover, the calf depends on its mother for survival, so uniting them in ownership most likely ensures the calf's survival. Every factor that goes into ownership design points here in a single direction. As one legal scholar summarized, the rule gives "a reward to planned production; is simple, certain, and economical to administer; fits in with existing human and animal habits and forces; and appeals to the sense of fairness of human beings in many places and generations."

If newborn farm animals are the easiest case—humanity's only universal attachment rule—then the boundaries of landownership may be the hardest. All the variables of ownership design are in constant conflict. More and more, landowners feel as if they are under siege from above and below and—as we will see—from the sides and within. But this is no surprise. Our attachment intuitions are often far from ownership reality. Ownership does not reach to heaven and hell. Your home is not your castle.

Ramblers and Gold Diggers

Nor is your country estate your castle, even if you are a celebrity couple like Madonna and Guy Ritchie.

In England, the right to roam has long been contested. A legendary incident galvanized the rambling community: in 1932 young factory workers in Manchester gathered by Kinder Scout, a mountain in the Peak District. Angered by a gamekeeper who had chased some of them off a few days before, hundreds of ramblers set off together to climb Kinder Scout. Cowed by the large number of trespassers, the gamekeepers gave way and the workers climbed the peak. On their way down, six leaders were arrested and five eventually sent to prison.

This mass act of civil disobedience led to a long struggle, resulting in an Act of Parliament in 2000 creating a right to roam. It was a victory, though only a partial one: the right applies in eight percent of the country. But the battle to extend the right to roam continues.

The highest profile encounter occurred in Dorset, where planning authorities determined that 380 acres of the £9 million country estate owned by the pop singer, Madonna, and film director, Guy Ritchie, would be accessible to the public. The couple challenged the decision and won a reduction on appeal, opening up 100 acres of the 1,200 acre estate.

By contrast with England, Scotland recognizes an ancient "right to roam." Ramblers have the right to wander over many private lands and sometimes even camp there. Many northern European countries offer a similar right. In Sweden, the national constitution specifically grants the freedom of *allemansrätten*, or "freedom to roam." In a clever publicity stunt, in 2017 the Swedish tourism board listed the entire country on Airbnb, citing the "Swedish law that gives all people the right to be free in Swedish nature." In countries that recognize the right, ramblers haven't needed permission to walk through, and sometimes forage on, rural uncultivated land.

For most of American history, foragers have been free to enter others' land and take away the wild plants they encountered. They weren't being sneaky; foraging wasn't theft. They had a right to roam that included using others' land. Historically, mushroom hunters, raspberry pickers, cherrystone clam diggers—and gun-wielding hunters—haven't needed permission to enter rural land that was not fenced, cultivated, or posted with no trespassing signs.

And this makes sense. In early America, wild-caught food was an important nutritional resource. So states favored labor and possession (*I worked hard to gather those wild raspberries*) over attachment (*Those raspberries are mine because they're attached to my land*). That right to roam was the universal rule at America's founding—a deliberate anti-aristocratic rebuke to England, which reserved rich hunting and foraging lands for large landholders and the Crown.

But times change. As we discussed in the Introduction, the invention of barbed wire in the late 1800s upended the meaning of landownership in America. Barbed wire was a cheap way to send a powerful message: *It's my land—and, by the way, the stuff on it is mine too. Keep out!* But people can climb barbed-wire fences or cut through them. So landowners pushed to change the law as well, using the attachment principle to create an invisible fence. Today the landowners' story has prevailed in half the states, and it's the growing trend. In those states, foragers and hunters are trespassers, even on unfenced, unposted land. The raspberries, clams, and deer belong exclusively to the landowners where the resource was harvested or shot.

The state of Maine hangs in the balance. Thomas Saviello, a Maine state senator, proposed a bill to ban foraging without permission. "This, to me, is a no brainer," he explained. "If you own the land, it's not my right to go onto your property and take something that belongs to you." What Saviello missed, though, is that foraging is theft only if the state decides to favor the landowner's attachment claim over the forager's competing claims rooted in labor and possession. Will the state stick with American tradition or join the new majority? Saviello's bill has stalled for now, but American law increasingly favors organized landowners over dispersed foragers and hunters.

Greg Corliss was grading the driveway for a new guesthouse on the Sun Valley ranch of Jann Wenner, owner of *Rolling Stone*. Greg looked down at the dirt and shouted to Larry Anderson, his friend and boss, "Larry—look, gold!" Larry ordered, "Put 'em in your pocket—we could split 'em." It was Greg and Larry's lucky day. They had just found ninety-six half eagles, eagles, and double eagles—gold coins minted between 1857 and 1914 and worth about $25,000 when they dug them up. A century back, when Sun Valley was a ragged mining outpost, someone had buried the coins in a mason jar and never returned for them. Greg shouted, "We'll get a reward! We are going to be on the cover of *Rolling Stone*!"

"Shut up," Larry muttered. "This is between you and me."

Larry held on to the coins while they considered what to do. Eventually, Greg demanded half the find. Larry worried Greg might resort to violence. Everyone talked. The story became Sun Valley gossip. Eventually, Larry handed the coins over to Wenner; Greg sued Larry; then both sued Wenner. As one local mining engineer said, "How dumb were these guys? Obviously, you split 'em and the split buys the other guy's silence—because Jann Wenner needs more money like a hole in the head."

The drama arose because Larry and Greg couldn't keep quiet.

Initially, Wenner offered Greg and Larry a big finders' reward. But he withdrew the offer when the lawsuits started, saying, "Greg Corliss is a ne'er-do-well who's milking this for all it's worth. He's a liar and an asshole." In reply, Greg was surprisingly understanding. "If you're wealthy, and some dickhead who found coins in your driveway is suing you—I can see Jann's side."

Fights over treasure troves go way back. People have been sparring over buried loot for millennia. In England, troves went to the Crown, even when found on private property. Today finders may receive half the value if they disclose the find—and jail time if they don't. When America was founded, states intentionally took an anti-aristocracy stance, as with the right to roam: treasure went to the finder, not to the landowner. Idaho followed this lead when it became a state in the 1860s. State law favored the fortune seeker. Even if you find treasure on someone else's land, it's yours, just like wild animals and plants.

Greg and Larry argued the state should stick with this tradition: it should reward the searchers, or treasure will stay buried or hidden, and everyone loses. This is an *ex ante* argument like the one we made regarding the Barry Bonds home run ball: award ownership to create incentives for future treasure seekers. Wenner countered by invoking the attachment principle: ne'er-do-wells should not be free to come onto his land and take away buried stuff, especially if they are his employees.

Judge James May, in the Idaho district court, sided with Wenner. He ruled the possessor of the land gets the gold, thus aligning Idaho law with what has become the majority rule in American states. Today landowners and employers (like Wenner) usually beat finders and employees (like Greg and Larry). We've circled back toward England.

Double eagles and foragers in Maine may be unusual cases, but the same rules that govern them operate everywhere—even in the realm of ideas. With copyright law, Congress legislated that the copyright holder automatically controls a host of additional rights—they attach to the original work. If you write a book, you own derivative rights, like the right to adapt the work into a play. The same attachment rules work for inventors: certain rights to improve on an invention attach to the owner of the original patent—even if those improvements would not qualify for patent protection on their own.

Attachment even drives recent heated controversies over cultural appropriation. Eighteen-year-old Keziah Daum tweeted a photo of herself at the prom wearing a traditional Chinese dress. The post went viral, and not in a good way. Jeremy Lam retweeted her post, writing, "My culture is NOT your goddamn prom dress." Daum felt she was engaging in cultural appreciation, not appropriation of something attached to, and therefore owned by, another. She explained, "My intention was to show my admiration for this culture." But the attacks on social media accused her of theft. Similar charges have been made about foods (Korean tacos), hairstyles (white people with cornrows), songs (Avril Lavigne's Japanese-themed "Hello Kitty" video), dance (non-Arabs belly dancing), parties (fraternities hosting Cinco de Mayo celebrations), and many other examples. E-mails from deans cautioning against cultural appropriation have become routine on campuses every October as Halloween approaches.

Companies also get involved in these disputes, as when Urban Outfitters marketed Navajo Print Fabric Wrapped Flasks and Navajo Hipster Panties. The Navajo Nation sued. Urban Outfitters won a round in court but then settled, with both sides agreeing to collaborate on a line of Native American jewelry.

Similar battles arise around biopiracy, when companies develop products without paying the indigenous and tribal peoples who identified special value hidden in local plants or animals. To give an example, French researchers patented a compound derived from a plant, *Quassia amara,* after they learned the traditional local culture of French Guiana relied on it for its antimalarial properties. The company's claim is based on productive labor; the community's on attachment.

All these conflicts reflect tensions between dominant and minority cultures: To what extent should communities own their traditional dress, food, art, and knowledge because it is closely connected to, and in part defines, the group? Whose stories count, and who decides what's theft? These are fights over the boundaries of attachment.

Attachment's Magnetic Pull

Attachment is a powerful core intuition for ownership. It's the principle that translates an airplane boarding pass into my wedge of space; a land deed into control of my crops, trees, animals, wind, solar, water, oil, gas, and countless more resources. Through attachment, the owner of an existing thing—whether land, cow, or copyright—comes to own new things plausibly connected to the original. But why is this so?

At the most basic level, we need straightforward rules that assign initial ownership of newly valuable resources. This helps keep people from fighting with each other too much in the scramble to claim the unowned. That's true not just for calves and buried treasure but also for drone flyways and fracked oil. For newly emerging resources, we often lack any preexisting rule at all. Attachment often fills that vacuum, first in practice, then as a matter of law.

Every ownership rule has pros and cons, winners and losers. Attachment is powerful in part because it can be cheap to administer and easy to understand: simply award the new resource to the owner of the already-existing, visibly attached one. The calf goes to the owner of the cow.

As Tom Merrill, the leading proponent of this broad view of attachment, explains, the principle addresses a key ownership design question: Who is likely to be the most productive manager of new resources? Existing owners of connected resources are at least as likely to be competent as any other plausible claimants. If adaptation rights don't attach to the book author, then someone has to figure out where else they should go. A simple attachment rule keeps disputes out of court. No judge has to parse who was the first in time to write the play. Or who penned the best adaptation. All they need ask is, did the owner of the book copyright authorize this adaptation?

But is attachment fair? Often, no. That's a big downside. As Merrill emphasizes, the principle "has built into its very operation a set of doctrines that mean the rich get richer." Wealth concentration does not always result, but attachment tends in this direction. If we grant new resources to established owners, there can be a multiplier effect where "those who already have significant property continually get more." Wenner, the landowner, got gold he knew nothing about and had no expectation of receiving. Attachment awarded him a windfall. Finders get nothing, not even a reward, so they are likely to dig less and hide more.

Attachment works like a magnet, attracting new resources to existing owners and repelling everyone else. The losers are the foragers and hunters, scavengers and clam-diggers, bird watchers and trappers, hikers and snowmobilers, screenwriters and garage tinkerers, and all the others who labor productively to find, uncover, and develop new useful resources.

With land, the trend is toward attachment and away from rewarding first-in-time, possession, and productive labor. Attachment is easy to explain. It often just feels right—especially to existing landowners. True, attachment doesn't always win, especially if there are sufficiently powerful advocates on the opposing side. Drones remain an open contest. Merideth argues for an expansive version of attachment, while delivery companies push for a different ownership story. But when attachment becomes the ownership baseline—when it starts to seem natural and inevitable—then it pushes aside our other stories. First-in-time, possession, and labor are cast as deviant exceptions instead of equally worthy choices.

People may complain about wealth inequality in America—everyone can point to causes, from tax policy to racial discrimination. But few think about the role of attachment, the ownership mechanism that tends to concentrate ownership in fewer and wealthier hands.

Dry Wells and Sticky Staircases

Charlie Pitigliano's grandfather, an Italian immigrant, moved to California's Central Valley in the 1920s. The land he bought was fertile, to be sure, but the real draw was the vast source of ancient groundwater that lay beneath. Farmers owned this water according to the attachment rule of the day. They could irrigate their fields with as much as they could pump. So they pumped, and pumped.

Today there are one hundred thousand wells across the Valley, watering farms that provide a third of the country's vegetables and two-thirds of its fruit and nuts. The next time you eat an almond, odds are it was grown in the Valley. The same is likely true for your next grape, asparagus stalk, pistachio nut, and other pricey items in the grocery produce section. Farmers like Pitigliano have pumped their way into your supermarket. Groundwater helped make the Valley the most valuable agricultural area in the world.

But there's a tragic flaw in this cornucopia—a flaw based entirely on badly designed attachment rules. When water was plentiful, attachment worked fine—as do most ownership rules when there's plenty to go around. But with scarcity, unlimited pumping proved disastrous. Decade after decade, farmers extracted groundwater faster than the aquifer could replenish it. Over time, the water table dropped, the soil compacted, and the land started to sink. In parts of the Central Valley, the land surface has dropped twenty-eight feet since the 1920s. Streets cracked, bridges buckled.

When farmers chase down a retreating water table, there are predictable consequences: the water table keeps on dropping, eventually falling below existing wells. This vicious cycle hit the small town of Monson, thirty-five miles from the Pitigliano farm, especially hard. The poor Latino farmworkers who live in Monson still have water beneath their homes and trailers, but they have no money to pay for drilling the ever deeper wells needed to reach the falling water table. One well could cost a year's salary.

During the most recent drought—one that lasted for six years— nearly one thousand wells started running dry in Tulare County, an area in the Valley the size of Connecticut. With a gurgle and then an ominous hiss, the water would stop flowing. Gladys Colunga, a mother of six in Tulare whose well ran dry, blames the farmers' pumping. "I understand that they need to get their crops as well, but then we're a family, we have children and we need that water. I mean, we can live without a TV, we can live without cellphones, but we can't live without water."

Dominic Pitigliano, the current operator of the family farm, spent over a million dollars putting in new wells to reach the water table, some one thousand feet down. It's expensive to keep chasing the receding water, but Pitigliano felt he had no choice: "You don't want to lose everything you've put your heart and soul into your whole life just disappear because you sat on your hands." Almond trees and the other crops need water, so farmers continue to pump. Each farmer takes advantage of individual water rights; collectively, they deplete the aquifer.

Groundwater pumping is a problem not just in California's Central Valley—strong attachment rules lead to a crisis anywhere water becomes scarce. Across America, landowners are sucking their neighbors' wells dry. These dilemmas may not be familiar to big-city dwellers who rely on piped water, but it's a constant concern for tens of millions who depend on well water.

Consider Bart Sipriano, a homeowner in Henderson County, Texas. He awoke one morning to discover his hundred-year-old well had run dry, and he soon learned why. The Ozarka water bottling company—now a division of Nestlé—had moved in nearby and started pumping ninety thousand gallons of groundwater a day to bottle as spring water and ship around the country. For Sipriano, suddenly, "it was like living out in the desert."

Harold Fain, Sipriano's neighbor, was next in line. Just days after Ozarka began taking water, the water level in Fain's well significantly dropped. He was stunned. "In my furthest dreams," he said, "I can't imagine doing something on my property that would hurt my neighbor. And if I could dream up something, I wouldn't do it." Fain and Sipriano sued Ozarka. These Texan neighbors had accidentally discovered a downside of attachment. The water in their wells felt like it was theirs—it had always flowed underneath their property—but a stranger could siphon it away.

The problem with natural resources is that we often design initial ownership rules when the resources are in abundance. There's plenty for everyone. If the land is yours, then the stuff underneath must be yours, too. How much water can you pump? As much as you can capture from under your land, by whatever means you choose.

And at first, attachment works fine. You pump, I pump, everyone has plenty. Lawyers call the groundwater regime a *rule of capture,* same as the rule for wild animals we introduced in Chapter 1. (Many modern ownership rules trace back to colorful old farm analogies.) With this rule in place, you can stand on your ground, stamp your foot, and proclaim, *It's mine all the way down.*

In setting this initial rule, though, we overlook the consequences of later scarcity. Attachment can work both ways—that's one of its important features. Your neighbors have the same right as you to stick their straws into the underground punch bowl. They own as much as they can suck out from under their land, including the water that would have flowed to your well. If you pause for breath and your neighbor keeps on sucking, you may be left dry. Literally. This is not a complicated race to understand. Almond farmers and water bottlers quickly realize they need to add powerful diesel motors that don't stop for breath. Soon the aquifer loses its capacity to replenish. Eventually there's nothing for anyone.

Shouldn't it matter that existing homeowners are left parched? How can it be that Fain owned the water in his well until the moment Ozarka pumped it away? Isn't that theft? No, not under Texas's attachment rules.

Fain's case went all the way to the Texas Supreme Court. He lost. Since 1904, Texas has awarded surface owners "absolute ownership" of underground water, so they can pump as much as they want, whether or not it sucks neighbors' wells dry. Subsequent court rulings have established that neighborly behavior—what Fain was asking for—is not required in Texas. Even though drilling one well can lower the water table and harm water quality and availability for neighbors, Texas courts have been unwilling to intervene. They say if you want to change the rule of capture, get the Texas legislature to pass a law.

The court's reluctance to intervene illustrates another feature of ownership design: *rule stickiness.* Rules that are productive and useful in one era can turn catastrophic in another, and yet they stick. Judges often hesitate to fix even the dumbest rules, sometimes passing the buck to legislatures, sometimes deferring to past court decisions, rarely taking the lead. Suspicion of change is a deeply ingrained legal habit. As William Blackstone wrote in 1787, in the first general and accessible synthesis of English law, property law "is now formed into a fine artificial system, full of unseen connections and nice dependencies, and he that breaks one link of the chain, endangers the dissolution of the whole."

On the other side of the divide, sharply critical of unquestioning deference to precedent, Supreme Court justice Oliver Wendell Holmes, Jr., wrote a century later, "It is revolting to have no better reason for a rule of law than that so it was laid down in the time of Henry IV. It is still more revolting if the grounds upon which it was laid down have vanished long since, and the rule simply persists from blind imitation of the past." Much of a lawyer's training involves learning tools for navigating between Blackstone and Holmes—between embracing the value of continuity and advocating for needed change.

Texas has opted for continuity, but its attachment rules were adopted long before anyone understood aquifers. The rule of capture may have made sense when people were digging small shallow wells that didn't much affect what happened to neighbors. No one considered the possibility that deep drilling and powerful diesel pumps could reach water located far beneath the surface and rapidly deplete entire water tables. Drilling technology and pumps changed the playing field, and not just by lowering it.

As Barry McBee, chair of the Texas Natural Resources Conservation Commission, argued, these old rules do not "protect private property rights at all, and the Ozarka case is evidence of that. Farmers and ranchers believe they should have absolute rights to their water. Well, the rule of capture says they have that—unless the guy next to them has a bigger pump. Their rights become quite ephemeral at that point." In

Texas today, attachment means surface owners own the groundwater flowing beneath, but only until another surface owner pumps it up.

When Texas considered improving its groundwater ownership design, big water users steamrolled the legislature. The Texas and Southwestern Cattle Raisers Association argued that requiring "reasonable use"—what Fain was asking for—takes away what's "always" been theirs. And that's a hard no in Texas. Echoing Blackstone's conservative creed, Ridge Pate, legal director of the powerful Farm Bureau, added "We're dealing with folks' property rights. When you take one away, where does it end?"

Notice Pate's strategy here: he's arguing for rule stickiness by deploying the *slippery slope* move, one of the most powerful (and often used) rhetorical devices in ownership debates. If you can cast needed reform as a slippery slope—or invoke variations like the "parade of horribles" or the "camel's nose in the tent"—then any proposed change to the existing regime, however small and reasonable, will seem to lead inevitably downhill to disaster. Better to keep the status quo, even if it's flawed.

Parents use this move all the time with little children. "No, you can't stay up another hour, because where would that end? After midnight." "No candy after school today or your teeth will rot."

Whenever you hear a sticky rule–slippery slope argument, recognize there is an equally strong reply: what we like to call the *sticky staircase* riposte. "Yes," you can concede, "the old rule has value." Then you pivot: "But it's not quite right, so let's make this one reasonable change. We'll take this one small step and stop safely on this sticky stair."

Tommy Knowles, with the Texas Water Development Board, argued the sticky staircase point, proposing alternatives like creation of water conservation districts with circumscribed powers to limit overuse, interbasin water markets, and "reasonable use" rules that allow unlimited consumption unless a neighbor's supply is threatened—sticky steps that could have big payoffs for neighborly relations and sustainable pumping. The ranching and farming lobby brushed aside these reforms, even though, as McBee pointed out, rural residents are the people most threatened by the rule of capture.

Rhetorical strategies aside, arguments over groundwater exemplify a recurring challenge for managing scarce resources. In the academic literature, this challenge is known as the *tragedy of the commons*—and it's one of the building blocks of modern ownership design. Every farmer knows the race to pump is a losing game, but why sacrifice for the greater good if there's no guarantee others will do the same? If you try to conserve water and others don't, then you're a chump. But if no one conserves, then the farmers destroy the resource for everybody. This race-to-pump dynamic can occur with all kinds of resources—groundwater and oil, fish and foxes, grass and pasture—whenever access is open to all. Every farmer, fisher, or shepherd is better off in the short term by consuming as much as possible as quickly as possible, and by investing as little as possible in conserving the resource. That's each individual's rational choice right now. But what makes sense individually in the short term is disastrous for all of us collectively over the long term.

Charlie Pitigliano knows farmers should cut back to prevent the losses he and others suffer from subsidence and empty wells. "To save our valley," he says, "we have to police ourselves." But no one wants to go first. What's the point of moderation if everyone else keeps drilling? The race to capture traps each farmer, the pumping continues, and everyone loses in the end.

Well, almost everyone. Unlimited capture is fine, for a while, for the very wealthiest and the most mobile—yet another instance of this rich-get-richer ownership rule. After Ozarka drains Henderson County's groundwater, Nestlé can redeploy its pumping equipment to aquifers in other rule of capture counties across Texas. Drain one dry, move on. Managers at Nestlé bottling plants don't care where the water tanker trucks roll in from, so long as they keep on rolling. Today the company is involved in water drilling disputes in Michigan, Florida, Maine, and other states.

Attachment, though, does not have to lead to tragedy. When we look up in the sky, planes fly overhead; landowners don't have claims to airways. Only a small, odd collection of states still follow the Texas rule for groundwater: Connecticut, Georgia, Indiana, Louisiana, and Massachusetts. Try to find anything else that unites only these states. Every other state, liberal and conservative, has adopted some or all of the sticky steps Knowles proposed for Texas—water conservation districts, water markets, reasonable use.

Even in Texas, it would not be hard to protect aquifers while respecting ranch and farm owners' views. How can that be? Look to oil and gas.

Black Gold

One hundred and fifty years ago, the oil industry was booming . . . in Pennsylvania. The first oil rush occurred in Titusville, Pennsylvania, back in 1859. Well drillers raced in, trying to get as much crude out of the ground as fast as possible. Photos from the period show a forest of wells crowding each other.

Drillers overpumped oil in Pennsylvania for the same reasons they overdraft groundwater in California: the rule of capture. So well drillers pumped as quickly as possible. The tragedy here was the waste of oil. When an oil field has too many wells, the pressure in the field drops, and much of the oil remains trapped underground. Better to have fewer wells and slower extraction. By carefully maintaining oil-field pressure, drillers can pump far more oil.

When oil was first struck in Texas, the state adopted the rule of capture. Each surface owner over a pool of oil could drill a well. Pump it or lose it. This seemed an unsolvable problem, destined for groundwater's tragic outcome.

But oil drillers in many states rapidly sidestepped a tragedy of the commons, not with new technology but through redesigning the meaning of attachment. When oil producers saw oil field pressure drop and wells quickly dry up, they lobbied to create *unitization*, a new form of oil and gas ownership designed to collect together overly fragmented interests.

How does unitization work? The details vary from state to state, but the basic idea is simple. All landowners above an oil field are joined together in a privately owned unit, like a corporation in which the owners are shareholders. Landowners give up the right to drill their own wells; in exchange, they get a share of the profits based on how much oil lies beneath their lot (and they retain rights to surface uses like ranching and farming). The unit hires a professional operator to maximize overall revenue by drilling enough wells to get oil out, but not so many that pressure drops; pumping more when prices rise, cutting back in slumps. In short, the unit operates the field to create the biggest possible pie for owners to split.

Unitization respects the principle of attachment—owning land means you own the oil underneath—but it transforms the practice. Your individual right to drill becomes a pro rata share in the unit's profit. Instead of competing to pump as fast as possible, thus shrinking everyone's pie, the neighbors now share a joint goal. All benefit from expanding the pie as much as possible, so each gets a bigger slice. Unitization has become the gold standard for operating oil and gas fields with multiple surface owners. It's ownership design that solves the tragedy of the commons.

Texas is the only oil-producing state not to require compulsory unitization—surface owners can voluntarily create a unit, but only if they all unanimously agree, and that's hard to achieve. Instead, Texas adopted and has stuck with a more collectivist ownership form to address the commons tragedy—an odd choice for a state that prizes individual autonomy. Since the late 1930s, the Texas Railroad Commission (by a quirk of politics) has controlled oil production through "proration" rules: the state agency sets production caps for individual owners each month and it enforces well-spacing rules. You can't dig a well if it's too close to someone else's existing well—a form of first-in-time. Proration is a less productive ownership form than unitization—it relies on information-poor state actors rather than on nimble private market operators, a cost that has become more apparent as drillers shift to deep drilling and horizontal fracking. It seems Texas lags behind the most market-friendly ownership solution because small independent operators—a potent political force in the Texas legislature—believe they can individually extract more by keeping their wells outside of unit control.

It doesn't have to be this way.

Back in California, the recent drought across the state broke the long-standing political stalemate on groundwater management. With a new law, California is redesigning ownership to keep more land from sinking and more wells from going dry. Maybe it takes a devastating drought to try something new.

Unitization and reasonable use rules are just a few of many ownership forms available to tame problems arising from the rule of capture and ensuing tragedy of the commons. We'll look at some more successful approaches in Chapter 7, but here's one that may seem radical: change the ownership baseline for underground resources. Maybe they shouldn't belong to the surface owner at all.

As it turns out, in most of the world, they don't. One hundred forty-two countries, including well-off ones like Japan and Chile, say underground natural resources belong to the state as part of the common wealth—flowing oil, gas, and water are like the air we breathe or the oceans we fish. Landownership means you control certain rights on the surface and close to it, but attachment does not reach much below ground. What seems a "natural" feature of private landownership in the United States appears to be a downright bizarre choice in most of the world's market economies.

In America, it's too late to change the ownership baseline for underground natural resources. Few argue that these resources should be publicly owned. Trillions of dollars have been invested in the expectation that some version of attachment will govern water, oil and gas, coal, uranium, iron, and other minerals. The United States is an exception and will remain so. While we routinely reengineer the practice of attachment—say, by switching to unitization—America won't abandon the principle for already-existing resources.

Following the end of Apartheid, South Africa actually switched rules. The 2002 South African Mineral Development Act rejected the prior rule that private parties owned the minerals beneath their property. Instead, minerals now come under state ownership and control.

For emerging resources, it's a different story: there, attachment has to compete with rival stories and ownership remains up for grabs. To experience the ebb and flow of these new resource conflicts, let's start at the beach.

Beach Nourishment and Concrete Islands

Linda Cherry lives in a three-story beachfront home on the white sands of Destin, Florida. In the 1970s, Destin was a quiet fishing village of two thousand residents. Now it's one of the most popular beach towns along the Gulf Coast, with 65,000 visitors arriving in peak season. Property values have skyrocketed. Locals proudly call Destin "the world's luckiest fishing village."

While her home might be in a crowded destination, Cherry didn't have to worry about tourists with blaring speakers and beach-spreading towels and tents. Her lot, like all Florida beachfront, extends from her back porch down to the waterline at the average high tide—dry sand is private; wet sand, public. Cherry loved her private beach. Like many neighbors, she put up NO TRESPASSING signs to drive home the point.

In the past, this rule worked well for Destin beachfront owners.

Beaches grow and shrink depending on sands carried by currents and storms. But in lucky Destin, the beaches simply grew with new white sand, year after year. Who owned the new sand? In Florida, Cherry did, along with her neighbors. Attachment can expand owners' lots horizontally, not just vertically. So long as the dry sand builds up *gradually,* private land expands—always touching the mean high-tide line. This is beachfront attachment.

But there's a problem: attachment also works in reverse. If sand slowly washes away, then Cherry's private beach shrinks. And shrink it did. Because of climate change, sea levels in Florida have risen about five to eight inches over the past century, and they will continue rising. Until now, being able to walk out your back door to the ocean proved a great investment. But going forward, beachfront owners are facing climate realities, and everyone is fighting for the remaining dry sand.

Starting with Hurricane Opal in 1995, Destin beaches started eroding, sometimes retreating up to five feet a year. Destin's most expensive homes were at risk of disappearing altogether. So wealthy beachfront owners pressured the city, which lobbied the state, to preserve the private beaches. How do you keep a beach from eroding away? The brute-force way is to add more sand, a lot more sand.

The idea of piling sand on beaches would have seemed crazy a century ago. Early Florida speculators bought beachfront land for less than a dollar an acre. Beaches were smelly waste lands reserved for fishermen who dried nets and for rough characters who hung around the boats. (Back in Chapter 1, Lodowick Post was chasing the fox on "unpossessed and waste land, called the beach.") Today, though, half of Americans live within fifty miles of a coast; a bungalow the size of a garage can sell for millions.

The practice of "beach nourishment" started with Coney Island in 1922. Today it involves moving extraordinary quantities of sand from offshore seabed dredging or inland quarry mining onto the shore. Florida alone has spent $1.3 billion to nourish 237 miles of its beaches over the past eighty years. In 2017 the U.S. Army Corps of Engineers dumped hundreds of thousands of tons of sand to shore up just one three-thousand-foot stretch of Miami Beach, with an $11.5 million price tag paid by local, state, and federal taxpayers. The most extracted mineral in the world today, exceeding by weight all the fossil fuels we pump, is sand and gravel, used for beach nourishment along with fracking, land reclamation, concrete, and glass. Sand has become scarce; extracting it is imposing ever-escalating environmental harms.

Beach nourishment pleases property owners and local businesses, but it is a losing game. Geologists point out the foolishness of trying to hold back the tide—literally. Rising seas and the next big storm will inevitably reclaim the beach. Biologists keep finding devastating new effects on marine life buried or destroyed by dredging. Taxpayers rightly see it as a perverse subsidy that temporarily protects the wealthiest homeowners. Yet the practice is growing: the well-off are good at extracting subsidies for their own benefit, and they frame the subsidy as protecting tourism, or the tax base, or property values. Whatever it takes. Beach nourishment is another instance where attachment favors the fortunate.

But who owns the new beach? If a private beach grows gradually and naturally, the new dry sand remains private. What if the government suddenly dumps tons of sand between your eroded beach and the ocean? Turns out, horizontal attachment has limits, just as we've seen for attachment up in the air and down underground.

Under Florida law, sudden expansions of beachfront land belong to the public, not to private beachfront owners. Florida follows a rule that traces back to ancient Rome: private ownership remains fixed at the old mean high-tide line following sudden changes like those resulting from hurricanes. And in Florida, the cause of the sudden change has always been irrelevant: beach nourishment by the state is like a hurricane. So when Destin added seventy-five feet of beach, the new dry sand was public, free for beach-spreading riffraff to wander across and set up their tents, smoky grills, and loudspeakers.

Cherry fought back. In her view, the city might be justified if it said, "We're doing this to protect the beach and to protect the upland owners." That was what the city said, but she didn't accept that as Destin's genuine motivation for nourishing the beach. "I'm sorry, you'll never in a million years get me to believe that. It was strictly to provide the public beach that they sought." Like #droneslayer Merideth, Cherry adamantly holds to her story of property rights. She and her neighbors sued, arguing that when the state adds sand, the gradual attachment rule should apply—and the new publicly funded beach should be fenced off as their private preserve.

The case went to the U.S. Supreme Court, which ruled unanimously that the Florida courts' interpretation of Florida attachment law was right: regardless of the cause, the state had indeed always limited horizontal attachment after sudden changes. Whether it was by a hurricane or a bulldozer, it produced the same result. Beach nourishment did not take anything from Cherry that had been hers to begin with.

For Cherry, watching the city add sand to her beach was a bitter experience: "It had to be how the French felt when they saw the German tanks coming across their property. It was an absolute, total violation of our constitutional rights." Perhaps a bit strong, but attachment brings out powerful emotions, particularly when it feels like something connected to you was taken. Remember the endowment effect in Chapter 2?

Horizontal attachment may seem trivial, of interest only to well-off beachfront owners, but it has pressing geopolitical, military, and economic consequences.

Nowhere is this truer today than in the Spratly Islands, a sprawling archipelago in the South China Sea. Named after a nineteenth-century British whaling captain, the Spratlys are tiny. Their combined surface area covers just three-quarters of a mile, scattered across more than 164,000 square miles of ocean. The Philippines, Indonesia, and Vietnam all lie within a few hundred miles of the islands, with China much farther away, about a thousand miles distant. Until recently, none of these nations paid the Spratlys any attention. They were inhabited by crabs, seabirds, and occasional fishing shacks.

Today, though, China is spending billions, rapidly converting the Spratlys' meager rocks and reefs into islands with permanent settlements and concrete airstrips. Many security analysts fear these fortified military outposts could trigger the next big war. Why is China taking such an interest in far-flung rocks? And how is attachment at the center of it all?

One of the oldest bodies of international law centers on who controls waters off shorelines. Coastal states have always wanted to keep the resource-rich waters for their own fleets, so they assert attachment: *The coastal waters are mine because they extend off my coast.* Seafaring countries insist on having access anywhere their boats can sail, demanding a reward for labor: *The fish belong to those who work hard to catch them.*

For centuries, countries observed the *cannon shot rule.* Coastal states controlled waters up to three nautical miles off their coasts—because that was about as far as land-based cannons could fire. The old law in Latin translates to "land's dominion ends where the range of weapons ends." It was a practical rule. Then, after World War II, countries with large outer continental shelves such as Chile and the United States extended attachment further—asserting national control over ever more coastal resources. Today coastal states can claim full territorial control of twelve nautical miles offshore, and, more important, an Exclusive Economic Zone (EEZ) for ocean resources up to two hundred nautical miles offshore. Russia, Canada, and other countries are currently jostling in the Arctic, trying to extend their control toward the North Pole as climate change melts polar ice, creates access to deep sea oil and gas, and opens shipping routes.

Attachment turns out to be the most important international law principle for acquiring and managing ocean wealth. Without attachment, most fisheries and deep sea oil fields would be in international waters—governed by the rule of capture and vulnerable to the tragedy of the commons. On the high seas, beyond national control, vessels compete to harvest as fast as possible and fish stocks decline. That's what happened to whales in the 1800s, when fleets sought blubber for lamp oil (overharvesting of whales is part of what created a market opening for land-based oil drilling). Marine biologists now monitor a long list of species that have been fished to near-extinction on the high seas.

Today states assert EEZ control over coastal waters that contain more than 90 percent of the seafood caught globally. Attachment makes it possible to solve part of the overfishing problem: with EEZs, nations can exclude foreign fishing fleets. But domestic fleets are just as capable of destroying fisheries, and fish do not respect EEZ boundaries. These problems have led to a wave of ownership innovations, which we explore in Chapter 7.

Island countries have been accidental beneficiaries of expanding EEZs. Minuscule territories in the Pacific now have sovereign control over resources, expanding out in two-hundred-mile-wide circles around each island. The archipelago nation of Kiribati, for example, has a land area of just 310 square miles, yet its EEZ controls the resources in 1.3 million square miles of surrounding ocean.

This is where the long-neglected Spratlys come in. Because of territorial control and EEZs, even barren atolls are suddenly worth fighting over. China asserts ownership based on discovery dating back perhaps two millennia (first in time). Vietnam notes it has ruled the Spratlys since the seventeenth century (possession). And the Philippines bases its claim on proximity (attachment).

An international tribunal dismissed China's historical claims, but China responded by erecting "fishermen's shelters" on the aptly named Mischief Reef, off the Philippine coast. These were little more than shacks awkwardly set on rocks. Over time China's building intensified, pulverizing coral reefs with massive dredging of sand; then the new land was stabilized with concrete structures. Now there are over 3,200 acres built atop the reefs, including airstrips, radar facilities, and other military installations.

Why the frenzied building? Under international law, for an island to claim offshore territorial control and an EEZ, it must be above water at high tide and capable of human habitation. On its face, this would not include most of the Spratlys, which consist of rocks jutting above high tide and atoll reefs exposed only at low tide. China's strategy is similar to adverse possession, which we discussed in Chapter 2: lay claim to the newly inhabitable lands, then bootstrap that claim with attachment for the surrounding waters.

U.S. Admiral Harry Harris has mocked the manufactured islands as the "Great Wall of Sand," but it is no laughing matter. The South China Sea has rich fishing areas as well as oil and natural gas reserves. Perhaps most important, it provides one of the world's most active shipping lanes, with over $5 trillion worth of goods passing through annually. The United States has warned China to stop creating islands in the South China Sea and repeatedly sent warships to the area.

While no shots have been fired, the war of words between the United States and China has been escalating. Admiral Harris stated that if China attempted to control air rights above the islands (vertical attachment), the United States would ignore the claim. Secretary of State Rex Tillerson raised the possibility of a naval blockade of the manufactured islands—an action usually interpreted as an act of war. Three years later, Secretary of State Mike Pompeo stated that "The world will not allow Beijing to treat the South China Sea as its maritime empire." The Chinese government-controlled newspaper, *Global Times,* has made the stakes clear, warning that "unless Washington plans to wage a large-scale war in the South China Sea, any other approaches to prevent Chinese access to the islands will be foolish."

Manufactured islands—plus expansive claims to attachment—are changing the global balance of power.

Boo Boo, Dockers, and Tulip

Attachment reaches not only above, below, and to the side, but also deeply *into* your home, as Natore Nahrstedt discovered to her dismay. Nahrstedt lived happily with her cats—Boo Boo, Dockers, and Tulip—in the Lakeside Village Condominiums in Culver City, California. But then she discovered that her neighbors' control extended, via attachment, straight into her living room.

The troubles began when a neighbor spotted Tulip sunning in a window and notified the Lakeside Village Condominium Association. The association reminded Nahrstedt of the pet restriction attached to her home, fined her twenty-five dollars, and ordered her to remove the cats. Nahrstedt refused. The association fined her again, and then again.

Brad Brown, the property manager, had no sympathy for the cute cats: "The [rules] come with the property. A lot of people bought property here because we have these pet restrictions." And the neighbors mostly supported enforcement. "I agree people have the right to have pets," said Ruth Faine, a condo owner, "but if that was so important to them they shouldn't have moved here, because they knew it was against the rules. There are plenty of condos where you can have as many pets as you want."

The fines continued to escalate, so Nahrstedt sued. How could the association possibly force her to expel her noiseless, indoor cats? "I will not get rid of these cats," Nahrstedt made clear. "They're my babies. I chose to have cats instead of babies. . . . If they were attacking your children, you'd go out and hire an attorney and do the same thing."

The case went to the California Supreme Court and received national attention. The stakes were high. If the court ruled for Nahrstedt, condominium associations could risk bankruptcy, potentially having to defend in court each routine enforcement decision against a disgruntled owner. On the other hand, if neighbors can reach that deeply into our most intimate spaces, then what's left of individual freedom?

Until 1960 *common-interest communities* were virtually unknown in America—no condo buildings, no golf course or marina communities, no gated residential subdivisions. Condos weren't physically complex to build, but they did require innovative ownership design. There was no simple way for an individual to own and get financing on "unit 10C," a box of space up in the air, separated from land; no simple way to share ownership and management of common features like elevators, gyms, and golf courses; no way to collect maintenance fees and enforce community rules. That ownership form had to be created—added to the *numerus clausus,* the limited number of ownership forms we allow. Puerto Rico was the catalyst. It adapted a version of old condo law from Germany; then the law jumped from Puerto Rico to the mainland, spread nationwide, and became wildly popular.

The meteoric rise of the residential association has radically altered how Americans live, work, and relate to one another. It's changed the meaning of community. Since 1960, we've gone from about zero to over 70 million people living in one of over 350,000 residential associations. Today three out of five new residential units are governed by a condo-like structure. In many cities, if you want to own a home, your only realistic choices are in a community with a homeowners' association in control.

This transformation is based on a form of attachment quite different from claims to groundwater or fish. Here attachment starts with a contract and ends as property. When a developer builds a new project, every initial buyer must contractually agree to the community's governing restrictions. The initial unanimous agreement binds all future owners—whoever is living in the condo—and not just those who signed a contract with the original developer. (The ability to bind nonsigners is what makes these restrictions a form of property instead of contract.)

The attachment point arises because these ongoing restrictions are reciprocal: owning your unit gives you control over what your neighbors do in their homes—and they get control over you: *I can restrict your activities inside your unit because it is legally attached to mine.* The homeowners' association is empowered, and indeed required, to enforce the agreed restrictions on behalf of the owners. They can and do reach into our most personal spaces, as Nahrstedt discovered through her lawsuit.

Homeowners' associations routinely pass rules that would be unconstitutional if publicly enacted: no Christmas wreaths, no brown lawns, no pickup trucks, no religious services, no day care, no indoor smoking, no solar panels, no lawn flamingos, no clotheslines, no political signs, no flags. Even kissing a date good night on your front stoop can be forbidden. In Rancho Santa Fe, California, Jeffrey DeMarco was fined for having too many rosebushes. When he sued and lost, he had to pay the association $70,000 in legal fees, and he lost his home. Pamela McMahan, an elderly owner in Long Beach, was fined and eventually forced to leave her condo for failing to carry her dog across the lobby—dogs' feet were prohibited from touching the floor. And all these restrictions are privately created, with little judicial supervision and less legislative intervention.

And what of Boo Boo, Dockers, and Tulip? They lost. In effect, the California Supreme Court ruled that if each cat got its day in court, condos would drown in litigation. So homeowners' associations get the final say, more or less, in applying the rules in their original, unanimously agreed restrictions. (Later-enacted bylaws, which do not require unanimity, get slightly less deference from courts.) If you want the benefits of condo living—more affordable space, like-minded neighbors, and shared amenities such as gyms or golf courses—then you have to accept neighbors' control. It's debatable whether your home was ever your castle, but your condo certainly is not.

Perhaps condo rules allow neighbors' ownership to extend too far into our intimate lives. Like all attachment rules, we have to decide the boundaries. When do condo restrictions—even those unanimously agreed upon—conflict with fundamental values around ownership? When should ownership rules free us from "freedom of contract"?

For Justice Armand Arabian, the no-pet rule went too far. Dissenting from the Court's ruling, he wrote, "More than simply embodying the notion of having 'one's castle,' [owning a home] represents the sense of freedom and self-determination emblematic of our national character. Granted, those who live in multi-unit developments cannot exercise this freedom to the same extent possible on a large estate. But owning pets that do not disturb the quiet enjoyment of others does not reasonably come within this compromise."

Justice Arabian did not persuade the court—the majority wanted a bright-line rule, not a mushy standard (an ownership design choice discussed in Chapter 1) under which courts would be forced to determine the reasonableness of each Boo Boo, Dockers, or Tulip. But Arabian's view on pets ultimately won the day. The state legislature created its own bright-line ownership rule for domestic pets regardless of the condo's contractual agreements. In California, keeping a cat is now a fundamental freedom that comes with owning a home (but not renting, as landlords can enforce no-pet rules). The reversal came too late for Nahrstedt. She and her cats had moved out.

The way to avoid condo overreach is to avoid condos. But even if you buy a stand-alone home, there's still no escaping attachment's reach inside your home—at least when it's a ghost that's attached.

Jeffrey Stambovsky decided to quit New York City for someplace quieter. At 1 LaVeta Place in Nyack, he found the perfect house, an old Victorian facing the Hudson, just twenty miles from the city. Helen Ackley was ready to sell. They struck a deal for $650,000. It was an ordinary real estate sale like millions of others each year—until Stambovsky learned that the house was inhabited by poltergeists, a reputation that Ackley had cultivated, even including the home on local haunted house tours. Ackley and her real estate agent did not, however, disclose the haunting when they listed the property for sale.

Stambovsky tried to back out, but Ackley refused, citing the old-fashioned rule for real estate transactions: *caveat emptor,* "buyer beware." After much legal to and fro, the court sided with Stambovsky: having promoted the poltergeists' attachment to the home, Ackley could not later deny their existence. The judges concluded that "as a matter of law, the house is haunted." Attachment inside the home can extend to ghosts and no-pet rules equally.

And house-haunting is more common than you might imagine. According to ghost investigator Linda Zimmerman, in Nyack alone many homes come with well-recognized ghosts attached. Ackley's home did not even make the list of the dozen most haunted places in the area. Luckily for Ackley, after Stambovsky backed out, ghost-loving home buyers made multiple offers for 1 LaVeta Place—so long as she could provide assurance that Sir George and Lady Margaret, the resident poltergeists, were strongly attached to the home and would continue haunting the place post-closing.

And it's not just ghosts that can attach to a home. Moving from the supernatural to the sepulchral, attachment can reach even to the grave. Over centuries, people have buried kin in backyard plots; millions more were interred in long-abandoned cemeteries. Still today their families may legally cross your land to pay their respects, even if the existence of the long-neglected grave is a complete surprise to you. The *graveyard right* attaches to the grave and gives the descendants of the deceased eternal access to your land. And if the grave turns out to be Native American, the attachment rights are yet more stringent, sometimes prohibiting any construction that would disturb the remains.

Attachment is the tool by which owners claim new resources plausibly connected to something they already own. And at the same time, attachment works reciprocally for condo neighbors, bereaved descendants, drone operators, beachgoers, and the state—reaching above your land, down below, from the sides, and through the past. Your home may be your castle, but it's never yours alone.

Earth, Sun, and Wind

We wrap up this chapter with a contemporary puzzle: trees versus sun. There's likely no better place to put up rooftop solar panels than the cheerily named town of Sunnyvale in northern California. Carolynn Bissett and her husband were environmentalists who drove a Prius and took pride in the eight redwood trees they had planted on their property. Their neighbor, Mark Vargas, was an equally proud green. He drove an electric car and installed solar panels on his rooftop. As his neighbors' redwoods grew, though, what had been a friendly eco-enclave began to resemble a reality TV show.

The redwoods started shading the solar panels. Vargas demanded that Bissett lop off the tops. She refused. "We're just living here in peace," Bissett said. "We want to be left alone." Vargas countered, "I think it's unfair that a neighbor can take away this source of energy from another neighbor." He sued.

Ownership rules regarding neighbors and sunlight have been around for a long time. In England, the "doctrine of ancient lights" dates from the 1600s and prevents a neighbor from blocking the path of sunlight into an already-existing window. British courts even developed a standard known as the Grumble Line—the point at which ordinary people would begin to grumble about a room's poor light. These rules, however, were universally repudiated when America created its own legal system. Here you could pretty much build what you wanted, sun-blocking or not. And for most people, most of the time, no one much cared. There was plenty of space and sun.

With the rise of denser communities and affordable solar power, though, access to sunlight is becoming a contested resource. Versions of the conflict between Vargas and Bissett are playing out across the country. Say you want to grow trees or add another story to your house, but that added height will shade your neighbor's solar panels.

Who should win? Here are some options, all consistent with the attachment principles explored in this chapter:

- Bissett can block as much light as she wants.
- Vargas has a solar right, free from tree shade.
- Bissett can block light but must pay to shade Vargas.
- Vargas has the right to light but must pay for Bissett's trees.

For Bissett, her home is her castle. Like William Merideth, the #droneslayer, she claims her lighthouse beam of ownership up to the sky. If she wants to grow redwoods on her lot, that's her right. It's an environmentally friendly choice as well. Live and let the trees live, she says. What's worse, Vargas installed his solar panels five years after she had planted the trees. Bissett's first-in-time claim strengthens her attachment one. Vargas should have known the redwoods would grow and shade his panels; he should have sited the panels elsewhere.

Vargas can make the same home-as-castle claim, just inverted: the sunlight falling on his solar panels is attached to, and therefore part of, his suburban kingdom. Bissett's redwoods are taking his solar energy. Even if Bissett acted first, first-in-time is just one ownership story among many. Times change, and states can shift the baseline for ownership to encourage what they believe to be more valuable use of scarce resources. To rule otherwise, the Supreme Court wrote in an analogous dispute from a century ago, "would preclude development, and fix a city forever in its primitive conditions." Technology advances, cities grow, values change, and we adjust ownership accordingly.

Each of these viewpoints has merit. Usually neighbors resolve such ownership conflicts by chatting over the backyard fence. But when goodwill breaks down and neighbors go to court, what happens? For physical intrusions, courts use a bright-line rule called *trespass*—you can evict and collect damages from someone who steps onto your land. But for non-physical intrusions, judges look to an old body of law known as *nuisance*. Nuisance law prohibits you from maintaining uses that are "unreasonable"—a standards-based approach. When your neighbor blasts ear-shattering heavy metal music at three a.m., that's unreasonable and a nuisance. In real life, though, it can be hard to decide what is an ordinary use and what is deviant—it depends on the ownership baseline. How about if neighbors blast country music at ten p.m.? What if it's soft classical music at supper?

Today nuisance law is a mess—its tests are mushy and unpredictable. What's reasonable to me may be an outrage to you. The question *What is reasonable?* has no objective, value-free answer. We seem caught between a rock and a hard place, between trees and sun.

There's an alternative *law and economics* approach, building on three insights by Ronald Coase, a Nobel Prize–winning economist. First, he noted, resource conflicts are always reciprocal—growing trees and installing solar panels are both ordinary uses; the problem arises only because they are next to each other. Asking if it's unreasonable to plant trees that shade a neighbor's solar panels misses the point that each use injures the other. If we decide to protect sunlight, then redwoods get chopped down and Vargas is harming Bissett. But if we choose to protect trees, then solar power is shaded and Bissett harms Vargas. Awarding ownership to either side harms the other. Each use seems reasonable or harmful depending on where we set the baseline. In this simple framing, someone, it seems, has to lose. That's life, right?

No. It does not have to be that way. Coase's next point is that ownership rules would not matter if we lived in a "perfect" world— which for economists means a world with no spite or other irrationalities, where everyone knows everything, bargaining is costless, and policing instant. According to the Coase Theorem—the single most cited theorem in law—in that perfect world, rational people would always negotiate to put resources to their most socially valued use, regardless of what the law says:

How does that work? Assume, for a moment, we were in that

perfect world and could know for certain that solar is more valuable than trees. If Bissett owns the right to grow redwoods, then Vargas will offer to pay Bissett more than tree value and less than solar value. Bissett will agree to cut the trees—and we get solar. Conversely, if Vargas owns the right to sunlight, Bissett will offer to pay him up to the amount she values the trees; Vargas will decline the deal (we've stipulated that solar is worth more than trees). So we get solar.

In other words, in the economists' perfect world, if solar is more valuable, we get solar, regardless of who the law says is the original owner. Payments go this way or that depending on who starts with ownership (so law affects the distribution of wealth), but resources always end up in their highest-valued uses.

There's a catch, though, as Coase himself emphasized in his third insight: we don't live in a perfect world. People are irrational, have deep emotional ties to things like trees and solar panels, often lack important information, aren't always good at bargaining, and are uncertain if agreements will be enforced. After Vargas sues, Bissett may be in no mood to negotiate, no matter the price. Then resources may be trapped in low-value uses, even if, in theory, there's a deal that could make everyone better off.

So back in the real world, ownership design really does matter: if we favor trees initially, we may end up with trees, even if solar is more socially valuable. And in the real world, the distribution of wealth matters, too. Our initial choices on ownership are sticky and consequential.

Coase's insights led legal economists to develop what has become an influential tool for ownership design. Instead of rehashing fights over what's "reasonable," they could ask questions like *When are negotiations likely to break down?* and *How can we set initial ownership so resources are more likely to end up in high-value uses?* Asking these questions helps open up ownership design beyond the two unsatisfying options described above: Bissett wins, renewable energy loses; Vargas wins, redwood trees are chopped down.

Imagine that we decided to reward Bissett's home-as-castle and first-in-time intuitions by assigning her ownership. Redwoods add beauty to the environment. But we also care about renewable energy. To signal that care, we could require tree owners to pay solar producers for the renewable energy they lose because of the shade. Now Bissett has to think hard about the costs her trees impose, because she has to pay that cost. If she really loves those trees, she can keep them, but she has to pay.

Or consider the opposite. Times have changed, and today renewable energy comes first. We do not want to "fix a city forever in its primitive conditions," as the Supreme Court noted. To reflect that, we could say that Vargas owns the stream of sunlight on his panels. But there's a catch here, too: Bissett did nothing wrong in planting redwoods (she was first, after all), and forcing her to cut them down may feel unfair. So let's require Vargas to pay Bissett for her loss. Now it's Vargas who has to engage in some deep reflection. Is it really worth paying to chop down the redwoods to ensure steady sunlight? Maybe he could more cheaply avoid the conflict by moving the panels elsewhere on his lot, to a spot where there would be no harm at all—then we get both trees and solar.

One problem with implementing this approach is that there's rarely reliable, on-point data to crunch, and even if there were, legal economists have no value-neutral way of assessing how much redwoods or solar energy are really worth. Who should pay whom how much? Ultimately, ownership requires choice among values.

Maybe we assign ownership to Bissett based on first-in-time or on a strong sense of fairness. If we believe neighbors are generally pretty good at bargaining around this type of localized conflict, then we let Vargas try to strike a deal with Bissett if he really values solar more. Conversely, if we strongly want to shift people toward renewable energy, then we can pick Vargas and let Bissett offer Vargas an appealing deal.

But if we think people will generally have a hard time bargaining around our initial ownership choice—maybe a hundred neighbors have a stake in the outcome, or just a few spiteful ones—then we can switch to a different rule: have a judge set the price for the solar or tree loss. The parties don't have to bargain. They can simply acquire ownership by paying the judge-set price.

So we end up with four options. First, decide whether Bissett or Vargas has the initial ownership. Then decide whether they must reach a voluntary private deal to shift ownership or can have a judge set the price. This type of analysis has shown up in thousands of scholarly papers. We have judges set prices if we're skeptical of neighbors' ability to bargain (bargains often fail), or we focus on setting initial ownership if we lack confidence in judges' ability to set prices (often they have no clue).

As between Bissett and Vargas, we think the right outcome probably would have been to favor solar to support the state's commitment to renewable energy *and* to require judge-set (or legislative) compensation in fairness to those who were there first, like Bissett.

These are not easy questions, but being explicit about them can advance ownership design. First, ask what's the preferred use—from the standpoint of collective well-being, or individual freedom, or whatever ultimate value you choose. Then consider, if you put initial ownership in the wrong place, which party can most cheaply avoid the costs of your mistake? And when is it worth the cost of having a judge step in to set a price?

Or we can just stick with the old-fashioned nuisance-law approach of deciding what's unreasonable. Legal economists gave up on the idea, but ordinary people usually know what's reasonable behavior and what's deviant. When your fist meets my face, we know who is harming whom. Perhaps trees and solar panels are a closer call—but that's true for both the nuisance-law and law-and-economics approaches.

Back in Sunnyvale, trees lost. California sided with solar panel owners and renewable energy. In 1978 the state enacted the Solar Shade Control Act that prohibited neighbors from shading more than 10 percent of a solar collector at any time between ten a.m. and two p.m., enforced by criminal prosecution and fines of up to $1,000 a day. Solar became the ordinary baseline use; redwoods were deviant when they shaded solar. Said Bissett ruefully, "We are the first citizens in the state of California to be convicted of a crime for growing redwood trees."

Bissett and her husband were not just the first people convicted of the crime of blocking a solar panel—they were the only people. Their case set off a national uproar, leading the state to amend the act in 2008. Now trees that preexist solar panels, like Bissett's, are totally exempt from the act, and violations are enforced through civil lawsuits, not criminal prosecutions.

After solar, which emerging natural resource is likely to spark the next big attachment battle? Look to the wind.

It's easy to imagine windmills just as quaint buildings alongside Dutch canals, but wind power has become big business. Giant wind turbines in Holland generate about 10 percent of the country's electricity. Wind provides over 15 percent of the electricity in Texas, more than in any other American state. Just as tall trees can shade solar panels, upwind turbines create "dirty wind" in their wake, making downwind turbines less efficient or impossible to operate at all. With more companies placing turbines around the country to take advantage of windswept terrains, conflicts are arising between neighbors "taking" wind.

Wind power, like solar energy and groundwater, pits different ownership claims against one another. Should it be a race to capture, where people can keep leapfrogging turbines upwind of each other? Or do we want to protect the first to put up a turbine? Most states do not yet have comprehensive laws to regulate wind conflicts. We are just beginning to see attempts at ownership design. Otsego County in New York now requires a "wake-based setback" so turbines do not interfere with each other's wind flows. Setbacks are analogous to well-spacing rules in oil fields, part of the Texas approach to preserving oil field pressure. But all oil-producing states (other than Texas) later realized that compulsory unitization was a superior ownership technology for this resource dilemma. Should states develop unitization for "windsheds"? Should they adapt reasonable use rules from water law? Or should they create another ownership rule altogether?

And don't forget airways for drones—another potentially transformative resource. What should we do about #droneslayers? We could protect William Merideth and his neighbors against trespass, letting them demand their own price for use of airspace above their land. But that attachment rule could create droneway gridlock, effectively grounding the nascent drone delivery industry. Alternatively, we could require drones to remain, say, two hundred feet above private land and ban hovering or circling overhead. But then irritated homeowners would have no simple mechanism to keep unwanted drones from flying by. The perceived unfairness and invasion of privacy might lead to even more drone-blasting.

Maybe we could design ownership rules so we get fast delivery of packages and pizza, vindicating the social interest (especially in pizza), and at the same time, we could compensate homeowners who suffer drone crossings, thus addressing our intuition that *My home is my castle* with its attached column of air. The technology already exists that would allow Amazon, UPS, and Domino's pizza to make micropayments for drone overflights. For particularly sensitive homeowners, we could reverse the cash flow, letting Merideth reject drone crossings altogether if he pays the delivery service to reroute its drones over homeowners who prefer the cash. Micropayments on smartphones may become our twenty-first-century equivalent of barbed wire. Ownership rules just have to catch up.

Chapter 5

OUR BODIES,
NOT OUR SELVES

The Robin Hood of Kidneys

For decades, Levy Rosenbaum ran a life-saving business. People dying of kidney failure came to him for help. He found willing donors and matched them up—for a price. "So far, I've never had a failure. I'm doing this a long time," he said.

Rosenbaum's services did not come cheap. He charged recipients as much as $160,000, of which perhaps $10,000 went to the living kidney donor and the rest to doctors, visa preparers—and his profit. He explains, "One of the reasons it's so expensive is because you have to *schmear* [bribe] all the time." It's also expensive because this business has been illegal since 1984, when America criminalized the live organ trade.

In 2009 Rosenbaum was caught in an FBI sting, pleaded guilty, and became the first—and so far, only—person convicted in America for selling living human organs. At his sentencing hearing, the courtroom was packed. The kidney broker was swarmed, but not by outraged victims. Well-wishers came to plead for leniency. One said, "There are no victims here. The donors are happy and the recipients are happy." Rosenbaum called himself "the Robin Hood of kidney transplants."

The government prosecutors argued, "There is only one thing that his story has in common with Robin Hood, and that is, it is fiction." Rosenbaum coached "donors" to lie to their transplant doctors and pretend they were making compassionate gifts. He carried a gun as he made millions brokering deals, sometimes threatening donors if they tried to back out. He ended up spending two and a half years in jail.

Prosecutors argued that jailing him put people on notice that selling kidneys is "an affront to human dignity." Almost every country in the world currently criminalizes organ sales, including kidneys. As one medical ethicist put it, markets in body parts are "simply too exploitative of the poor and vulnerable. The quality of the organs is questionable. People lie to get the money. The middle men are irresponsible and often criminals."

Maybe. But each person has two kidneys and needs only one for a full and healthy life. The law says it's fine—even noble—to give away a spare kidney. Thousands of people make that gift every year. So why can't you sell one? Transplant doctors profit, hospitals profit, so why not the providers of the raw materials? Is your spare kidney different, in some essential way, from spare kidney beans you can sell from your garden?

Certainly, paying for kidneys may exploit vulnerable sellers. Perhaps it degrades our sense of common humanity. But if we are serious about saving patients with organ failure, experience suggests that allowing some limited form of sale is the only sure path to people's survival. Voluntary donations and organ donor checks on driver's licenses don't produce nearly enough kidneys. Neither does encouraging young people to ride motorcycles (called "donorcycles" by emergency room doctors). Categorically prohibiting sales ensures the premature deaths of an estimated 43,000 people annually in America, the same death toll, as one study puts it, "as from 85 fully loaded 747s crashing each year." By contrast, in Iran—the only country that currently allows sales—no one dies waiting for a kidney.

Which is the worse "affront to human dignity," markets or death? Is Rosenbaum a villain or a hero?

We all have an intuitive understanding that some things should not be for sale. They are priceless—not in the sense that there can be no price, but that they should not have a price. In this sense, our bodies are the quintessential *sacred* resources, the core of self-ownership. These resources are constitutive of our very humanity, our "personhood," as one author puts it. On the other end of the spectrum lies the *profane,* all the ordinary things we buy and sell in markets, like bicycles and baskets. Drawing the line between self-ownership and ordinary ownership, between sacred and profane, has been a centuries-long struggle.

Today we have arrived at near-universal self-ownership for every person, a recognition of our equal dignity and worth. At the same time, though, medical advances are making it possible to sever organs and cells from our bodies, creating new resources that were science fiction just years ago. Should we treat those bodily resources as sacred, profane, or somewhere in between?

The answers are all over the map. Literally. Today in Montana, you can sell your bone marrow cells, but only up to a maximum of $3,000, while in neighboring Wyoming, the sale is illegal. In some Nevada counties, you can sell sexual services, even your virginity, but in next-door Arizona that's prostitution and a crime. In Illinois, you can rent out your womb to gestate another's embryo, but not across the border in Michigan. For bodily resources, the boundaries between sacred and profane are sharp—and they are often state lines. These geographic differences cannot be explained by looking at red versus blue states, North versus South, or any other familiar divide like wealth or race. Religious believers and atheists stand on both sides, as do economic conservatives and progressive feminists.

Though the rules for self-ownership may appear haphazard, they are not. This chapter will show you the forces that shape every self-ownership debate. We can't tell you whether you should view Rosenbaum as a villain or a hero, but we can give you the tools to unpack the debates and decide for yourself on solutions for some of our most challenging resource dilemmas.

Head and Master

When we invoke self-ownership, we are asserting, *It's mine because it comes from my body.* Self-ownership is the root of all other ownership—it's the reason you can make claims based on possession, first-in-time, labor, or attachment.

In turn, self-ownership has two components: first, it's the freedom not to be owned by another. Put bluntly, you are not someone's slave. Second, it's the power to be an owner on equal terms with everyone else. This combination—being able to own and not to be owned—is the prerequisite to human freedom, dignity, and equality; it's the foundation on which you write the story of your own life.

Slavery is the antithesis of self-ownership. It's the original sin of ownership in America. Millions of Africans were brought to America unable to own, but were owned by others. Many of our self-ownership debates today are echoes—sometimes direct, sometimes faint—of the brutal ownership of African American bodies. Even after the Civil War, Jim Crow laws enforced direct analogues to slavery like sharecropping and debt peonage (a widespread practice in the South, persisting until the 1990s) that coercively denied full self-ownership to millions of African Americans.

Today around the globe, slavery has been abolished in law. But not in practice.

Born in the Philippines, Eudocia "Lola" Tomas Pulido lived and died as an enslaved person. Her owner, Alex Tizon, wrote, "She was 18 years old when my grandfather gave her to my mother as a gift, and when my family moved to the United States, we brought her with us." For almost sixty years, Pulido prepared the food, cleaned the house, and served Tizon and his siblings and parents. He says his parents never paid her. They beat her. When Tizon's mother died, he inherited her. "Pulido came to live with me," he wrote. "I had a family, a career, a house in the suburbs—the American dream. And then I had a slave."

Here's the surprising part of this story: it's not ancient history. Pulido was brought to America in 1964; Tizon inherited her in 1999. During all those years, she was able to make only one trip home, on her eighty-third birthday in 2008—and learned that almost everyone she once knew there had died. She returned to Tizon's home and passed away in 2011. When Tizon recounted Pulido's story in a 2017 *Atlantic* article, readers expressed justified outrage over the injustices she had borne.

But Pulido's story is not that unusual. By some estimates, and using various definitions, there are between 60,000 and 400,000 enslaved people in America today (and perhaps up to 40 million globally). Men, women, and children are held in debt bondage by sex traffickers or are forced to work without pay in restaurants, farms, salons, and other businesses. You may have encountered them without realizing it—perhaps the manicurist at a nail salon, a food delivery person, or a neighbor's housekeeper, like Pulido.

Self-ownership is not just about ending the practice of people owning people. It also includes expanding who can own what. When governments restrict certain groups' capacity to own, the results can be deadly. Starting in 1933, after Hitler took power in Germany, the Nazis passed more than four hundred laws directed at Jews, many of them addressing rights of ownership. Jews were first forbidden from owning farmland, later required to report what they owned, and then "Jewish property" was confiscated without compensation. In Germany, taking the ability to own was a prelude to taking lives.

In America, parallel laws ended in Japanese dispossession and internment rather than genocide. A century ago Frank and Elizabeth Terrace tried to lease a farm in Washington state to a Japanese immigrant, N. Nakatsuka. (His first name does not appear in the records.) None of them knew the state had made the transaction illegal. At trial, the judge enforced Washington law and made clear his view: Japanese immigrants were potential enemies and could not be trusted with land. The Terraces lost, then lost again before the U.S. Supreme Court. Nakatsuka was kicked off his farm. During World War II, he was interned at the Tule Lake Relocation Center.

Nakatsuka's story was not an isolated example. The Washington law was based on California's Alien Land Law, passed in 1913, which prohibited Japanese and Chinese people from owning or leasing land so they wouldn't compete against farmers of European descent. California's law remained in force until 1952, when the state supreme court ruled it unconstitutional. Washington's law stayed on the books until 1966, despite multiple attempts to remove it. Today Florida is the only state that has not repealed its version of the law—it's still on the books but is not enforced. The U.S. Supreme Court has never ruled these racist laws unconstitutional.

During the same period, private developers created and enforced ownership agreements known as *racially restrictive covenants,* designed to reserve entire neighborhoods for white residents. These widespread covenants primarily excluded African Americans, Asian immigrants, and Jews, along with Mexicans, Greeks, Catholics, and many other groups, depending on local prejudices. In the landmark 1949 case, *Shelley v. Kraemer,* the U.S. Supreme Court finally struck down enforcement of these covenants, but they still appear in millions of deeds, carried forward from sale to sale. Studies have shown their mere existence in a home's "chain of title" continues to have a strong effect on who lives where.

Women in America have faced analogous struggles to achieve self-ownership, often seeking inspiration from African Americans' fight, sometimes a step ahead, sometimes behind. When Elizabeth Cady Stanton and Lucretia Mott organized the 1848 Seneca Falls Convention—America's first women's rights gathering—they focused on securing ownership rights as much as voting rights. Back then, when women married, they effectively stopped being self-owners under old "coverture" rules. In 1869 Harriet Beecher Stowe, author of the famous antislavery book *Uncle Tom's Cabin,* wrote, "The position of a married woman . . . is, in many respects, precisely similar to that of the negro slave. She can make no contract and hold no property; whatever she inherits or earns becomes at that moment the property of her husband. . . . She passes out of legal existence."

Without self-ownership, wives had few options to direct their own careers or to leave unhappy, abusive marriages with any assets. "Man is, or should be, woman's protector and defender," explained an 1872 Supreme Court decision. "So firmly fixed was this sentiment in the founders of the common law that it became a maxim of that system of jurisprudence that a woman had no legal existence separate from her husband, who was regarded as her head and representative in the social state." The justices concluded, "This is the law of the Creator."

And *head and master* laws continued in force until recently. Through most of the twentieth century, statutes in several American states gave the husband authority over all jointly owned property. Even if a woman paid for the family home and her name was on the deed, the husband could sell it without her knowledge or consent. Louisiana, the last state to abolish these rules, did so only in 1979, in the shadow of federal court compulsion.

Unmarried women did not necessarily fare better. Until Congress passed the Equal Credit Opportunity Act in 1974, banks could deny women credit cards if they did not have male co-signers.

The arc of self-ownership has bent toward greater inclusion. African Americans, Asian immigrants, Jews, women, and others were once restricted from specific types of ownership because of their group identity. Yet over time, their capacity to own has steadily increased. We call this the *universality impulse,* and it is an unremarked feature of ownership design: after a form of ownership is made available to one group, usually white men, pressure builds over time to include others, until the form is equally available to all. Universality is not inevitable; achieving and then maintaining it requires constant struggle. Same-sex marriage is the most recent instance, extending equal ownership rights to gay and lesbian couples that have long been available to heterosexuals.

For all of us, self-ownership starts with control over our own bodies, then extends to include the power to amass assets, to build a future better than the past, to invest in our families and vocations, and ultimately to participate as full citizens in a democracy. It means the ability to write and rewrite the story of our own lives. These are hard fights, with new fronts always emerging.

Golden Eggs

Wendy Gerrish is an accomplished acupuncturist who runs her own business. Well educated, she holds a master's degree in integrative medicine. Gerrish supplements her income by selling her eggs for $20,000 per "donation." Her eggs have resulted in ten living biological children, aside from a son who lives with her. Over ten thousand children are born annually from similar sales, driving America's $80-million-a-year egg-donor market. If you pick up a student newspaper, you'll see ads recruiting donors.

Gerrish is what's known in the trade as a "premier donor," paid extra because lots of buyers want eggs like hers. Shelley Smith, director of a Los Angeles–based egg broker agency, says prices are "usually based on higher education, great SAT scores." As Smith points out, "When we put up a really beautiful donor who is also probably smart and has other qualities, we get calls immediately. I call it the 'feeding frenzy.' No one ever comes in and says, 'I really want a dumb, ugly donor.'"

Smith's top donor received $100,000 for her eggs, a fee typically paid only to blond, blue-eyed, athletic Ivy League students. Asian and Jewish women also command a substantial premium. Smith finds this type of discriminating taste perfectly appropriate. "When you pick someone to marry," she notes, "you are picking the genetics for your child as well. . . . Why can't you kind of look for those qualities in an egg donor who is going to help you build your family?" One study found that donor compensation advertised in university newspapers increased by $2,000 for every hundred-point increase in the school's average SAT scores.

Until the 1980s, this market did not exist, for the simple reason that there was no way to fertilize an egg outside a woman's body. The development of in vitro fertilization (IVF) changed that. Now one in eight IVF attempts uses donor eggs. True, some of those eggs are donated altruistically, perhaps to help infertile friends and family. But most are sold for cash, even though egg brokers studiously continue to refer to sellers as "donors" to avoid triggering debates about sacred and profane ownership.

High fees can be an effective motivator. Donating eggs requires weeks of self-injections of powerful drugs to boost the number of eggs produced; then surgery under anesthesia to extract those eggs. The process can be painful and risky: fertility drugs may hyperstimulate ovaries, releasing too many eggs; rare complications from surgery and anesthesia can lead to infertility, blood clots, even death. "It's not like you're just like, 'Okay, yeah, I'm going to take my eggs out, and give them to you,'" Gerrish said. "You're dedicating months of your time to these people, sacrificing part of yourself, your body."

Egg buyers are the other side of this market. For them, the transaction can feel miraculous. Michelle Bader got married at forty-three, immediately started trying for children, and soon discovered her own eggs were not viable. She went shopping for a donor. "It's like I was dating online," Bader said. "And really early on, I saw a girl that spoke to me. She looked like an angel to me." Two years later Bader had twins, at a cost of $7,000 paid to her "angel," and another $13,000 for medical, legal, and broker fees. To Bader, it was worth "every cent." For many male same-sex couples, buying an egg is the only route to parenting a biologically related child.

Every country has to decide, should self-ownership include the power to sell one's eggs? Are eggs sacred—constitutive of our personhood, like our bodies—and not for sale? Or are they profane, like other commodities we sell in markets? Should they be analogized to spare kidneys or to kidney beans?

American fertility doctors tried to split the difference, facilitating sales but imposing price caps. Doctors' organizations published guidelines, saying payments for eggs over $5,000 "require justification" and payments above $10,000 are "not appropriate." They argued higher prices could lead vulnerable donors into taking unjustified health risks and exclude needy buyers from fertility treatment—creating a market that was at once exploitative, degrading, and exclusionary.

To egg donor Lindsay Kamakahi, though, these reasons sounded contrived—less high-minded ethics than self-serving excuses that allowed fertility clinics, rather than donors, to fix prices and pocket the profits. So she sued to overturn the price caps. If women's bodies were to be mined for raw materials, Kamakahi wanted to be paid in full, not in small change. Shelley Smith, with the Los Angeles egg agency, agreed, saying, "Doctors don't have a cap to what they get paid. They can charge whatever they want. . . . Agencies certainly make money at it. Why do the donors have to have a certain amount that's right for them to get paid, when nobody else has any kind of cap?"

Fertility doctors soon capitulated and settled with Kamakahi. Now regular eggs are sold at regular prices, premium ones at whatever the market will bear. In America, there are plenty of eggs for sale despite the injections, surgery, and other risks—and despite potential consequences for our shared understanding of human dignity and equality.

The Dimmer Switch of Ownership

Fifty years ago, when folks said, "You look like a million bucks," they intended it as a compliment. Today, though, it may be more of a cold accounting. In addition to eggs, we can sell our hair (up to $3,000, for redheads), blood plasma (up to $5,000 per year with frequent donations), sperm (up to $10,000 per year for determined donors), breast milk ("pumping for profit" can yield $20,000 per year), and clean urine ($40 per sample, more on the black market). And after death, there's a gruesome, lucrative, and largely unregulated market in parts of human cadavers. Your body really is becoming a gold mine.

Except for the big-ticket items needed for live transplants. Apart from Iran, national laws prohibit people from selling spare organs like kidneys, regenerative organs like livers, and partly transplantable organs like lungs and intestines. Looking from head to toe, we face a puzzle: how to explain the mosaic of rules governing which parts of our body we can and cannot sell.

The answer is: we have been framing our choices the wrong way. For resources derived from our bodies, we tend to imagine ownership as an on-off switch. The on position is what we've been calling the profane—allow trades in markets. When we toggle the switch to off, it says the resource is integral to our humanity—"Yes, the resource is yours, but not for others to buy." And for millennia, these two options more or less sufficed.

With human hair the switch has always been on. Maybe such sales are not contested because hair grows outside our body, can be painlessly cut, and regenerates quickly. Markets in hair date back to ancient Egypt. Some nineteenth-century European villages held annual "hair harvests" where poor girls sold (or were forced to sell) their tresses; today the global trade exceeds $1 billion annually. Though hair markets may exploit sellers, we don't hear many calls to ban sales, trace where the hair originates, or improve compensation for those who sell their locks. Just the opposite: unregulated sales of new products like hair extensions are booming.

By contrast, for babies, the switch seems to be off. Parents may not sell their infants. We recoil from baby-selling for the same reasons we reject slavery. Even if baby sales were free, fair, and fully informed— with sellers and buyers both unequivocally better off—most of us would still reject baby markets. Why? Because their very existence would degrade "the texture of the human world," as the property scholar Peggy Radin memorably put it. And such markets would disrespect the newborn's self-ownership—its inherent freedom, dignity, and equality. Imagine learning that your parents bought you on Amazon, and your stork was a UPS drone. To protect these core values, we flip the switch to off. Individuals are sacred—they cannot be sold to others.

But there's a catch. The switch is not quite all the way off. It may be true, as Thomas Jefferson wrote in the Declaration of Independence, that adults are "endowed by their Creator with certain unalienable rights." Children, however, are not so endowed. Parents have some ownership rights in kids. True, they cannot sell them, but they can give them away—we call this adoption. The law has long framed parental rights in part as ownership—*Charlie? She's mine*—to an extent consistent with children's well-being. So, just as with kidneys, the on-off switch doesn't quite apply.

We measure our transition to adulthood in no small part by our increasing independence from parental ownership. For many, our teenage struggles included some version of the classic argument, "You're not going out dressed like that." "Oh yes, I am. It's my body and I'm old enough to choose." For a while, parents win those fights, but, soon enough, children tend to prevail. Self-ownership means you can get a buzz cut, pierce your navel, or ink a dragon tattoo. In time kids become full self-owners; for parents, the ownership switch moves to off.

Between hair and slavery—that's the contested terrain for claims to bodily resources deriving from self-ownership. Markets for body parts used to be the realm of science fiction or horror movies. But now, thanks to medical advances, doctors can sever an increasing number of bodily resources (more or less) safely for valuable uses.

Many of these new resources have an in-between quality. It's here that the on-off switch image blocks our thinking about ownership design. There is a better approach: let's upgrade our image from a switch to a dimmer. *Flipping a switch* lets us see only all-or-nothing ownership solutions. *Setting a dimmer* makes visible a range of options between completely on (unrestricted sales in markets, profane) and all the way off (absolutely no transactions, sacred).

And this debate reaches far beyond self-ownership in our bodies. When people view tangible resources as especially constitutive—that is, as essential to who we are as free and equal people—they often receive distinctive legal protection. This is why we sometimes defeat market forces to keep people in their homes using rent controls, homestead preservation rights in bankruptcy, and "partition in kind" of co-owned land (which we come to in Chapter 6).

Whenever any new resource appears, ownership is ambiguous and contested. We need an initial rule to determine who starts as the owner and what it is they own. To see how the dimmer can work, let's return to Levy Rosenbaum's stock-in-trade: kidneys. Spare kidneys are capable of saving lives if sold in freewheeling markets, and they are partly constitutive of our humanity. But the on-off switch doesn't allow us to address this in-between nature—instead it forces us to one extreme choice or another.

When transplants first became medically possible in the 1950s, most patients died. Demand for kidneys began to increase only twenty years later after better antirejection drugs increased survival rates. In 1983 H. Barry Jacobs, a Virginia businessman, spotted a business opportunity: there was no legal bar to commercial kidney sales. So he set out to create a market, letting sellers name their price, finding buyers, and reserving broker's fees for himself.

To help set the initial rule, people often *reason by analogy,* one of the most widely used tools for ownership design and for legal reasoning in general. That was how states set initial ownership for oil, gas, and water—deciding they were analogous to foxes and importing a rule of capture (as discussed in Chapter 4). One feature of this tool is that it dovetails easily with the on-off-switch image. We just need to ask: Is selling a kidney more like selling hair or selling people?

In response to Jacobs's business plan, the Virginia legislature analogized organ sales to slavery and banned the practice. Congress then extended Virginia's ban nationwide with the 1984 National Organ Transplant Act (NOTA)—the law that sent Rosenbaum to jail. For many people, the idea of selling body parts was simply intolerable, indeed akin to slavery, treating a class of people as subhuman. If that's your view, then maybe stick with NOTA. Forbid sales to protect human dignity and prevent exploitation of the poor and vulnerable.

The problem is, analogies that work for some purposes mislead for others. They are a rhetorical device, not a matter of logical proof. Kidneys do not have their own autonomous self-ownership interests. Nor are spare kidneys essential to survival—altruistic donors can lead full and healthy lives, and they are rightly celebrated for the gifts they make to family members, friends, even strangers. Kidneys are not really the same as the people in which they reside. These differences matter and could push you toward allowing kidney markets.

Reasoning by distinction can be as powerful a tool as reasoning by analogy in ownership design. Moving to the dimmer image lets us design ownership with both analogies and distinctions in mind. Perhaps we can set the dimmer to create profane markets that guard the resource's sacred qualities. If so, we can save thousands of people every year from dying of kidney failure . . . and at the same time protect human dignity and prevent coercion.

How would this work for kidneys? For starters, if you fear poor donors will become spare parts banks for the rich, then prohibit sales on the open market. Say no to eBay auctions. We could limit the pool of buyers to hospitals and insurance companies and require that the kidneys they purchase go to those, rich or poor, at the top of doctor-determined transplant lists—as already happens with many donated organs today. The sales price might not reach auction levels, but hospitals and insurance companies could still form a robust pool of ready buyers. And the poor could benefit as transplant recipients, instead of remaining tethered to dialysis machines.

If your concern is that unhealthy donors will sell bad kidneys, then require intense medical screening—as happens already for donors giving away kidneys. Or if your worry is that selling a kidney puts disadvantaged donors at risk of later health issues, then mandate guaranteed lifetime health insurance as part of compensation—a rule for gifted kidneys the New York legislature considered adopting in 2019.

If your concern is that selling a kidney coerces the most vulnerable people, consider the alternatives. Poor people already work extra shifts and take dangerous jobs that risk their health—they translate their self-ownership into hard labor and then into cash. Why deny adults the ability to pay off a mortgage by selling a kidney instead of working in a coal mine or convenience store? Liberals often insist on "my body, my choice" when it comes to abortion, but flinch at kidney markets; similarly, conservatives may extol "freedom of contracts," but object to letting people contract around bodily integrity. Put differently, why shouldn't trade-offs between kidney sales and coal mining be the individual's choice—assuming (and this may be a heroic assumption) we can create safe, fair markets that protect against exploitation and degradation?

If your worry is that kidney sales are a slippery slope to slavery, well, no, we can make it a sticky staircase (a tool introduced in Chapter 4). Why not take one life-saving step—introducing highly regulated, protected markets—and then stop?

And you shouldn't be naive about the virtues of the current rule. As with liquor in the Prohibition era, organ sale bans just drive markets underground. Brutal illegal kidney markets exist around the world where "donors" get no protection and little or no cash. The wealthiest patients—not the neediest—know where to go and whom to pay to save their own lives. The rest die, and many more suffer on dialysis, knowing the kidneys they need exist, people are willing to sell them, and insurance would pay (because transplants are so much cheaper than dialysis), but NOTA and similar rules around the world put the organs out of reach.

Finally, the idea of carefully designed kidney markets—pushing the dimmer halfway down—is not so fanciful. In 1984, NOTA also banned sales of stem cells, which were then harvested painfully from bone marrow via hip surgery. But today these cells can be easily filtered from your blood. In 2011, one federal appeals court covering nine western states changed the analogy for stem cells, describing them as more like blood plasma, which can be sold, than kidneys, which cannot.

But the judges did not push the dimmer all the way up to full sales, either. Potential sellers must join the national donor registry. Doctors make matches based on medical need and cell compatibility, so sellers cannot auction their cells to desperate patients. Sellers have no direct contact with patients. Payments are capped at $3,000 to limit undue influence on vulnerable potential sellers—a cap like the one doctors tried to impose on egg sales. Using a dimmer to move between the sacred and the profane—between no sales and unrestricted sales—has the potential to save many of the three thousand people who die annually awaiting stem cell transplants. But the only potential sellers are in states like Montana, covered by the 2011 court ruling. Across the border in Wyoming, the dimmer is pushed all the way down. Paying for stem cells remains banned, a crime like selling a kidney.

NOTA is not set in stone. The law is less than fifty years old. When Congress passed NOTA, it was concerned "that human body parts should not be viewed as commodities." Since then, the costs of

NOTA have become more apparent: medical need for organs keeps increasing while voluntary ways to nudge up supply have failed. There are many good objections to kidney sales—the coercion and dignity objections give us pause—but perhaps smart ownership design can address each concern directly. We can set the ownership dimmer partway up if we choose.

If you want to uncover the rules of ownership, there's no better place to start than by mastering the art of reasoning by analogy and distinction. That's what the Montana court did with stem cells, and it's a tool available to all of us in everyday life. Whenever you hear someone reason by analogy—"kidneys are like people"—consider distinctions—"kidneys don't have identities; they don't think for themselves." Persuasive distinctions can make the difference between life and death.

Golden Eggs, Revisited

Now let's circle back to Wendy Gerrish and her golden eggs. When IVF first made egg sales possible in the 1980s, we had to set the initial rule. By analogy, are eggs more like kidneys or sperm?

Courts in America picked sperm and jump-started a vibrant market. Indeed, eggs are similar to sperm in some ways. After they are extracted, there are plenty more left. And each has the capacity to create life when joined with the other and gestated in a womb. Both raise concerns regarding involuntary parenthood (when used against the donor's will, say after divorce or death) and potential parental obligations to the resulting offspring (who may want to know their biological donor, or need to know for medical reasons). These factors counsel for treating sperm and eggs equally—and for pushing the dimmer a notch away from unregulated sales.

But distinctions matter as well. Sperm is easily collected and quickly regenerates, like hair. Eggs, by contrast, are more painful to

extract, with injections, surgery, anesthesia, and potentially dangerous complications, perhaps more like kidneys. Vulnerable or reluctant
egg-sellers may be desperate for a big influx of short-term cash while
discounting too much the emotional and health risks; motivated sellers can't necessarily afford follow-up care; and coercive middlemen
may lie to donors to capture most of the profits. These differences suggest we push the dimmer further down for eggs than sperm, requiring
more counseling and follow-up care, perhaps imposing more limits
on sales.

On the other hand, concerns about gender equality may suggest
pushing the dimmer up for eggs—despite the added risks—back
toward parity with sperm and market sales. Egg sales first became
possible in the 1980s, at a time of generational change, when many
women were battling to assert control over their own bodies and to
be treated as equals in the marketplace. That's what Kamakahi was
fighting for when she challenged fertility doctors' price caps. Today, if
we are going to set the ownership dimmer differently for women and
men, we need compelling justifications.

Where should we set the dimmer? Our deepest (and often unex-
amined) moral commitments influence how we make this decision.
Assume we could guarantee that eggs sales were completely safe, fully
informed, noncoercive, free and fair. Some people might still object,
not necessarily to impose gendered roles, but out of a commitment to
preserve a particular understanding of our common humanity. Their
point is eggs should not have a price at all in a decent society.

To sharpen this concern, consider the ads that routinely appear
in elite student newspapers recruiting egg donors. The ads offer large
sums for eggs specifically from tall, athletic, white or Asian women
with high SAT scores. For the past fifty years, federal law has made it
illegal to advertise for a "white roommate" or a "pretty female" flight
attendant—because those ads legitimize and perpetuate a culture of
discrimination even if particular landlords and tenants, employers

and workers, agree to the deal. So why is it okay to print similar ads for egg donors?

Reasonable people can differ on egg sales. America opted to move the dimmer most of the way up, with its attendant challenges. Canada, China, and most liberal European countries have gone the other way, prohibiting commercial sales. In England, donors are allowed to receive only token reimbursements, like taxi fare to the clinic. As a result, few English women donate, and the country has a multiyear wait for eggs. Today a global influx of "fertility tourists" come to America to buy eggs and start families.

Even within a family that otherwise agrees on big-picture "God and country" questions, you can often fire up robust disagreement on markets in body parts. Some may push the dimmer down if they hold certain views on sanctity or coercion; others push it up if a particular vocabulary of freedom or markets is their touchstone. Views also shift depending on which analogies and distinctions come to mind first and how the question is framed. (Recall the psychology of ownership we explored in Chapter 2.) That's why rules on self-ownership do not easily align with red or blue states, North or South, high- or low-wealth regions, within groups of religious conservatives or secular feminists, or around the dinner table.

Thinking of self-ownership as a dimmer is challenging, but it can move us past a simple tug-of-war over the on-off switch. Instead, we can design ownership to address each core value directly on its own terms. It may be possible to create win-win solutions. But for this, we need access to one more crucial ownership design tool, and that's where we turn now.

Moore and Less

Your body may be a gold mine, but you are not always the miner. Others may extract resources from your body for their profit. John Moore learned this the hard way.

While working on the Alaska pipeline in the 1970s, Moore was diagnosed with hairy-cell leukemia, a rare cancer. He sought treatment from David Golde, a leading cancer researcher at the University of California in Los Angeles. Golde successfully removed Moore's diseased spleen. For the next seven years, Moore made regular return visits to Los Angeles to give samples of his bone marrow, blood, and semen. He tolerated these difficult trips, assuming they were part of his follow-up care. Moore did wonder, though, why a doctor in Seattle couldn't have taken the samples. Moore began to get suspicious when Golde offered to pay for his flights to Los Angeles and to lodge him at a fancy hotel, the Beverly Wilshire.

At one visit, Moore refused to sign a consent form asking him to grant the University of California "all rights" in any potential product developed from his blood or bone marrow. Golde followed up immediately, calling Moore three times to ask why he had not given consent. When Moore stalled, saying he must have forgotten, Golde sent letters to Seattle pestering him to sign. Moore hired a lawyer.

He learned that the white blood cells from his cancerous spleen were special, overproducing a particularly valuable protein. After the surgery, Golde and his colleagues began devising a way to isolate that protein and generate it in large quantities for sale. They used Moore's spleen to develop a new cell line—cells that survive in a petri dish, reproducing independently and in perpetuity. Moore realized that some of the seven years of postsurgery procedures he had endured were meant to increase Golde's wealth, not Moore's health.

Soon after Moore refused to sign the consent form, Golde filed a patent claiming ownership of the "Mo" cell line. Golde had already received over $3 million in value from a biotech company and stood to earn many times more—at the time, the value of the Mo cell line was forecast at several billion dollars. Moore got nothing. He told a reporter, "It was very dehumanizing to be thought of as Mo, to be referred to as Mo in the medical records: 'Saw Mo today.' All of a sudden I was not the person Golde was putting his arm around, I was Mo, I was the cell line, like a piece of meat."

Moore sued Golde and UCLA for stealing his cells and demanded payment, arguing his self-ownership should include at least as much right to profit from his spleen as was claimed by the doctors who commercialized it without permission.

Moore's case is not unique. You may recall the tale of Henrietta Lacks, made famous by Rebecca Skloot's gripping book *The Immortal Life of Henrietta Lacks* and the HBO movie starring Oprah Winfrey. While Lacks was dying from cervical cancer in 1951, researchers at Johns Hopkins University took her cells and used them to create HeLa, the first self-perpetuating human cell line. It is no exaggeration to say that HeLa revolutionized modern medicine and underwrote many biomedical industry fortunes—making possible, to give just a few examples, chemotherapy, the polio vaccine, and the IVF techniques that jump-started egg donation and gestational surrogacy markets.

One patient, however, did not fare so well. The doctors who treated Lacks never asked permission to use her cells and never paid her. Lacks's husband and children discovered HeLa's existence only years later when researchers contacted them for tissue samples to help refine the cell line. Elsie, Lacks's oldest daughter, died indigent; her son Joe was imprisoned; another daughter, Deborah, was a teen mum who suffered from arthritis and depression. Lacks's family would have led different, likely better, lives had they received even a tiny fraction of HeLa's profits.

Lacks never got to assert claims based in self-ownership. She died soon after her cells were removed. Moore, however, lived long enough to sue, and he pursued his claim all the way up to the California Supreme Court. Did UCLA scientists steal cells from him? For the court, the answer depended on whether Moore owned the cells when Golde took them.

The court relied on the on-off-switch approach, reducing the conflict down to one stark choice over who owns the cells: Moore or Golde. If the switch is on, Moore wins, the cells are his to sell; off, Moore loses, the cells are protected from the market to support other fundamental values. For the court, the key value was promoting scientific innovation—they were not so concerned with Moore's personhood. Allowing patients any control over excised tissues would, the court feared, bog down doctors in expensive and lengthy negotiations, turning "every cell sample a researcher purchases [into] a ticket in a litigation lottery." The net result would "hinder research by restricting access to the necessary raw materials." And the simplest way they thought to avoid this outcome was to flip the self-ownership switch to off. So Moore lost.

He died unpaid in 2001 at age fifty-six.

The court's solution is puzzling. It's true, promoting scientific research is an important value. Golde worked hard to develop the cell line—and his productive labor may deserve an ownership reward. But labor is not all we care about. Why shouldn't Moore have a countervailing claim to valuable resources derived from his body? And how about protecting vulnerable patients during surgery? The court's concern for "access to the necessary raw materials" translates to doctors strip-mining people's bodies for their profit. That doesn't sound so respectful of human dignity.

In effect, the court told Moore that his body is so sacred, he's the only one who won't get paid from the Mo cell line.

The justices failed to consider an ownership tool that allows us to reconcile Moore and Golde's claims—letting us set the dimmer to reward self-ownership and labor, dignity and scientific progress, all at the same time. Lawyers call this tool the *rights-remedies distinction*. It's a two-step process. Here's how it works.

First, we set Moore's rights in the excised cells. Most people would agree that, at a minimum, Moore's self-ownership should include the right to say, *No. Hands off. Burn the cells after surgery.* This baseline aspect of self-ownership explains why no one accuses you of being a kidney-hoarder if you keep your spare in your body, even though your choice condemns—with near certainty—some other identifiable person to death. Similarly, by analogy, you are not a cell-hoarder if you decline to advance medical research, even if the noblest doctor pleads for access to your particular cells because of their extraordinary scientific value. But if self-ownership only includes the right to say no, then many valuable body-derived resources may be lost to science.

By contrast, if we push the dimmer up somewhat, then patients have more reason to say yes to making their cells available. One response could be to push the dimmer up but only a little, allowing Moore to give the cells away, like giving away a kidney or placing children for adoption. Why shouldn't Moore be able to direct his body's bonanza to the hospital or charity of his choice? Or slide the dimmer further up, allowing restricted sales like with stem cells in Montana. Or push even further, giving Moore a reason to say, *Yes, take the cells you want, if you can meet my price,* like Ivy League eggs today. In each case, Moore's rights derive ultimately from self-ownership—*It's mine because it comes from my body.*

Here's the challenge: as we push the dimmer up, it seems we give patients more ability to control the direction of research, perhaps letting them block science that saves millions of lives. Are we trapped in a tragic choice—caught between respecting patients' self-ownership and enabling scientists' labor?

No, the solution appears as we move from *rights* to *remedies*. After setting Moore's rights, then we have to make an independent choice:

what remedy should we give Moore if Golde takes the cells without permission? (We touched on remedies in Chapter 3, when describing the damages-injunction distinction.) Rights and remedies together make up ownership—neither is meaningful without the other. Can we design a rights-remedy combination that promotes scientific labor while valuing patient autonomy and human dignity? Assuming we grant Moore ownership rights in his cells against Golde's unconsented use, and Golde takes the cells anyway, here are a few remedy options:

- Golde pays Moore one dollar.
- Golde owes Moore fair market value for the cells.
- Golde transfers all patents and profits to Moore.
- Golde pays Moore a mandatory licensing fee.

We could require Golde to make a one-dollar payment as a remedy. As a matter of law, a dollar respects Moore's right not to have his cells used without permission. It just doesn't respect that right very much. Judges call this *nominal damages,* a remedy they use when the harm caused by the rights infraction seems relatively trivial, symbolic, or hard to measure. This remedy acknowledges that something was taken from Moore in principle, but it says other values are more important in practice. Nominal damages would be a light slap on the wrist to Golde. The message for future deviant doctors would be "rummage away."

Next, consider awarding Moore *fair market value.* The word *fair* is right in the name of the remedy—what could be wrong with that? The problem is the fair market value of Moore's cancer cells might well be zero or a billion dollars—it depends on how the judge evaluates the proportional contribution of Moore's cells to the overall value of Golde's patented cell line. And on whether the judge values the cells before the surgery or after the cell line is in view. In the future, doctors may gamble, take the cells, pay fair market value, and keep the patents and profits. Or maybe they will be too uncertain how judges will rule, so they will discard the cells, and science will suffer.

There's a simple way to remove uncertainty. Transfer all Golde's patents and profits from the Mo line to Moore. Lawyers call this remedy *disgorgement.* In theory, disgorgement removes the incentive to unjustly enrich yourself at another's expense. Why bother taking in the first place if you have to hand everything over, including the value from your own labor? Along these lines, an even tougher remedy would be to impose a criminal penalty and jail Golde. This remedy would send the strongest message: *Don't break into people's homes and steal stuff; don't break into patients' bodies and take away "raw materials."*

Realize, though, that the stronger the remedy we use to vindicate Moore's right, the less likely future doctors will be simply to take cells. (This is the *ex ante* effect we discussed in Chapter 2.) Instead, researchers will be more likely to try to negotiate deals in advance with patients. But that's just the outcome the court most feared: miring researchers in endless negotiations, exposing doctors to lawsuits if they secured the wrong permission (or nuisance suits even if they got the right permission), and shifting patient-doctor relations in an unseemly direction. Do we really want surgeons haggling with vulnerable patients over the price of their body parts just before going under the knife?

Ownership design is more art than science. There are many more options available than the ones just discussed, including, as it turns out, one nicely tailored to our dilemma. It's called a *mandatory license.*

Mandatory licenses are how radio stations play the songs they want without negotiating in advance with every Madonna, Kanye West, and a hundred thousand other music copyright owners. Radio stations tote up their playlists, multiply the number of songs by a preset mandatory licensing fee, and send periodic checks to payment clearinghouses (including ASCAP, BMI, and SoundExchange for aficionados). The clearinghouses aggregate those payments—along with payments from nightclubs, restaurants, karaoke bars, and digital streaming services—and then send one check to each artist based on the number of times their songs were played. It's not perfect—some songs are a lot more valuable than others—but it's easy to administer. The mandatory license means no negotiations, no gridlock, no lawsuits. Everyone pays; everyone gets paid.

We could adapt this remedy for excised cells. Recognizing patients' self-ownership rights in resources derived from their body parts shows respect for human dignity and autonomy. Some patients may prefer to say, *No, you may not use my cells,* and that should be their right. But we want them to say, *Yes, let's advance science.* To encourage that, we can protect self-ownership rights with a simple, easy-to-administer mandatory remedy—such as a small fixed percentage of resulting patent royalties. This dimmer setting means that if scientists make a billion dollars, then patients—self-owners who can choose to provide or destroy the necessary raw materials—also get paid.

All these choices are becoming more urgent as scientists combine big data with individualized medicine. A recent *New York Times* headline reads: WHY DIDN'T SHE GET ALZHEIMER'S? THE ANSWER COULD HOLD A KEY TO FIGHTING THE DISEASE. Stories like this never even consider whether we should view genetic mutations as anything other than raw materials, whether we should treat patients with greater respect than Moore or Lacks received.

You may well reject an in-between dimmer setting, like patient self-ownership coupled with a mandatory license. That's reasonable. Many prefer the on-off options: these extremes are straightforward to explain and even easier to administer. But understand the stakes. If you flip the switch off, individuals have little affirmative reason to choose to advance science. You limit the sick and vulnerable to making altruistic donations to profit-seeking scientists. If you choose the on setting, perhaps you see brokers hawking body parts to scientists in a ghoulish free-for-all. Neither option looks good. By contrast, savvy ownership design lets you set the dimmer so patients are neither slaves nor tyrants.

The dimmer image explains why control of body parts varies so much; the rights-remedies tool shows how to reconcile conflicting values. Last, we come to the most decisive question: Whose unseen hand is on the dimmer, setting rights and remedies? Who should decide these rules?

Womb for Rent

The law is surprisingly silent on ownership of bodily resources. In America, the 1984 National Organ Transplant Act is an exception. NOTA bans selling kidneys for transplantation, but it's silent on sales for research and experimentation. It bans surgically extracted stem cells but is unclear on blood draws. And what are the rules for patients like Moore and Lacks when deviant doctors treat them as raw materials? No one knows for sure. When and how can people say yes to selling bodily resources?

The answer: each of the fifty states makes its own rules. Every time you cross a state border, unseen hands move the ownership dimmer. The variety is striking.

Consider *gestational surrogacy*, an evolving market based on self-ownership. In 2018, following the birth of their third child, Kim Kardashian West and Kanye West posted their thanks: "We are incredibly grateful to our surrogate who made our dreams come true with the greatest gift one could give." California makes surrogacy relatively easy for the Wests and other wealthy people who want to rent another woman's womb. By contrast, until February 2021, New York banned surrogacy. Well-off New Yorkers—whether infertile couples or same-sex ones—had to travel to acquire their babies.

New York Times Magazine writer Alex Kuczynski crossed the Hudson River. "Exhausted by years of infertility, wrung emotionally dry by miscarriage, my husband and I decided we would give gestational surrogacy—hiring a woman to bear our child—one try," she wrote. "It was a desperate measure, to be sure, and one complicated by questions from all the big sectors: financial, religious, social, moral, legal, political." Luckily for Kuczynski, she had plenty of cash and an ability to travel. A womb broker led her to Cathy Hilling, a forty-three-year-old Pennsylvanian, mum to three children, and recent surrogate for another infertile couple.

Kuczynski and her husband created an embryo that they had implanted in Hilling. Nine months later Hilling delivered baby Max and returned home with her $25,000 fee. The Pennsylvania county clerk named Kuczynski and her husband as Max's legal birth parents, meaning they did not have to adopt the boy from Hilling, who actually gave him birth. As soon as Max was born, Kuczynski could bring her baby home to New York.

The most surrogacy-supportive states—California, Connecticut, Delaware, and a few others—give "intended parents" like Kuczynski certainty up front regarding their parental rights. New York took the opposite view, along with an odd assortment of states—Arizona, Indiana, Louisiana, and Michigan. If you want to rent a woman's womb in America, you must pay exceedingly close attention to where the contracts are signed, the embryo is implanted, and the baby born.

Variation also exists across countries. While some American states are relatively favorable to surrogacy, Western Europe is more uniformly hostile. When Thomas Reuss and Dennis Reuther, a German same-sex couple, wanted a baby, they, like Kuczynski, traveled to Pennsylvania. Their surrogate bore them Nico, their first son, and later carried twins for them. In Europe, "We regard surrogacy as exploitation of women and their reproductive capacities," says one German fertility doctor. "In our view, the bonding process between a mother and her child starts earlier than at the moment of giving birth." Unless you can afford to fly to America.

Surrogacy in America is not cheap. Prices start at $100,000 and escalate from there—$10,000 to secure an egg from the intended parent (more if the egg is premium), $30,000 to the fertility clinic and doctor, $20,000 for the surrogacy agency, and $10,000 for lawyers, along with insurance, travel, and many other expenses. The gestational surrogate earns perhaps $25,000—often enough to make a substantial difference in her life by paying for school, a mortgage, or family support. The intended parents must pay most of these expenses even if the surrogate does not become pregnant or suffers a miscarriage. The costs can mount quickly, but the result is you can custom-craft your own child today with purchased sperm and eggs and a rented womb.

Some couples have tried to lower the expense by traveling to India, Laos, Thailand, Mexico, or elsewhere, but they risk worse medical care, less healthy surrogates, and an uncertain legal environment. India shut down its billion-dollar surrogacy market in 2017. Now it allows only altruistic (unpaid) surrogacy, and only for heterosexual, childless Indian couples. Banning the paid market drove it underground—as with kidney transplants. Indian women are still implanted with embryos for pay, but they are flown to Nepal or Kenya to give birth and hand over the babies. Similarly, after Cambodia banned surrogacy, brokers began flying Cambodian women to Thailand to give birth.

According to one fertility lawyer, "anyone who can afford it chooses the United States." American states are cornering the legal market in womb rentals, and the country now runs a trade surplus in gestational services.

The IVF technology underlying gestational surrogacy (and egg donation) is recent, built on the HeLa cell line derived from Henrietta Lacks's body and refined only in the 1980s. As soon as gestational surrogacy became medically possible, people began asking: Should it be allowed? Where should we set the dimmer for market access to our body's *capacities* and not just for its *components*?

As with eggs and kidneys, we often reason by analogy. For many, the closest analogy is *traditional surrogacy*, where the surrogate is also the biological mother. For most of human history, this was the only viable form. And not surprisingly, intrafamily conflicts often ensued.

In Genesis, Sarah comes to Abraham and says, "God has kept me from bearing a child; please lie with my handmaid; maybe I shall have a son through her." Hagar then gives birth to Ishmael. Disputes between the descendants of Sarah and Hagar, Isaac and Ishmael— Jews and Muslims—continue to this day. In *The Handmaid's Tale*, Margaret Atwood gives us a dystopic vision of traditional surrogacy, updated as reproductive rape and slavery.

The first American court ruling on surrogacy came in the 1985 *Baby M* case. Mary Beth Whitehead, a traditional surrogate, contracted to deliver a baby to Elizabeth and William Stern. Then Whitehead changed her mind and tried to keep the child, fleeing the state with the infant. The Sterns sued. Some feminists supported a woman's freedom to sell womb services; others, including Betty Friedan and Gloria Steinem, argued that surrogacy dehumanized the birth mother, reducing her to a mere commodity. Conservatives split along similar lines.

For the New Jersey Supreme Court, the question was: Who decides the boundaries of self-ownership? Can individuals set their own rules via contract, or should public self-ownership values override private choice? The court said no to private choice. Surrogacy contracts are "illegal, perhaps criminal, and degrading to women," wrote the chief justice. "There are, in a civilized society, some things that money cannot buy." The *Baby M* decision had a powerful influence, leading New York to ban surrogacy contracts—at just the moment IVF was making gestational surrogacy possible.

Should we set the self-ownership dimmer for gestational surrogacy at the same place New Jersey set it for traditional surrogacy?

Before you decide, consider what's analogous and distinctive about the practices. Many of the most wrenching challenges are analogous: What if an intended parent wants to abort a seriously ill fetus and the surrogate refuses, or vice versa? How much medical risk should the surrogate be expected to bear for the fetus's health?

But there are important distinctions as well. Genetically, the embryo is unrelated to the surrogate who gestates it—a biological difference that changes how many people view the legal, ethical, and emotional relationships among the parties. It's easy to frame the baseline story as "my surrogate is gestating my embryo." One can imagine the embryo as a tenant with a nine-month lease—and the intended parents are paying the rent. From this perspective, maybe gestational surrogacy is nothing more than womb rental.

If you accept this analogy, then it's straightforward to allow surrogacy contracts while imposing safeguards, just as we do with other landlord-tenant arrangements. Surrogacy agencies and intended parents seek women they believe will be stable "womb-lords"—usually, educated middle-class women who have already had children, completed their families, and report at least partly altruistic motives for becoming surrogates. There are medical checks and required counseling. With these safeguards, gestational surrogacy could become an ordinary, thoughtfully regulated feature of women's self-ownership, not necessarily more coercive or degrading to our common humanity than the experience of renting an apartment in someone else's home.

Surrogacy is perhaps a close case, with reasonable views in rapid flux. It should be no surprise that states keep sliding the ownership dimmer to different settings. Nor is it surprising the settings do not track a simple red–blue or North–South divide—legislators grab for simple on-off analogies rather than doing the hard work of ownership design.

And when states flip, their choices interact with other states' decisions. After New Jersey became more supportive of paid surrogacy in 2018, the shift affected New York. New York women could not earn surrogacy income like their counterparts across the Hudson. And more to the point, wealthy New Yorkers like Alex Kuczynski still faced the inconvenience of having to travel to hire surrogates. So the politics in Albany changed, and the state flipped its rule.

Ownership design is always an ongoing battle between competing and overlapping levels of government—federal, state, county, and local. Historically, state legislatures have been the central actors. They are our so-called laboratories of democracy. But sometimes Congress imposes national uniformity, as with NOTA, and overrides state-level experimentation. And sometimes courts chart their own path, like when the appeals court allowed sales of stem cells in western states, despite NOTA's prohibition.

Who should be making these choices? In America, there is no simple answer. Say a majority in a California town opposes surrogacy. Should they be able to ban it within city limits even though the state allows it? Or should a city be able to allow it contrary to a state ban? What if it's banning plastic shopping bags, or marijuana, or guns? At its core, the tension is over whose hand should control the ownership dimmer. As governments experiment with ownership, innovations spread—a virtuous learning circle for some observers, a vicious one for others.

Sometimes states end up as *ownership outliers*. Since its nineteenth-century mining days, Nevada has been the only state in which self-ownership may include the right to sell sexual services. The state authorizes smaller rural counties—but not Las Vegas and Reno—to license brothels. The argument is that prostitution will happen anyway, so why not legalize and regulate it to empower people who choose sex work, to limit coercion, increase safety, and generate tax revenue? That's the theory. The practice, however, is often seen as exploitative and degrading. No state has followed Nevada's lead.

Nevertheless, a single state's self-ownership choices can have nationwide effects. Consider the phenomenon of virginity auctions, which are occasionally advertised online. When a twenty-two-year-old

Sacramento State University student, going by the name Natalie Dylan, decided to auction her virginity to pay for graduate school, she turned to the Moonlight Bunny Ranch, a brothel in Carson City, Nevada. "I feel people should be pro-choice with their body, and I'm not hurting anyone," she said. "It really comes down to a moral and religious argument, and this doesn't go against my religion or my morals." In olden days, fathers owned their girls and traded their virginities for marriage dowries. Dylan's position was that if virginity still has value today, why shouldn't she be the one to cash in?

Dylan and Nevada would push the dimmer up. What sense is there in allowing prostitution but banning virginity auctions? After all, auctioning certain intimacies is already a staple of the celebrity charity circuit. Kissing George Clooney cost the winning bidder $350,000 for AIDS research; a $140,000 charity auction bid secured a twenty-second kiss with Charlize Theron. For Dylan, the brothel fielded ten thousand bids and settled on a $3.8 million offer with a $250,000 deposit, before the deal fell through.

Most people outside Nevada, though, can and do distinguish between selling a kiss for charity and virginity auctions. Every other state pushes the dimmer for prostitution, including virginity auctions, all the way down, removed from market sale. But in a sense, Nevada overrides those states' policies toward self-ownership because Nevada-based websites reach everywhere.

Dylan argues, "There's no right or wrong to this." We disagree. Getting self-ownership right really matters for virginity auctions, kidney sales, egg sales, and surrogacy. This is why legislatures and courts, businesses and individuals fight so hard to control the dimmer. Each of us must choose among competing commitments to freedom, coercion, and the good society as we shape our plans for action. This is what we meant in Chapter 1 when we wrote that "ownership is not like deciding between chocolate and vanilla ice cream." What happens in Vegas does not stay in Vegas.

The Curt Flood Act

We close with a contemporary puzzle: Who should own athletes' careers and, by extension, yours?

When fans name the greatest baseball players of the twentieth century, stars like Joe DiMaggio, Ernie Banks, and Ted Williams stand out. Looking back at their careers, one unifying trait is their loyalty. DiMaggio played his entire career, thirteen years, with the Yankees. Same for Banks—eighteen years with the Cubs. Williams played all nineteen years with the Red Sox, even returning after service in the Korean War. Quite a contrast from today, when superstars seem to jump teams for a bigger paycheck every few years.

But DiMaggio, Banks, and Williams were loyal because they had no choice. Starting in 1879, teams placed a "reserve clause" in every deal, giving owners the power to extend player contracts indefinitely with only modest pay increases. The breakout star player never got a big payday. If DiMaggio wanted to play in Major League Baseball, he would be a modestly paid Yankee unless the team decided otherwise. The Yankees owned his talent and could play him, bench him, or trade—that is, sell—him. That's what happened to Babe Ruth in 1919, when Red Sox owner Harry Frazee sold him to the Yankees to finance some Broadway theater productions.

Then Curt Flood challenged the baseball lockup system. He had been an All-Star outfielder for the St. Louis Cardinals through the 1960s. When the team tried to trade him to Philadelphia in 1969, he refused. He demanded to be treated as a "free agent," able to field competing offers from other teams. Flood wrote poignantly, "After twelve years in the major leagues, I do not feel I am a piece of property to be bought and sold irrespective of my wishes. I believe that any system which produces that result violates my basic rights as a citizen and is inconsistent with the laws of the United States and of the several States." To critics who said he should be content with his all-star status and just play, he replied, "A well-paid slave is still a slave."

As one commentator noted, "One way to think about slavery is as a history of confinement and the struggle of movement—being moved against your will or seeking to break free of those chains. A connection can be made to what we're seeing in the league today." Football, basketball, and hockey leagues more or less followed the baseball model when they were created, as did European soccer leagues, locking up talent, buying and selling players.

Flood pursued his attack on the reserve clause all the way to the U.S. Supreme Court. Though he won two World Series, he lost his case, then played one last year and ended his career as well. His cause, however, ultimately won out. After baseball players formed a union in 1975, they soon negotiated to eliminate the reserve clause. Finally in 1998, Congress passed the Curt Flood Act, prohibiting owners' total control over baseball players' careers.

There are still, however, plenty of restrictions on professional sports players. The National Basketball Association has team-wide salary caps for players—but no caps on owners' profits. When National Hockey League players wanted to represent their home countries in the Olympics, the team owners refused to let them participate. Leagues mandate what clothes and shoes players may wear, and how they may behave, even in their private lives.

Control also extends to university players. When television networks agreed to pay NCAA schools $9 billion in their latest contract, players saw none of that money. Spencer Haywood, a basketball Hall of Famer, commented, "You can't expect people to continue to work for nothing on a false hope of, 'Well this is about education, we are getting you an education, we will feed you.' It sounds a little like 400 years ago, like slavery." Former Indiana star player Isiah Thomas agreed, saying of the NCAA, "Their business model is based on a plantation business model. . . . And it's probably the only plantation that's allowed to exist legally in the United States right now."

By contrast, coaches, usually white, are able to move freely between teams and can be paid extraordinarily well—often more than university presidents.

After pressure mounted against the NCAA, it finally relented. Starting in the 2021–22 season, student players will be able to earn money through endorsements, social media deals, and other uses of their names, images, and likenesses. The NCAA had little choice: California passed a bill that would have allowed players to sign endorsement deals; other states were quickly following suit, and Congress was considering national legislation. The new NCAA rules come with many limits—no payments directly from the universities, no use of school or conference logos—but they will bring student athletes much closer to their professional counterparts in terms of self-ownership. "It's starting to beg the question," said sports agent Cameron Weiss. "If we're going to allow this at the college level, what about the high school level?"

Leagues argue for the lockups not to enslave their players but for a more prosaic reason: they say unless they can reap the reward, they won't have incentives to invest in long-term player development—farm teams, minor leagues, injured reserves for the pros; education and the amateur ideal for universities. Sports fans also are often not sympathetic to players' complaints. After all, professional players get to compete in the game they love, and student players do get (some) education. You can almost hear the snide remark on a sports radio call-in show, *For a million bucks a year, sign me up.*

So should we push the dimmer up, allowing players to sell entire careers freely in exchange for training, cash, and certainty? Or should we push the dimmer a little bit down, allowing athletes to sign multi-year contracts but still ensuring they retain some freedom to renegotiate their life paths? In other words, should career-long lockups like the reserve clause be a part of ordinary sports markets or rejected as akin to modern slavery?

Before you answer, consider that it's not just elite athletes who are facing this self-ownership dilemma. When Krishna Regmi first started working in Pittsburgh as a home health care aide, his employer gave him a stack of paperwork to sign. "They just told us, 'It's just a formality, sign here, here, here,'" he recalled. He discovered the power of the *noncompete agreement* when his employer sued him for trying to move jobs.

About 20 percent of American workers are currently subject to a noncompete agreement, and almost 40 percent have signed one at some point in their working lives. Hospitals lock up doctors so they can't move to competitors; same with actors on television series, and coders in tech companies. And it's not just highly paid professionals whose capacities are tied up—the restrictions often cover temp warehouse workers, hair stylists, yoga instructors, even teenage camp counselors.

Fast-food restaurants often use a related tactic, called *no-poach* and *no-hire* clauses, to lock employees out of higher-paying jobs in businesses nearby. Jarvis Arrington worked as a ten-dollar-an-hour line cook at a Burger King in Dolton, Illinois. When he tried to get a higher-paying job in Chicago, he learned that no other Burger King franchise would hire him. Many janitors, landscapers, and other low-skill, low-wage workers are covered, and like Regmi and Arrington, they rarely know the rights they've signed away. Check out your employment contract. You, too, may be bound.

Many employers routinely insert noncompete clauses into employment contracts even in states where they are unenforceable. Why? People often wrongly believe their signature binds them, even to illegal terms. Companies take advantage of this psychological vulnerability to deter consumers from asserting their rights, just as landlords insert unenforceable clauses in leases to scare tenants. Most people are afraid to be sued, cannot afford legal help, and don't know the terms don't bind them. The result is that even unenforceable restrictions can tie employees to jobs for years, preventing them from seeking higher wages or escaping abusive bosses.

Would the same sports fans who were okay with the reserve clause for athletes be so confident if they knew noncompete restrictions also apply to the folks flipping burgers at fast-food restaurants and the janitors cleaning up late at night? Would you be okay if you learned these clauses might bind you to your job? How much of our body's capacities should we be able to sign away, consistent with respect for self-ownership? Here are some options:

- Permit self-enslavement again.
- Allow fully informed noncompetes.
- Accept limited noncompetes.
- Ban noncompetes.

The self-enslavement option hardly seems worth discussing. But for centuries, Americans understood it as perfectly consistent with self-ownership. Before Independence, half of white settlers from Europe came to America as indentured servants, bound for years to their owners. People indentured themselves for boat passage to America, to bring over close relations, or to support their families. This was a harsh deal: during the indenture, they could be sold like enslaved people or pledged as collateral for loans.

The Thirteenth Amendment banned indentured servitude, not just slavery. No one argues for self-enslavement today—allowing you to sign away your whole life to another, even for a few years. Any justifiable notion of self-ownership requires concern for our future selves—for the ability not just to write one contract one time, but to rewrite essential aspects of the story of our lives. Enslaving ourselves is outside the bounds of choice in a free society because it gives too little weight to our future well-being.

But how about the second option, pushing the ownership dimmer down enough to allow fully informed long-term noncompetes for a specified capacity? The problem is that writing fair deals is costly and time-consuming. Even star athletes with teams of expensive agents and lawyers have a hard time anticipating life's contingencies. Maybe fully informed deals are okay if we restrict them to the most highly paid workers? But even then, there must be limits, as the players' unions argued when insisting on free agency. And these deals are often renegotiated anyway when circumstances change a few years in.

The third approach, of limited noncompetes, results from the American practice of allowing states to define self-ownership. There is no federal law as yet, though Congress keeps circling around possible legislation. We see wide experimentation and constant flux in state law, just as with surrogacy. For years, big employers have been pushing to expand the grip of noncompetes as unions have weakened. They justify noncompetes by saying lockups motivate investment in training low-wage workers. Why invest in employees if they can immediately take their skills to rivals? Yes, they concede, noncompetes may lock in workers, but in exchange, they produce higher-skilled workers who earn higher wages.

The tide is turning, and now noncompetes face a backlash. As one state attorney general declared, "Non-compete agreements for low-wage workers are unconscionable. They limit mobility and opportunity for vulnerable workers and bully them into staying with the threat of being sued." The range of state approaches is striking. Seven states have banned noncompetes for low-wage workers. Oregon limited their enforceability to one year. Hawaii banned them for workers in the technology field; New Mexico banned them for health care workers. Massachusetts now requires employers to pay half of the former employee's salary during the period they are restricted from employment, absent a contrary agreement. Turns out, many states have noticed there's often more coercion and less wage-growth benefit for workers than employers promised.

Recently, some big employers have been reversing gear even in states that allow noncompetes. Amazon agreed to remove noncompete clauses that prevented warehouse workers from going to rival companies for eighteen months after leaving their job. Jimmy John's

Gourmet Sandwiches agreed to remove noncompetes preventing employees from making sandwiches for nearby rivals for two years. Did ending the lockups decrease employee wages or their training in sandwich-making? Probably not.

Finally, some states categorically refuse to enforce noncompetes. For over one hundred years, California, North Dakota, and Oklahoma have just said no—no to fully informed noncompetes, no to limited noncompetes. Employers in these states may use employment contracts to protect confidential information and trade secrets—so employees don't walk off with client lists—but not much more than that.

Here's one data point in support of the refuse-to-enforce-any-noncompete approach: Silicon Valley emerged, not by MIT in Massachusetts, but next to Stanford in California. Several studies attribute part of the difference between these tech hubs—and this is trillions of dollars in value and hundreds of thousands of jobs—to noncompete clauses. Silicon Valley thrives because workers can and do easily move from job to job, pollinating ideas from company to company and turbocharging innovation. That is harder to do in stodgy Massachusetts, where noncompetes have long locked workers in place.

Even in California, companies like Apple and Google fought to lock up their key employees. But they lost, and now the Valley helps power the global economy. At least in the tech industry, personal freedom dovetails with economic dynamism, the sacred with the profane.

Chapter 6

THE MEEK SHALL INHERIT VERY LITTLE

Valuable things rarely stay put for long. They move around from one owner to another. But how do they move? Most of the time, by purchase and sale. But where did the sellers get their things from? Yet another seller. And so on. For every single thing, we can trace a chain all the way back to the root of ownership. To the person who first made it *mine*—not by swiping a credit card, bartering some chickens, or unwrapping a gift, but by asserting a claim to original ownership.

We've explored five of these original claims. This chapter rounds out the ownership toolkit by looking at the sixth claim, one based on family ties—*It's mine because it's in my family.* A lot of property changes hands at critical moments in family life. Death is one such moment. Family members may claim things the deceased leaves behind. Marriage is another. Assets (and debts) often join at the altar and split on divorce.

Ownership within families spans a vast terrain, full of opaque rules that quietly build mountains of wealth high above plains of poverty. We provide just a peek at this landscape, exploring three inheritance tales and one divorce puzzle.

John Brown's Farm

As law professors, we often hear insightful stories from students in class who link personal experiences to the legal doctrines they are learning. Some years ago Heller was teaching about shared ownership of inherited land—a rather dry subject—when a Black student recounted the tale of her family farm. As a child, she had attended reunions that brought relatives from all over the United States to an old farmstead in Mississippi. Meals were presided over by an elderly aunt who had never left the land. The student cherished her aunt and the farm.

At one point, however, a distant cousin with a trivial ownership share in the farm wanted cash, so he sold his share to someone outside the family. That buyer then forced a sale of the whole farm using ordinary American *partition* law—the rules for how we break up co-owned land. These rules create a business opportunity for unscrupulous buyers: track down distant heirs, buy their tiny share, and use it to trigger partition sales. These sales often take place in rigged markets with little information and few buyers. And that is exactly what happened to the student's family farm. It was auctioned on the county courthouse steps for a lowball sum. After the sale, the student's family did not hold another reunion. And they were not alone.

At the end of the Civil War, General Sherman promised freed slaves "forty acres and a mule." When the North failed to fulfill its promise, freed slaves took matters into their own hands, working in earnest to buy their own land. By 1920, almost a million Black families owned farms; they formed an integral part of the rural southern economy up through the 1930s and '40s.

Today Black families own fewer than nineteen thousand farms nationwide—a drop of 98 percent in less than a century, and a stark contrast with white-operated farms, which dropped by only half over the same period. Why the difference? In part, because of the consolidation of inefficient small farms and intense racial discrimination in farm lending, along with outright violence and intimidation.

But obscure family ownership rules also played a key role.

Here is one family's story. In 1887 John Brown bought eighty acres of land in Rankin County, Mississippi. He was part of the great wave of freed slaves who invested their life savings in farmland. John lived a long life. When he died in 1935, he did not leave a will. Ownership of his land split among his wife and nine children. In time they all died, also without wills, so the land was split further among grandchildren. One of John's children, Willie Brown, began consolidating ownership in the land by buying the shares held by relatives. By the time Willie passed away, he had accumulated over half the ownership interests in the family farm, which he left to his wife, Ruth.

In 1978 Ruth Brown asked a court to divide the farm so she would own her share of the land outright—a manageable forty-five acres out of John's original eighty. The other sixty-six Brown heirs would still co-own the balance, in shares ranging from $\frac{1}{18}$th of the farm down to a tiny $\frac{1}{19,440}$th. The court agreed to partition the parcel, but not by physically dividing the land. Instead, the judge ordered the entire farm sold and the money partitioned among the heirs according to their ownership fractions.

As often happens in such forced partition sales, a single outside company was the only bidder. In Brown's case, it was a local white-owned lumber company that wanted to cut the timber.

Even though the family collectively valued the farm far above its auction price, neither Brown nor any other heir placed a bid. Why? Partly because state law often requires the bid to be fully or substantially paid in cash on auction day, a rule that makes bidding impossible for most ordinary owners. Partly because there was no simple way for the Brown heirs to organize a joint family bid that pulled together resources from the scattered owners. Many heirs did not even know they were owners. And no single Brown heir could top the lumber company's lowball bid. This is commonplace. When a judge orders land auctioned on courthouse steps, the deal is final, even though the price is usually far below what is considered fair market value in an ordinary transaction.

Brown got a little cash from the auction, but not nearly enough to replace the forty-five acres she hoped to farm. And the family got nothing to compensate for losing its place of remembrance and gathering.

The Brown family story tracks the arc of Black farmland owner-ship in America. When John Brown bought his farm, Black families were rapidly accumulating land. By the time Ruth Brown lost it a century later, Black landownership in the United States was in rapid decline, a decline that has continued through today. Currently, Black farmers constitute less than 1 percent of American farmers, and Black families continue to lose farms at a rate three times that of whites.

The cause of this dramatic farm loss starts with inheritance law, in particular the consequences for family ownership when someone dies without making a will. Many poor Black farmers in the South were suspicious of local white lawyers, and for good reason, so they never made wills. This suspicion continues today, even among some wealthy Black people. Aretha Franklin and Prince could well have afforded the very best attorneys, yet both passed away without mak-ing wills. Overall, three-quarters of Black people do not have wills, more than double the percentage of whites.

The result for Black-owned land in the Southeast is that over a quarter is now *heir property*, averaging eight co-owners, five of whom live outside the region. Amazingly, more land in Mississippi is owned by Black people living in Chicago than by those living in Mississippi itself. One expert calls heir property "the worst problem you never heard of."

Inheritance law imposes enormous costs on Black people—indeed, on anyone who does not write a will. When you die without a will, the state splits ownership among people the law designates as heirs, in a specified priority: spouses and children, grandchildren, parents, siblings, and then more remote relatives. "Many assume that not having a will keeps land in the family. In reality, it jeopardizes ownership," said one heir property researcher.

Partition sales (like the one that cost Brown her land) are the primary way that most heir property is lost. Under state law, when land is co-owned, as with heir property, many management decisions effectively require unanimous consent. But if the goal is to operate a farm successfully, then a decision-making rule that requires unanimity is a terrible approach.

Maybe this strikes home. If you have a family vacation house, perhaps you inherited it, with your siblings as co-owners. Your parents probably hoped the cabin would maintain your bonds after they were gone. Often the kids do get along well enough, despite disputes over paying for a new roof and summer rentals. But for grandkids, and the generation after that, disputes intensify. People move away, and family members have ever-weaker ties to each other and to the land.

Here is the key to the whole unraveling, in sharp contrast with rules in most European countries: American co-ownership law offers no effective support for managing shared property. Just the opposite. It assumes people will want to split from each other so they can have their own separate property, and it encourages them to do so. In American state law, if one grandkid fixes the leaking roof, there's no way to force the others to chip in. The repair cost can be recovered from the other owners only after the home is partitioned and sold. So that's what happens.

American law, building on traditional UK common law, makes everything about managing co-owned property difficult, not just repairs. It can be impossible to get a loan with just a partial ownership interest, so the land remains undeveloped. Often you can't get disaster relief either. Following Hurricane Katrina, up to $165 million of recovery funds went unclaimed because of difficulty in proving ownership of heir property. As a result, heir property often remains rundown and unimproved.

If any heir wants out of this co-ownership mess, then partition is the only solution, either by voluntary agreement or by court order. Historically, the law was written to prefer physical partition, like Ruth Brown sought. She wanted a forty-five-acre share of John Brown's eighty-acre parcel. But physical division can be a challenge to implement: land surveyors and appraisers are expensive; improvements on the land can be hard to divide; and the resulting lots are often too small to be economically useful. In practice and often in law, courts usually prefer to order the land partitioned by auction sale, especially if there are many heirs. Money is easier to split.

But this administrative ease comes at a cost. According to one analyst, the purchasers at these sales "are almost always white persons, frequently local lawyers or relatives of local officials, who make it their business to keep abreast of what properties are going to auction and who attend the auctions prepared to buy."

The U.S. Department of Agriculture says such sales are "the leading cause of black involuntary land loss." As a recent magazine feature on this practice explains, in one North Carolina county, "forty-two per cent of the [heir property] cases involved black families, despite the fact that only six per cent of Carteret's population is black."

The costs to Black families are high. Today median wealth among white families is about ten times higher than among Black families. The history of Black land loss is one of the contributors to this racial wealth gap. Says one heir property researcher, "If you want to understand wealth and inequality in this country, you have to understand black land loss."

The costs run deeper still. Selling a farm often breaks an intangible web of connections within the family, as happened to Heller's student when her Mississippi reunions came to an end. When a farm remains intact, an older family member might let some children settle on the land, and later the children might offer care in return. Landless elderly people are less able to mobilize this support and more likely to suffer lower living standards. The tragedy for the Browns was not only the lowball price and the wealth destruction but also the loss of the special value their farm held within their family. Lost family cohesion may be hard to measure in dollars, but it is a real cost.

Partition sales are not just of historical interest. Across the South, heir property currently makes up a third of remaining Black-owned farmland—roughly 3.5 million acres worth about $30 billion.

What can be done to prevent future loss of heir property farms? Ownership design, which created the problem, is the key to solving it. Many European countries have social policies and laws that help keep family farms intact. German law requires immediate reimbursement when one co-owner makes essential repairs, in sharp contrast with the American rule that reimbursement comes after partition. The German rule encourages maintenance and continued co-ownership rather than decay and partition. Even UK law—which had long been uniquely unsupportive of co-owned property—has recently shifted gears and moved closer to the cooperation-enhancing German approach. The details are complex, but the bottom line is that UK law now far surpasses its American progeny.

In America, the German model helped inspire the Uniform Partition of Heirs Property Act—a proposed reform developed by the U.S. Uniform Law Commission in 2010 and offered to state legislatures for enactment. The act is aimed at Black farm families who are land rich and cash poor, a combination that makes it difficult for them to get a loan from a bank or bid for the land in a sale. It sends most sales to the open market rather than to auctions on courthouse steps, gives family members the first option to buy, and requires judges to seek alternatives to sale if it will cause eviction or affect historic properties. For families who want to keep working together, these reforms can make it easier to keep the farm intact.

Seventeen states have passed some version of this law. For example, South Carolina now gives farm family members "rights of first refusal." And when "heritage land" is auctioned for a low price, family members have forty-five days to raise matching funds to buy it themselves. But eight southern states have failed to pass reforms—including North Carolina, the state with the most heir property.

Also, the legal reforms do not address the core management problem for heir property. Requiring unanimous consent creates classic ownership gridlock (see Chapter 3). In response, some public interest law groups have pioneered a solution to the gridlock dilemma by offering to help create family farm corporations for heir property. With a corporate structure, the new CEO—perhaps the elderly aunt still on the land—has the power to manage the farm, take loans or lease out the land, and host reunions or pay dividends to the other share owners. Family corporations are a better ownership technology than background co-ownership rules. But for most Black people, these potential solutions are too little, too late. Relatively few are left able to heed Toni Morrison's plea in her Nobel Prize–winning novel, *Song of Solomon:*

> Grab this land! Take it, hold it, my brothers, make it, my brothers, shake it, squeeze it, turn it, twist it, beat it, kick it, kiss it, whip it, stomp it, dig it, plow it, seed it, reap it, rent it, buy it, sell it, own it, build it, multiply it, and pass it on—can you hear me? Pass it on!

"A Meaningless System of Minute Partition"

The decline in Black landownership is not some strange anomaly. Native Americans have suffered a similar fate. The tragic stories of unjust wars, broken treaties, and forced migration are well known. Few, though, are aware how American inheritance law has diminished remaining Native American landholdings. Like heir property, much Native-owned land sits idle today, impossible to farm, mortgage, sell, lease, or use in any productive way.

How did Native Americans get stuck in this dismal ownership regime? In the 1880s, Congress decided to replace the "backward" practice of tribal landownership by dividing up reservations. The plan was that individual private ownership would speed tribal assimilation and disintegration. Native heads of households were "allotted" 320 acres; individuals received 160 acres of tribal lands. Not coincidentally, allotment left large tracts of "surplus" reservation land that could be distributed to white settlers.

To prevent allotments from quickly ending up in settler hands, the United States held these lands in trust ownership for Native American owners. The trust came with many restrictions on transfer. At first, ownership of the lands could not be transferred at all, even deliberately through sale or a will. Instead, when an owner died, the land was required to be split among heirs. After one generation, a parcel might have three owners; after two generations, maybe nine owners; after three, maybe twenty-seven. The government eventually allowed transfers by will but did not offer funds to pay to write them. For most Native American landowners, shares continued to be split among heirs.

As early as 1928, Congress realized that the allotment program was a disaster. One Congress member, in a speech on the House floor, said that "good, potentially productive, land was allowed to lie fallow, amidst great poverty because of the difficulties of managing property held in this manner." During a reform attempt in 1934, another member of Congress said, "The administrative costs become incredible. On allotted reservations, numerous cases exist where the shares of each individual heir from lease money may be 1 cent a month. The Indians and Indian Service personnel are thus trapped in a meaningless system of minute partition in which all thought of possible use of land to satisfy human needs is lost in a mathematical haze of bookkeeping."

Since the 1930s, no new lands have been added, but the millions of acres already allotted have continued to fractionate. Congress attempted to tweak the system in the 1980s by having tiny fractional shares revert to the tribe when an owner died. Sadly, the Supreme Court struck down this sensible reform, even though the justices understood that fractionation had become "extreme" and "extraordinary":

> Tract 1305 [on a Dakota Reservation] is 40 acres and produces $1,080 in income annually. It is valued at $8,000. It has 439 owners, one-third of whom receive less than $.05 in annual rent and two-thirds of whom receive less than $1. . . . The administrative costs of handling this tract are estimated by the Bureau of Indian Affairs at $17,560 annually.

The justices made a mistake. Instead of allowing Congress to unlock value through ownership design, the Court further entrenched the government-imposed "meaningless system of minute partition." A significant portion of the Bureau of Indian Affairs budget has long been consumed in tracking fractional shares rather than supporting Native American education, employment, or infrastructure.

The fractionation tragedy is not only an ownership disaster but also a failure of judicial reasoning and political will. Until recently, about 6 million acres of Native American land have been tied up in 100,000 fractionated tracts, owned by 250,000 landowners, holding 2.5 million fractional interests. In the past few years, a $1.9 billion buyback program has restored about one-third of those interests to tribal ownership. The buyback funds come from tribal money the federal government agreed to repay to settle one of the largest class-action lawsuits in American history. But even with the buybacks, much allotment land still serves as a frustrating reminder of loss rather than as a source of livelihood and connection.

You know the biblical passage *The meek shall inherit the earth.*

This ownership maxim misleads, like all the others we've explored. On earth as we know it, the meek often inherit very little.

And that's no accident. Why did Ruth Brown lose her Mississippi farm? Why does Tract 1305 on a Dakota reservation generate such frustration? Partition and lost inheritances result from too much focus on *exclusion* at the expense of good *governance*. The *exclusion-governance* balance is a central lever of ownership design.

Our gut reaction to the "what is ownership" question often comes from a place of exclusion. It's the KEEP OUT sign we nail to the barbed-wire fence. In the enduring words of William Blackstone, the great codifier of English law, writing in 1763, private property itself is "that sole and despotic dominion which one man claims and exercises over the external things of the world, in total exclusion of the right of any other individual in the universe." *If it's mine, it's not yours.*

Much old-fashioned American law (and UK law, until recently) assumes that sharing is the problem and exclusion provides the solution. So when states see co-owners—like Ruth Brown and her relatives—they offer partition to aid them in quickly separating from each other.

The mythic virtue of sole ownership runs deep—and is deeply misleading. The reality today is that, overwhelmingly, wealth in market economies is held not by individuals focused on exclusion but by groups of people working together. Think about marriage, condominiums and cooperatives, unitization, trusts, partnerships, and corporations. All these are successful examples of what Heller and Hanoch Dagan call *liberal commons* property—ownership designed to help groups of owners cooperatively govern scarce resources while preserving the essential autonomy of every individual. Liberal commons forms are also at the frontier of ownership innovation in environmental protection, like the catch share and cap-and-trade programs we discuss in Chapter 7.

While *exclusion* concerns the conflict between owners and strangers, insiders and outsiders, *governance* focuses on rules for how people who want to work together can do so successfully—not just for economic gain but also for social, even spiritual, reasons. When governance is well designed, individuals feel safe trusting each other, binding themselves together for their most important life projects— whether as spouses starting a family, condo owners sharing common space, law partners serving clients, or corporate investors creating a business.

To be successful, every enduring liberal commons must address three trade-offs. The first is the trade-off between individual choice and group authority. What can I do without asking the group's permission? Can I buy a big gift without clearing the expense with my spouse? As we'll see shortly, the answers vary across states (as they do across marriages). The second is the trade-off between enforcing majority decisions and respecting dissenting views. How should condo boards deal with Nahrstedt's defense of Boo Boo, Dockers, and Tulip (Chapter 4)? The last is the trade-off between protecting group values and allowing individual freedom to exit. Should there be a cooling-off period before divorce is final? How hard should it be to disown the group?

With exclusion and governance in mind, we can see why Black land loss has been so severe. The intersection of American co-ownership law with heir property makes governance virtually impossible; when co-ownership decisions require unanimity, partition and exclusion are the only practicable solution to almost any dispute among co-owners. Even a willing majority of Brown family co-owners could not get loans, make leases, or be repaid for repairs—in stark contrast to the cooperation-enhancing liberal commons form found in German co-ownership law.

America subjects its poorest and most vulnerable citizens to exclusion-oriented law that systematically thwarts efforts by co-owners, like Ruth Brown, to work things out. Over time these harsh rules have fragmented into oblivion what little wealth rural Black and Native American families struggled to accumulate. Weeds grow instead of crops.

For the rich, it's a different story.

"Only Morons Pay the Estate Tax"

On February 1, 1995, eighty-three-year-old Chester Thigpen testified before Congress—about as unlikely a setting as the tree farmer from Montrose, Mississippi, might possibly have imagined. The grandson of slaves, Thigpen had started farming at the age of seven, struggling with a mule to plow his uncle's cotton fields for thirty-five cents a day. His uncle managed to avoid the threats of partition and heir property, keeping the family farm intact.

In 1940 Thigpen purchased eighty-five acres from his uncle and slowly built up his holdings. With Rosette Thigpen, his wife, they gradually converted the cotton and row-crop fields into a working tree farm. Their attention to erosion control and wildlife habitat made the farm an environmental model for others. Thigpen was named National Tree Farmer of the Year, the first Black person to win the award.

But he was worried about the future of the farm and had come to Congress to express his fears. He testified not about pests or flooding but about the estate tax—a tax people pay the government on death for the privilege of being allowed to pass on property to a new generation.

"We also want to leave the tree farm in our family," he said simply. Hard work and careful stewardship over more than four decades had built the business. "Right now, people tell me that my tree farm could be worth more than $1 million. All that value is tied up in land or trees. We are not rich people. My son and I almost do all the work on this land ourselves. So under current law, my children might have to break up the tree farm or sell off timber to pay the estate taxes."

His closing lines spoke for future generations. "We just planted some trees on our property a few months ago. I hope my grandchildren and great-grandchildren will be able to watch those trees grow on the Thigpen Tree Farm—and I know millions of forest landowners feel the same way about their tree farms. We applaud estate tax reforms that will make this possible."

But here's the catch. Thigpen's farm was worth less than the minimum taxable threshold. After he passed away, his estate never paid anything; his family inherited the land tax-free. And according to his son, Thigpen had not drafted his own testimony—lobbyists against the estate tax wrote it for him. Thigpen was "the perfect poster child for the repeal campaign," law professor Michael Graetz has noted, "a front for wealthy white families who were financing the repeal machine." Repeal seemed a fool's errand at the time, but if successful, the effort could keep many billions of dollars in families backing the repeal campaign, headed by Charles Koch, Joseph Coors, and their wealthy friends—and help preserve their economic control down through the generations.

This was pure class warfare waged by billionaires through newspapers they owned, think tanks they supported, and legislators they funded. Their joint strategy was to telegraph concern for everyday Americans, while diverting attention away from the super-rich who alone paid the estate tax (and paid for its repeal). The master stroke for this campaign was a concerted effort to rebrand the debate as one about the "death tax." Frank Luntz, a political operative on the repeal payroll, later revealed that this rebranding "kindled voter resentment in a way that 'inheritance tax' and 'estate tax' [did] not."

To control the ownership narrative, the repeal campaign relied on personal stories that activated people's fears. That's why Thigpen was not alone testifying on the panel. With him were Bill McNutt, owner of Collin Street Bakery in Corsicana, Texas; Jim Turner, a rancher in Florida; and Robert Lange, a farmer from Malvern, Pennsylvania.

Each expressed concern that their family businesses would need to be sold to pay estate taxes. The key for pro-repeal lobbyists was that nearly 40 percent of Americans mistakenly believed they were in the top 1 percent, or soon would be, and thus were potentially subject to the tax.

Thanks to the lobbying campaign, Thigpen's story went viral. Luntz and his hired associates transformed a tax that affected fewer than two out of every hundred Americans into a seemingly populist cause. As one commentator notes, "Thigpen's story was repeated over and over again, and its racial undertones implied that the tax disproportionately impacts Black families. The only problem? It was a complete lie."

But the lie was effective. A *New York Times* story on the estate tax revealed that the proponents of repeal were unable to find a single farmer who had lost his or her business to the estate tax. Ironically, Thigpen's fellow small business owners would have been protected simply by raising the exemption limit a small amount—but that didn't suit the families behind the scenes who were paying for change.

When the campaign started, the federal version of the tax applied to estates worth over $600,000, with rates starting at 37 percent. In 2001, Congress started phasing out the tax; then in 2010 it raised the exemption to $5 million per individual. After President Donald Trump's 2017 tax bill, the individual exemption was boosted again, to $11 million. Today a married couple can accumulate over $23 million before their estate pays even a dollar of tax (and they can hire advisers to help them use specialized trusts and tax planning to cram in millions or tens of millions more under the tax-free limit).

If you are that rich, it gets even better: in many cases, not only is your wealth (and the extra crammed-in wealth) passed free of estate taxes upon your death, but much of it is not taxed during your lifetime, either. More than half of the biggest estates consist of stock, art, and real estate with *unrealized capital gains*—assets rich people accumulate that have appreciated in value. The capital gains are not taxed while you are alive (because there's no sale to trigger a tax); nor are they taxed when you die (because the assets are repriced to their value on the date of death and the lifetime gain disappears). This is an extreme version of the attachment principle we discussed in Chapter 4, applied to capital: wealth magnetically attracts wealth and—with sufficiently expensive lobbyists and advisers—repels taxation.

Today the estate tax applies to just two of every thousand people who die. It is a laser-targeted tax focused on those who can most easily afford to pay. Yet repeal continues to enjoy popular support—up to 70 percent. As Graetz says, this untaxed transmission of extreme wealth is "one of the most effective legislative campaigns in recent times." Lobbyists for the billionaire families and their multimillionaire allies certainly earned their extraordinary fees—successfully diverting the obligation to pay for government services onto everyone except those most able to do so. For the wealthy backers of the repeal campaign, investing in family ownership rules paid off handsomely, with a far higher rate of return than building actual businesses.

But estate tax repeal is just a start. The billionaires' club has a more elaborate game plan. The story starts one thousand years ago at the time of the Norman Conquest and the creation of England's aristocracy.

No Titles of Nobility

For much of human history, individuals didn't matter so much for ownership. Wealthy "owners" were merely their generation's guardian of family estates, obligated to transmit their ancestors' landholdings down to descendants. Though this may be hard to imagine today, in an important sense, the family was the owner, not any individual member.

Think about the popular TV series *Downton Abbey.* Set in England just before World War I, the story centers on Robert Crawley, Earl of Grantham, whose landed estate supports his family's refined lifestyle and the dependent economy of the local tenant farmers and villagers.

Life is good as lord of the manor, but Robert faces a problem. Under England's family ownership rules, his hands are tied. He doesn't fully own anything. *Entailment* means he controls the family estate as his generation's guardian—he could add to the family estate, but not sell or will away any part of it. *Primogeniture* requires that only his eldest male heir can inherit the land, house, and title in their entirety. Entailment and primogeniture were ownership tools that rich families developed to make sure they stayed rich. Historically, aristocrats like Robert could not vary this outcome by writing a will.

Because Robert has three daughters but no son, upon his death Downton Abbey will go automatically to Matthew Crawley, a distant third cousin and closest male heir who is (horror!) a middle-class lawyer in Manchester. Even worse, Lady Grantham (Robert's wealthy American-born wife, Cora) has been caught up in the family ownership dilemma. The large dowry she brought from New York has become inextricably part of the Downton Abbey estate under old "coverture" rules (noted in Chapter 5). When Robert dies, Cora's money, necessary for the estate's upkeep, goes to Matthew as well. Much of the show's first season turns on the family's efforts to bring Matthew together with the Granthams' eldest daughter, Lady Mary Crawley. If they marry, then the family will escape being booted off the estate on Robert's death. (The same marital imperative motivates Jane Austen's *Pride and Prejudice*.)

Until the industrial revolution, most wealth was held in land. Primogeniture was a powerful tool for aristocrats aiming to avoid fractionation among heirs, the outcome inflicted on Black and Native American owners—and on the Irish. Fractionation was in part responsible for the Irish Potato Famine and the resulting wave of immigration to the United States. Following the Popery Act of 1703, England did not allow primogeniture for Catholics in Ireland, so their farms fractured as generations passed. Plots shrank to the point that planting a diversified range of crops became impossible. Eventually, potatoes were the only viable, nutrient-dense food that could be farmed. When a blight killed that sole crop, there was no alternative. A million Irish people starved to death; an exodus of survivors came to America.

England's primogeniture rules also punished women—they were married off. And it left out younger brothers—they were shipped away to the military and the ministry. The rules even affected Julian Fellowes, the creator of *Downton Abbey*. Fellowes's wife, Emma Kitchener, could not inherit her uncle Earl Kitchener's title. Because the earl had no male descendants, the title would die with him. "I find it ridiculous," said Fellowes, "that a perfectly sentient adult woman has no rights of inheritance whatsoever when it comes to a hereditary title—I think it's outrageous, actually." Nevertheless, for English nobility, these costs were tolerable compared with the benefits: rewarding a single male heir meant the family could carry forward the entire estate intact from generation to generation.

It doesn't have to be this way. Some societies have favored the youngest son, while others have preferred daughters. But overwhelmingly, cultures have favored inheritance by the eldest son. Even in the mythical world of *Game of Thrones*, primogeniture vies with dragons in the ultimate claim to the Iron Throne. The key point is that every inheritance rule creates distinct winners and losers among descendants, either maintaining the estate intact or dividing it over time. There is nothing natural or preordained about who should inherit what—or even whether inheritance should be allowed at all. It's all contested.

Through careful ownership design, England's wealthiest families were able to perpetuate themselves as an elite class that has endured for centuries. A recent study showed, remarkably, that many of the most powerful English family names in 1170—decades before the

Magna Carta—still enjoy high social status more than eight hundred years later. And England is not alone: the richest families in Florence, Italy, today substantially overlap with the richest in 1427.

But this has not been the rule in America. Here inheritance is not a right that inheres in ownership; rather, it's a privilege the state chooses to offer—a distinction the U.S. Supreme Court explained when it first ruled the estate tax to be constitutionally permissible. From the Founding, Americans rejected family ownership rules that supported hereditary aristocracy. Entailment was substantially abolished. Primogeniture was never part of American law. The Constitution explicitly forbids "titles of nobility." *Downton Abbey* has an American audience, but it is not an American story.

As a historian observed, "Of all the potential perils to the new American republic, the prospect of concentrated power . . . troubled the intellectual leaders of the Revolutionary generation. Familiar as the founders were with old Europe . . . they understood why the accumulation of inherited wealth led to inequities and imbalances that inevitably corrupt any system of government." Passing vast wealth from generation to generation has long been denounced in America as a feudal and aristocratic affront to the country's civic ethos.

Nevertheless, by the end of the nineteenth century, America had drifted far from a country of yeoman farmers. It increasingly resembled the aristocracy and landed estates of England. The Gilded Age—lorded over by John Rockefeller, Cornelius Vanderbilt, J. P. Morgan, Andrew Carnegie, and other robber barons—concentrated wealth to an extent that the country had never before seen and that the Founders had labored to prevent.

Fears over the political power wielded by this small group of super-wealthy sparked a backlash. Teddy Roosevelt, making full use of his bully pulpit, called for both a progressive income tax and an inheritance tax. In 1916 Congress passed an estate tax, eventually setting the rate at 25 percent for estates over $10 million (worth over

$230 million in today's dollars). The tax helped pay for the U.S. war effort in World War I, and it achieved Roosevelt's goal to tame what he called "the really big fortune, the swollen fortune."

Politicians and the public understood the estate tax as a moral imperative. As Franklin Delano Roosevelt made clear, "The transmission from generation to generation of vast fortunes by will, inheritance or gift is not consistent with the ideals and sentiments of the American people." The president believed, as did most Americans, that each generation should stand on its own.

Even England came around on this point, abolishing both entailment and primogeniture in the 1920s and, following World War II, imposing a heavy inheritance tax. The real Downton Abbeys of the day were forced to sell their family holdings or become museums to afford "death duties," as the taxes were called there. By the early 1990s, in both England and America, it was well accepted that children should not inherit all their parents' wealth, that justice and morality require paying the state a substantial share for the privilege of being allowed to inherit at all and to help level the playing field in each generation.

But shared wisdom can change quickly. The recent increase to a $23.4 million estate tax exemption is just one small part of how rich families pass on privilege. We are well on the way to a second Gilded Age. You can now see why Gary Cohn, the former head of Goldman Sachs and chief economic adviser to Donald Trump, memorably said, "Only morons pay the estate tax" or "rich people with really bad tax planning." Gutting the estate tax is just one step in creating the conditions for the big prize: a perpetual American aristocracy.

That step recently happened in, of all places, South Dakota. Yes, the same South Dakota that Laura Ingalls Wilder described in the *Little House* books.

"A Real Boutique Place"

Aristocrats, as a rule, want to pass on family wealth indefinitely, locking in privilege forever. In England, along with entailment and primogeniture, the key building block that the wealthy used for wealth transmission was the *trust*—perhaps the single greatest ownership invention of Anglo-American law. Scholars attribute a substantial measure of the economic dynamism and dominance of the British Empire, and now the American one, to the power of the corporate form, a close relative of the trust.

Trusts are masterpieces of flexible governance.

In simple terms, a trust separates legal ownership from practical benefit. Imagine a wealthy owner places stocks, bonds, art, and real estate in a newly created trust to benefit family members. The owner appoints a trustee (a family member or paid professional) to manage the trust on behalf of the beneficiaries. The trustee is the legal owner, able to buy and sell the trust assets to ensure a prudent return; the beneficiaries receive the cash.

One advantage of trusts for wealthy owners is that they allow fine-grained control over beneficiaries' lives via instructions enforced by the trustees: "You get paid only if you graduate from college," or "if you join the family business," or "not if you marry Henry," whatever. Second, trusts shield beneficiaries from many of the challenges and responsibilities of their wealth. And third, trusts can last a long time, enduring as initial beneficiaries die off, and continuing to pass on wealth to later generations of beneficiaries.

But all trusts must expire. An old law, known as the *rule against perpetuities,* eventually brings them to an end. The English Crown put the rule in place in the 1600s, in part to beat back the rising aristocracy. Kings and queens did not want families to be able to hoard so many resources that lesser aristocrats could challenge the throne itself. Perpetuities law carried over to the American states.

The rule is the law students' nightmare; applying it on exams is tricky. But its effect is simple: it ruthlessly limits how long the dead can control the living. More or less, the rule allows people to tie up resources for the lives of people they know, usually their kids, and then for twenty-one years afterward. When the grandkids reach adulthood, the trust dissolves and the remaining assets are distributed outright to beneficiaries—free from trustee control. Liberating assets is good for the ultimate beneficiaries (who can direct their own lives), good for the Crown (which avoids too-powerful nobles), and good for society (the indolent rich are free to fall out of the ruling class, leaving space so others can rise).

Aristocrats, and wannabe aristocrats, did not love the rule against perpetuities. It was a roadblock to dynastic stability. What to do? Abolish the rule. For centuries, this has been a quest of the super-wealthy, the impossible dream, the Holiest Grail.

Enter South Dakota.

The story begins with credit cards. In the late 1970s, Citibank was going broke, hampered by "usury" limits—a biblically inspired cap on interest rates that lenders could charge. South Dakota governor William "Wild Bill" Janklow was looking to make a mark. He made a deal: if Citibank relocated its credit card division to the state, bringing four hundred jobs, the state would lift its caps on credit card interest rates. Then, because of an obscure 1978 Supreme Court decision, Citibank could export its sky-high South Dakota rates nationwide, along with a host of other deceptive and abusive lending practices. Other credit card companies followed, setting up small South Dakota outposts with national reach. That's why, to this day, you probably mail your credit card payment to a South Dakota P.O. box (or maybe to Nevada or Delaware, which gutted their usury laws to compete with South Dakota).

Thus was born America's trillion-dollar consumer debt overhang—debt that exceeds the future capacity to repay, and that blocks consumers' ability to borrow more, even for their own worth-while new projects.

Building on this success, Janklow turned to lifting the cap on intergenerational wealth transfers. With a brief law—just nineteen words—he abolished the rule against perpetuities for assets nominally held in South Dakota trusts. As journalist Oliver Bullough wrote on South Dakota's emergence as a global tax haven, "Aristocracy was back in the game."

South Dakota began advertising itself as the place to set up *dynasty trusts,* offering families the ability to perpetuate their wealth while helping them to avoid inheritance taxes. Suddenly South Dakota became the premier global money magnet. "To some, South Dakota is a 'fly-over' state," said the chief justice of the state supreme court, speaking before the legislature. "While many people may find a way to 'fly over' South Dakota, somehow their dollars find a way to land here."

This sounds almost gleeful, but who benefits in South Dakota? Almost no one. Certainly not South Dakota residents, if they even know that the perpetual-trust business exists. The change resulted in no tourism or investment bump. The wealthy set up these trusts from afar—typically they never even visit the state to sign papers. Nor does any of the money come to South Dakota in any meaning-ful way; it resides there solely as a matter of law. The trusts and their beneficiaries pay no income tax, capital gains tax, or inheritance tax to the state.

The only in-state benefits flow to the small, tight-knit group of lawyers, bankers, and accountants who sponsored Janklow's law and who now create and manage the trusts locally. One state leg-islator commented, "The voters don't have a clue what this means. They've never seen a feudal society, they don't have a clue what they're enabling. . . . I don't think there are 100 people in this state who understand the ramifications of what we've done."

South Dakota's success in enriching local elites caught the attention of family wealth lobbyists in other poor states with pliable legislatures—not just Nevada and Delaware but also Alaska and Wyoming. Today about a dozen states have entered the trust administration game.

In 1997 Alaska started marketing the *self-settled asset protection trust,* an innovation in which the trust creator can also be the beneficiary—you give yourself your own money in trust. This maneuver effectively puts a firewall between the wealthy owner and those owed money. The assets are legally owned by the trustee, often out of reach of creditors—including ex-spouses and children owed support by ex-husbands (usually), businesses trying to collect debts owed by the owner's failed ventures, and injured patients trying to collect on malpractice judgments against the doctors who harmed them.

Threatened by this competition from Alaska, South Dakota raised its game. Janklow created a task force to ask the wealthiest families, What more can we possibly give you? A South Dakota version of the self-settled asset protection trust soon followed, but with even more generous provisions for the donor. Nevada then upped the ante. This back-and-forth sparked a "race to the bottom" of ever more extravagant giveaways to the rich. South Dakota lets you add a *spendthrift trust* provision, under which trustees can choose when and where they pay beneficiaries. Creditors cannot intercept these payments ahead of time and find it nearly impossible to track the money later on. This provision allows trustees to keep getting cash to irresponsible beneficiaries who crash their Maseratis and stiff their victims. The state even offers special *purpose trusts* to direct money in dodgy ways that are disallowed elsewhere on public policy and morality grounds (like bestowing a fortune on your dog). Finally, South Dakota's nondisclosure rules let you keep much of this super-secret from people you have wronged.

As one financial adviser commented, South Dakota has "done a pretty good job in making themselves unique; a real boutique place."

By 2010, South Dakota trust companies had raked in about $60 billion in assets. By 2020, this passed $350 billion, coming not just from the new American aristocracy but also from corrupt oligarchs, drug kingpins, third-world despots, and others with hot money to shield, responsibility to deflect, and dynasties to build.

South Dakota is crushing Switzerland, the Cayman Islands, and other traditional tax-avoidance and banking-secrecy havens. If you are super-rich, you already know this; if not, it may be a surprise to learn that the globe's excess wealth spigot now drains into South Dakota trusts.

Historically, states did not undermine shared values and the national good so unilaterally, but long-standing norms of comity and forbearance are breaking down, with South Dakota leading the way. Advisers for the wealthy realized that America's decentralized ownership system creates an opportunity: a state can be as deviant as its average uninformed voter will tolerate, and then that state can impose those extreme views nationwide. Money is mobile. Add in a passive Congress, and states face almost no federal oversight.

No one in South Dakota complains about dynasty trusts because the harm falls on federal taxpayers and on people in faraway states like New York and California, where services are curtailed because of lost tax revenue. With South Dakota trusts, really rich people get the best of both worlds: they can live where they like without paying their fair share, while their money lives in South Dakota shielded from responsibility.

As baby boomers die in the coming decades, roughly $30 trillion will be passed on, the largest wealth transfer from one generation to another in human history. Most will be shielded from estate taxes. And most will go to children and grandchildren who did not earn their wealth but are protected from the consequences of their irresponsibility. Why? Because as a matter of trust law in places like South Dakota, the dissolute offspring don't "own" any assets, only the trust does.

By contrast, people who have the bad judgment to earn a paycheck—rather than inheriting it in an asset protection trust—are not so lucky. If you, a wage earner, injure someone driving your Honda or if you refuse to pay child support, the state will garnish your wages; that is, they will intercept your paychecks until you have paid off the court judgment. Not so for the super-rich. Freedom from garnishment is a special privilege reserved to those who inherit via spendthrift trusts.

When this inequity first began emerging in the 1890s, John Chipman Gray, America's then-leading property lawyer, railed against it. "That grown men should be kept all their lives in pupilage, that men not paying their debts should live in luxury on inherited wealth are doctrines as undemocratic as can well be conceived," wrote Gray. Allowing spendthrift trusts would create, he feared, "an aristocracy, though most certainly, the most contemptible aristocracy with which a country was ever cursed."

The first Gilded Age, when Gray was writing, spurred the adoption of income and estate taxes to battle harms from extreme inequality and to prevent the entrenchment of family dynasties. The hope was to return America to a more egalitarian time. And indeed, for decades, the tax scheme worked. The country became substantially more equal at the same time it became enormously wealthier.

But now the second Gilded Age is leading in the opposite direction. Already the richest 1 percent of Americans own about 40 percent of the nation's wealth (by comparison with about 23 percent in England and France and 35 percent in Germany). And that share is increasing, while the incomes and wealth of nearly all the rest are stagnating or dropping.

A century before Gray, America's Founders were already well aware of this danger. They would be dumbfounded today that we are passively tolerating the creation of a new Gilded Age. In an 1813 letter to John Adams, Thomas Jefferson argued there was a meaningful distinction between America's "natural aristocracy" founded on "virtue and talents" and its "artificial aristocracy, founded on wealth and birth." The key for Jefferson was that "the artificial aristocracy is a mischievous ingredient in government, and provision should be made to prevent its ascendency."

In reply, Adams argued that the American political institutions they had created were more robust than Jefferson feared. When "honor, wealth, and power are made hereditary by municipal laws and political institutions," wrote Adams, "then I acknowledge artificial aristocracy to commence, but this never commences till corruption in elections becomes dominant and uncontrollable." The key for Adams was that "we, to be sure, are far remote from this. Many hundred years must roll away before we shall be corrupted."

Jefferson was right on the danger; Adams on the timeline; and Gray on the consequences.

A country created in opposition to inherited status now tolerates states like South Dakota and Nevada whose legislatures affirmatively promote dynastic wealth and responsibility evasion. This is not a progressive position, certainly. But neither does it fall within any intelligible version of American conservatism, a political tradition committed to individual freedom, opportunity, and markets.

Today's artificial aristocracy radiates an above-the-law attitude. You hear the contempt not just from economic advisers like Cohn, who says only morons pay estate taxes, but also from real estate billionaires like Leona Helmsley, known as the "Queen of Mean" for suing her contractors and stiffing her service people. Before being jailed for felony tax evasion, Helmsley famously uttered what could be the rallying cry for creators of South Dakota trusts: "We don't pay taxes. Only the little people pay taxes."

To drive home her point, when she died in 2007, Helmsley left $12 million in trust to support Trouble, her Maltese dog, on a diet of Kobe beef and crabcakes. During the uproar that followed the trust's disclosure, Donald Trump, Helmsley's longtime rival and ally, came to her defense, saying, "The dog is the only thing that loved her and deserves every penny of it." Nevertheless a New York court found the trust amount to be contrary to public policy. The trust then relocated to South Dakota, which eagerly welcomed the fees associated with harboring Trouble's doggy-treats money.

Creating today's dynasties does require some cash up front. You have to retain lawyers, bankers, advisers, and lobbyists, along with a stable of pliable legislators. When South Dakota trust lawyers proposed even more giveaways to dynastic families during the 2018 legislative session, the chair of the Judiciary Committee, Mike Stevens, sped up passage by shutting down debate. Said Stevens, "No more questions. I didn't understand perpetuities in law school, and I don't want to understand it now." Family dynasties banked on Stevens's continued ignorance.

South Dakota has made tiny tweaks to arcane ownership rules, but the consequences are vast. They help create the paths through which America sustains the most unequal distribution of wealth of any major country on earth. Make no mistake: this transformation is not happening by accident, by magic, through the free market, or just naturally. It's a brilliantly designed heist, engineered by family-dynasty lobbyists and accomplice legislators. And lower taxes for the super-rich mean higher taxes for everyone else.

The 1 percent of the 1 percent have their hands firmly on the remote control of trust law. They count on you not knowing it even exists.

A Brief Exhortation

Most of us will not be hiding our money in South Dakota dynasty trusts. Nor do we individually have the means to fight the harms that these trusts inflict—that will take the joint efforts of an informed electorate. But there is something practical you can do. Every year Heller devotes a class to "How to Be a Grownup." The bottom line:

create your own estate plan. It may be scary to think about, but it's not hard to do.

Every parent of a minor child needs a will, if for no other reason than to designate the child's guardian. If you die without a will, the state will decide who raises your kids. Every older person needs a will, too, even if you don't have significant assets. Writing a will is a kindness to survivors so they know who gets what. Too many families are torn apart fighting over objects with sentimental value—like Arthur and Mildred's rocking chair, discussed in the Introduction—even when the cash value is negligible.

While you're at it, fill out an *advance directive* (perhaps called a living will and a health care proxy, depending on where you are) specifying medical treatments you do and don't want if you are too ill to speak for yourself. The importance of these documents was highlighted during the early days of COVID-19, when doctors were rationing who got the scarce available care. But even in ordinary times, this document is essential—unless you want others guessing your preferences at a life-or-death moment.

There are a few more simple documents to create as well, like a *durable, or lasting, power of attorney,* so someone can manage your finances if you can't. There are even some easy-to-create trusts available that can substantially improve the lives of those who survive you. If you don't want your minor children to receive an unrestricted pile of cash when they turn eighteen, you need a trust, as you do if you want to provide for a family member with special needs. Finally, document your passwords for financial and social media accounts, along with contact info, so that in an emergency, the right people know where to look and what to do.

When you write these documents, put in some thought about what your wishes really are. Talk with the people who will serve as your executor, trustee, guardian, and proxy—they can be different people. Make sure they know what you want. And update all this every few years, especially when you experience a life cycle event like marriage, children, or divorce.

Estate planning is an area where it is reasonable to spend money on a lawyer. Laws vary by country, and it's important to follow the rules precisely for your documents to be valid. Planning can provide closure, both emotional and practical, to family members at a particularly vulnerable moment. And you don't necessarily need a lawyer, if that's what is holding you back. You can look up online how to create most of these documents easily, legally, and at low cost—all in less than a weekend. It's worth it.

From Shared Sacrifice to Self-Sacrifice

Wills and trusts are important, but they are just a part of family ownership. Claims of *mine* arise throughout our lives and often play a larger role than we may realize in our most intimate relationships.

Jurisdictions vary dramatically in how they govern ownership between spouses, with each rule inescapably reflecting an implicit endorsement of the ideal marriage. In some, the spouse whose name is on the title has sole authority to manage that asset or fritter it away. This ownership baseline tends to favor the economically dominant spouse, usually still the husband in a conventional marriage.

Others insist on a baseline rule of more egalitarian asset management, so spouses share equal control of the home or bank account regardless of whose name appears on the deed or account. This baseline automatically requires more deliberation between spouses about important life decisions. Making a large investment, like taking out a mortgage on the house, requires joint agreement (and gifts to mistresses are disallowed).

Can you guess which baseline operates where? By quirks of American geopolitics and history, New York has the husband-dominant rule during an intact marriage, and Texas now has the more egalitarian rule. Most people don't realize how much family ownership rules vary as they cross state borders—until things go awry. Then it can become painfully apparent.

While American states have a lot to say about ownership within an intact marriage, they are even more focused on what happens on divorce—as the great mezzo-soprano Frederica von Stade discovered to her surprise. When the curtain fell at Carnegie Hall on April 22, 2010, the audience burst out in thunderous applause, threw bouquets of flowers onstage, and demanded four encores. A triumphant farewell concert for von Stade. In a career spanning four decades, she had appeared at famed opera houses around the world, performing in concerts with the world's greatest orchestras and conductors.

Early on, von Stade made ends meet singing in bars where "customers weren't expected to listen, and didn't." On a fifty-dollar dare from a friend, she applied to a music conservatory; later, she was selected in the Metropolitan Opera's recruitment competition, started with small roles, and moved up.

In her rise to operatic stardom, her husband, Peter Elkus, was there for every step. They had met as conservatory students. A promising baritone singer, Elkus put his own career aside to focus single-mindedly on building von Stade's. Elkus served as her vocal coach, managed the household, and directed her press. The partnership worked. Her annual earnings increased from $2,250 in the year she and Elkus wed to $622,000 in the year they divorced—a 275-fold increase as she rose to opera's peak.

Their divorce had an unusual twist: Elkus argued that the "increased earning capacity" that von Stade had acquired during the marriage was itself a "marital asset," making him a part owner of the economic value of her enhanced career and celebrity. So he asked the court to divide this marital asset, giving him an equitable share of her future earnings.

On the other side of the country, Anne Graham made a similar demand, though she was neither famous nor wealthy. For six years, she had been married to Dennis Graham. During that time, she worked as an airline stewardess, providing 70 percent of the couple's income, much of which went to paying for his MBA tuition at the University of Colorado. During their marriage, she worked to put him through school.

He finished his degree, secured a high-paying job—and then divorced his wife. With no tangible property or investment portfolio, they had no assets to split; no kids meant no child support. And because both had jobs, no alimony, either. Instead, Anne Graham asked for half the value of their sole marital investment—her husband's increased earning capacity associated with his MBA.

Though worlds apart in glamour and wealth, both Peter Elkus and Anne Graham claimed an ownership interest based on their investment in their spouses' careers. Both had sacrificed their own careers and spent money to increase the overall economic potential of the marital community. Should this increased earning potential be something the marriage owns, divisible on divorce? Or should it be separately owned and not split? What does it mean, anyway, for one ex-spouse to own part of the other's increased earning potential?

Whether a supporting spouse can own another's earning potential after divorce may seem a technicality of family law, but the implications run deep. Here are three options for what supporting spouses get:

- Half the increased earning potential.
- Reimbursement for expenses.
- Nothing.

To Peter Elkus and Anne Graham, the issue was simple. Both sacrificed present pleasure, income, and opportunity to support the long-term financial success of the marriage. They could have invested in real estate or stocks—and if they had, any increase in value would have been split with their spouses upon divorce. But they invested in human capital (the spouse's career) instead of built capital or financial capital. The principle is the same: they gave up current consumption, expecting joint benefit later on. It seems unfair for Frederica von Stade and Dennis Graham simply to reap all the reward from the joint marital efforts.

Indeed, New York adopted this reasoning. The court ruled for Peter Elkus—a landmark case in the state.

There is a compelling moral logic to the New York approach. Equitable division of increased earning capacity conceives of spouses as equal partners who jointly decide how to combine their earning power within the protective solidarity of the marital community. This approach rejects the notion that courts should peer inside marriage to determine who contributed what, who deserves what. Instead, it signals that the state believes marriage to be about sharing the good and the bad together as a single unit, as equals.

Given America's still-pervasive gender inequality, this equal partners principle erases—at least during marriage—men's greater power in the market. It sends a signal that equal division of career success is an entitlement of marriage, not a social welfare handout.

But the New York rule can be tricky to implement. When a judge orders ongoing payments to the ex-spouse, that may lock together spouses who want nothing more than to separate. Expert appraisers can certainly quantify increased earning capacity, but what if they are wrong? What if von Stade decides the Met is not for her and quits to join the Peace Corps? Does she have to go back to court to reduce her payments? Elkus should no more be able to determine the trajectory of von Stade's life than the St. Louis Cardinals should have been able to control baseball player Curt Flood's (as discussed in Chapter 5).

There's a second approach to dealing with increased earning capacity on divorce: reimburse supporting spouses for their investments.

This is the rule in New Jersey. Supporting spouses get back their contributions to earning spouses' enhanced careers, plus interest.

Under this rule, the court effectively erases the spouses' joint life decisions. Reimbursement imagines a world as if the joint undertakings of marriage never happened. When the marriage ends, the debt is repaid, and that's it. The supporting spouse receives zero upside benefit from the marital choices; all that goes to the earning spouse. By contrast with New York's equal partners approach, New Jersey sends a message that spouses should keep individual accounts of married life, with reimbursement available for certain expenses. Is that the kind of Excel spreadsheet marriage you want?

But there is an upside—and this is key. The New Jersey rule is easy to administer. Reimbursement avoids the difficulty of estimating the value of a future career. There's a (usually small) onetime repayment and no future ties.

Most of the country rejects both the New York and New Jersey approaches. They follow a third ownership rule for increased earning capacity acquired during marriage: the capacity is not marital property or even property at all. The supporting spouse gets zero back as a matter of right (though judges may factor in the imbalance elsewhere when equitably dividing other assets).

That's what the Colorado courts decided in the Grahams' case. In the judges' view, the husband alone went to classes, wrote papers, and studied for exams. They could not understand how increased earning capacity could be owned at all—even though New York had a long tradition of doing just that. And the expert in the Graham case had no trouble putting a number on career enhancement from the MBA. He calculated that Anne should receive a onetime payment of $82,000.

The zero-ownership rule enforces a harsh vision of marital life. The losers are usually women in a society where married men are still the primary earners and hold most marital assets solely in their own names. This rule helps explain why—even after decades of reforms—women's financial status continues to plummet after divorce, while men's rises. The Grahams represent the run-of-the-mill story, not Elkus and von Stade. States use ownership design to reinforce an old-fashioned vision of marriage: it's a gamble—for the supporting spouse. Is that what spouses expect when they marry today? For most, likely not.

As with wills and trusts, marital ownership is a powerful form of social engineering, quietly steering couples in their most intimate relationships. Today shared sacrifice to create future earning potential becomes self-sacrifice of the noncareer spouse, usually the wife.

This story has an important coda. In 2016, New York abandoned its commitment to egalitarian treatment of enhanced earning capacity. The state changed its rule to join the rest of the country: zero marital ownership of increased future earnings; zero split upon divorce. Maybe rich New York City bankers and lawyers—or state legislators in Albany—got fed up paying spouses they had left behind. The result: New Jersey still reimburses the supporting spouse for expenses, but today no state treats increased earning capacity as a marital asset to be divided upon divorce.

Marriage Menus

Surprisingly (at least to us law professors), few couples tailor marital ownership to their liking. They spend months designing floral centerpieces and picking the first dance for their wedding reception, but they accept whatever off-the-rack version of marital ownership their state happens to offer. It doesn't have to be that way. Well-off people get not only the caterer and wedding band they prefer; using prenuptial agreements and trusts, they can also get most of the marital ownership rules they want.

Why shouldn't states make at least some of the key choices meaningfully available to everyone, automatically and at low cost?

Hundreds—yes, hundreds—of *mandatory* and *default* ownership relations shift at the instant of marriage. To note just a few, you and your spouse now share retirement savings and pensions; federal and state income tax benefits; tax-free spousal gifts; Social Security, veterans, military, and disability benefits; equitable or equal division on divorce; elective shares on death; and inheritance rights as next of kin. With every marital property rule, the state imposes its preferred story on your most intimate life.

The choice between mandatory and default rules is an important feature of ownership design. When the state makes a rule mandatory, it says, *We really mean it.* You can't avoid it if you're married, and you may not be able to acquire it if you're not. Default rules allow couples to work around them, but generally the rules are sticky. The state says, *We prefer this rule.* And few people think to change it (recall the endowment effect discussed in Chapter 2). Much of ownership (and contract) design involves evaluating the moral worth and practical consequences of making rules mandatory or default.

Sounds complicated? Well, so is the tax code. Yet 40 percent of Americans file returns every year online. Software prompts you to answer a few simple questions such as Are you a veteran? Do you own a farm? If you answer yes, you get more information and can make more choices. If software works for filing taxes, maybe it can help you redesign ownership in your own marriage as well.

And note, this is not a one-and-done decision. Ownership rules in your marriage can shift radically even after seemingly mundane events, like when you relocate. Failure to update marital ownership can be devastating, as Dorris Hanau learned.

Dorris married Robert in Illinois. During their marriage, Robert earned money, bought stock, and registered it in his name. The couple then moved to Texas, where Robert died, leaving the stock to his children, Steven and Leslie Ann—and not to Dorris.

If Robert had died in Illinois, Dorris could have exercised something called an *elective share.* This is the tool Illinois uses to protect spouses who are cut out of a will. Simply by virtue of being his wife, Dorris could have elected to take a third of his estate (or half if Robert had no descendants). About forty *common law* states—states whose law derives from England—use this tool to protect disinherited spouses.

Texas is not a common law marital property state. Instead, it follows *community property* rules that trace back to Mexican law and before that to Spanish law. Historically, community property was America's most patriarchal marital regime: the husband managed the couple's property under head and master rules (discussed in Chapter 5). By 1970, however, Texas flipped, making spouses equal managers of community property during the life of the marriage and splitting it equally on divorce or death.

Community property includes most of the assets a couple acquires *in* the state, during their marriage. It protects spouses from disinheritance by automatically making them both present and equal owners, no matter whose name is on the deed or account. On divorce or death, each spouse simply gets half. Today if you happen to live in one of the nine community property states, you are automatically enrolled in America's most egalitarian marital ownership regime.

But not Dorris. Robert had acquired his stock portfolio in Illinois and titled it in his name, as his separate property. The character of property does not change when the spouses relocate (unless they affirmatively agree to make the change). So the stocks remained Robert's separate property when the Hanaus moved to Texas. Division of marital property is governed by the state where the spouse dies. Texas does not have an elective share, so when Robert died there, he could pass all his separate property through his will to his children, and nothing to Dorris. By moving, Dorris lost the protection of Illinois's elective share, but she did not gain the protection of community property. Why? Because the couple acquired no community property while residing in Texas. There was no community to split. The bottom line: Dorris got nothing.

She fell into a gap between English and Spanish law—the two regimes that automatically govern most marriages in America. She could have protected herself had she addressed the risk before leaving Illinois. But that would have meant knowing the problem existed and hiring a lawyer to solve it. It makes no sense to demand this level of vigilance from ordinary couples. Some states have implemented small technical changes to protect certain migrating couples. In California—also a community property state—Robert's stock portfolio would have been treated as "quasi"-community property and equally split. But Dorris didn't think to relocate west.

If online software can help you amend your taxes, why can't it help you amend ownership in your marriage as well? States could offer marital ownership menus so people could choose the essential elements of their own marriages—initially, before their wedding day, and later, during the life of the marriage.

In 1998 Alaska—a common law state—started this menu approach, allowing couples, including out-of-state couples, to elect community property rules for some or all marital assets. But the state expanded the marriage menu for the wrong reasons, and to bad effect. They were not concerned at all with helping Alaskans better align their marriages with their most intimate values.

Alaskan lawyers and bankers persuaded the state legislature to offer the community property option as a tool to attract trust business from wealthy out-of-staters. Because of a glitch in the federal tax system, if you own a large, highly appreciated stock portfolio, it's better to die with those assets governed by community property law than by common law. Your surviving spouse and later beneficiaries avoid certain capital gains taxes. Alaska lets you retitle precisely the assets that maximize tax avoidance—and you don't have to be married in Alaska or even bother visiting the state. But this dodge costs a lot in local professional fees. And generating those fees was the point of adopting the marriage menu. Watch out, South Dakota.

The potential downside of these trusts—as Alaskan lawyers caution their (mostly male) clients—is the built-in egalitarian nature of community property. The price for avoiding taxation is that, on paper at least, husbands give wives an equal say in managing the particular marital assets sheltered in the trust.

As we see it, Alaska's marriage menu is a smart concept, executed poorly. The option targets exactly the wrong people. Few Alaskans are rich enough to benefit from this complex tax-avoidance scheme, but it's possible a fair number would prefer a marital ownership regime, like in California or Texas, that treats spouses as relatively equal partners in their marital journey.

What if Alaska simplified the choice? Allow couples to check either a community property or common law box when they get their marriage licenses, like the choices couples make when they click through pro-or-con screens regarding options for tax deductions. No lawyers, no bankers, no fees. The marriage menu could perhaps extend further. Maybe let couples choose their preferred rule on increased earning capacity and other key aspects of marriage. Maybe let couples amend their selections after major life events.

A well-crafted menu would allow all marrying couples—not just the wealthy—meaningful choices in writing their own marital story. The mere act of choosing, and the intimate discussions that accompany choice, could make for stronger, more intentional marriages. If we trust couples to select appetizers and entrées from their wedding caterer's offerings, why not extend the options to their joint lives beyond the wedding day?

Maybe it's time to consider marriage menus.

Chapter 7

THE FUTURE OF OWNERSHIP—
AND THE WORLD

Pick any newspaper. We're 100 percent confident there's a major headline today—the day you are reading this chapter—whose meaning snaps into focus if you understand the hidden rules of ownership. We wrote this book so you can have more of these "aha" moments.

How can we be so sure about predicting today's news? Because ownership is the scaffolding that society uses to structure every struggle over the things we all want. That's a lot of things. And where should we look to see the future of ownership? Anywhere people are chasing scarce resources. That's everywhere, really.

As we write this chapter, the biggest headlines that touch on ownership concern threats to the natural world and at the digital frontier. The stories highlight blows to the environment—unchecked climate change, loss of tropical forests, and crashing fisheries. And they describe perils to individual freedom from tech giants and governments online, through data tracking, algorithmic discrimination, and pervasive surveillance. Even though these are challenges at a national and even planetary scale, they are basically the same as fights over Knee Defenders and droneways, parking chairs and line-standers. All are fights over who gets what and why. Only the stakes are higher.

Remember that we are all using the same ownership toolkit. It contains six contested pathways to claiming ownership: *first-in-time, possession, labor, attachment, self-ownership,* and *family*. And it contains a small handful of design tools including: *ex post–ex ante, rules–standards, exclusion–governance, baseline setting,* and *liberal commons.* This same toolkit controls both the trivial and the epic.

Looking to the future, the challenge will be to mix and match this limited number of pathways and tools as we seek to address seemingly unsolvable dilemmas at the ownership frontier. It turns out that paying careful attention to how we make things *mine*—whether greenhouse gases or clickstream data—may be our best chance for saving the planet and preserving our freedom.

The Greatest Water on Earth

New Yorkers are rarely a soft-spoken group, particularly when boasting about their city. *Time Out* magazine lists fifty reasons why New York is the "greatest city in the world"—greatest skyline, greatest theater, and on and on. These brags should come as no surprise. Everyone has heard of the Empire State Building and Times Square. But you may be surprised at what the magazine lists as the number-one reason New York is so great.

Its drinking water.

And you don't need to take the magazine's word for it. New York tap water routinely wins blind taste contests against even the priciest bottled water.

While New Yorkers may know their tap water tastes great, few know that it comes from 125 miles northwest of the city; and even fewer know that innovative ownership design lies at the heart of providing over a billion gallons of safe and refreshing water to nine million people every day. But Al Appleton knows.

Appleton is a bear of a man with a quick wit and disarming candor. In 1990 he became commissioner of the New York City Department of Environmental Protection and director of the city's water and sewer system. He immediately faced a dilemma. Unlike most big American cities, New York did not have treatment plants for its tap water. Showing great foresight in the early 1900s, the city had laid huge pipes from the undeveloped Catskill Mountains, far to the north and west, to bring the region's pristine water down to giant reservoirs near the city. Apart from mechanical filters at the collecting reservoirs to keep out sticks and leaves, and chlorination to kill bacteria, the water went almost directly from the mountains to faucets in apartments in Manhattan and homes in the Bronx.

Starting in the 1980s, though, small farms in the Catskills watershed came under economic pressure. They increased fertilizer use and began selling land to residential subdevelopers. As the population grew and land use intensified, the clean water that New York City had taken for granted came under threat. Coupled with a revision to the Safe Drinking Water Act, it looked like New York would need to build a huge treatment plant for Catskills water with a price tag up to $4 billion, along with $200 million more annually to operate the plant.

Instead of going ahead with construction, though, Appleton took a step back and looked to the ownership toolkit. Most everyone assumed a new treatment plant was inevitable. But Appleton reframed the problem. The watershed's vegetation and soil had been doing a great job breaking down contaminants, trapping sediments, and filtering toxics. The result was admirably high-quality drinking water. Instead of spending enormous sums to treat water downstream, how about investing instead to restore the upstream landscape? Was it possible to avoid spending money at all on a big plant? As Appleton put it, "A good environment will produce good water."

Thus began an eighteen-month process of more than 150 meetings with local groups in the Catskills, negotiating land-management practices to ensure water quality. One participant described the endless meetings as similar to a "rolling Thanksgiving dinner with relatives you only want to see once a year." The final agreement was signed by sixty towns, ten villages, seven counties, and environmental groups. New York City committed to spending $1.5 billion to acquire sensitive lands, restore stream corridors, and fund partnerships that would foster water quality and support economic development in the watersheds.

The results have been impressive. Water pollution dramatically declined. New York City payments have proven popular with rural upstate landowners. And the Environmental Protection Agency was persuaded that the watershed initiatives would provide safe drinking water, so the federal government has repeatedly waived the requirement that New York City build the multibillion-dollar treatment plant. As a result, in purely financial terms, New York came out ahead by investing in natural capital rather than in built capital, investing in green rather than gray infrastructure. The program has paid for itself many times over.

But what does all this have to do with ownership?

We tend not to think about ownership when we are talking about the environment. The benefits we receive from nature—the clean air we breathe, a stable climate, fish schooling in the oceans, scenic vistas across landscapes—seem like they must be goods common to all. That's a lovely notion, but it's also a problem.

Common ownership works well when resources are abundant, but it often fails as populations grow and technology changes. When valuable resources are free for the taking, we tend to take too much—the tragedy of the commons discussed in Chapter 4. The result of common ownership is that we're overfishing the world's oceans, cutting down tropical forests, and overusing the atmosphere by emitting greenhouse gases at historically high levels, driving climate change. At this rate, the world of our children and grandchildren will be very different from the one we grew up in, and not for the better.

Just as the Catskills watershed provides clean drinking water, nature provides all kinds of critical services that we take for granted. Insects pollinate our crops. Microbes in soils break down waste and create fertile fields for farming. Coastal marshes protect against storm surges and provide habitats for young fish. These are all examples of common resources that benefit everyone and are owned by none. We all enjoy the wild birds and butterflies flying around us. But the landowners who provide the habitat for this wildlife receive no compensation in exchange. If they don't own the resources and can't charge for them, then they have little economic reason to protect or invest in them.

Wetlands, for example, may protect towns by slowing floodwaters or filtering drinking water. If landowners convert wetlands into homes or farms, they may benefit financially, but the community is made far worse off by flooding and dirty water. Because no one owns wetlands' services like flood prevention and water purification, landowners don't take the value of those services into account when deciding how to use their land. If the choice is to earn a living by draining the wetland to grow crops or to earn nothing by preserving it, then the choice is simple. Drain the wetland.

Appleton's great insight was to innovate around the attachment principle we described in Chapter 4. He told Catskills landowners that New York City would deal with them as if they owned the environmental services attached to their land. We don't think twice about paying for potatoes or coal attached to land, so why not pay farmers for improved water quality? Appleton crafted an ownership tool in which wealthier downstate city dwellers would pay poorer upstate farmers to preserve a clean environment. He showed that *as-if attachment* can motivate people, even in the absence of state law giving people ownership over the environmental benefits their lands provide.

This approach of creating what we call *as-if ownership* in nature's bounty has exploded in recent decades. Salzman has been working with governments around the globe for decades to develop payment schemes that compensate landowners for providing natural services. In recent work, he identified more than 550 active programs around the globe with an estimated $42 billion in annual transactions.

The strategy is being used to try to save the world's rainforests. Tropical forests contain most of the world's species diversity and capture vast amounts of carbon from the atmosphere, playing a critical role in slowing climate change. Deforestation is responsible for up to 20 percent of global warming. As this chapter is written, swaths of the Amazon forests, often called the lungs of the planet, are burning.

The basic problem is that people who live in these forests don't own the environmental services they provide. They can't charge for wildlife habitat or storing carbon. Even though these resources are critical to humanity, we receive them for free. Not surprisingly, owners and squatters in forests focus instead on things they can sell. They burn forests to clear them for grazing, logging, and agriculture. The challenge is to make trees worth more standing than cut down.

Norway is doing just that, trying to offset some of the climate harm it has caused by extracting North Sea oil. Thanks to its sovereign wealth fund—profits the country accumulated from oil sales—Norway has been able to spend tens of billions of dollars paying people in the Amazon, Indonesia, and Mexico for their efforts to reduce local deforestation rates. If the rate of forest loss slows, more trees are left standing and more carbon is captured from the atmosphere.

China has made an even larger investment. Environmental payments have become a central component of the country's nationwide environmental-protection strategy. China has already paid over $50 billion to farmers and households to increase forest cover. By planting trees instead of chopping them down, China gets flood protection, wildlife habitat, and water quality—all shared goods that come along with investing in trees.

So can we use ownership design to steer people to conserve nature rather than despoil it? Absolutely. Around the world, new types of ownership to promote environmental services are changing the behavior of farmers and forest dwellers, timber companies and big landowners. They now compete to protect the environment, and they make money in the process.

With a billion-dollar program here, a billion there, ecosystem-services ownership begins to add up. While substantial already, these programs are not yet nearly big enough. The key to addressing some of the world's greatest environmental challenges may be to encourage people to call ever more aspects of nature *mine*.

The Not-So-Deadly Catch

Clambering around high stacks of metal crab traps, the crew of the trawler *Time Bandit* works late into the black night of the Bering Sea, far from the comforts of their home port on the Alaskan coast. They have to focus just to keep their balance on the pitching deck. It's nasty weather, but that's a given for this part of the world. Howling winds throw cold spray over the crew. Without warning, a thirty-foot rogue wave crashes over the port bow, bursting across the deck. The crew regain their balance, shake off the water, and look around.

Then one starts screaming, "James! James!"

The bow hand, James Tommy, is nowhere to be seen. If he has been swept overboard into the freezing seas, it's over for him.

On the bridge, Captain Jonathan Hillstrand mutters, "Okay, James . . ." Barking on the intercom to the deck, he orders, "Body count. Body count."

The only response is more frantic calls of "James!"

Hillstrand can do nothing but watch from the safety of the bridge, swearing to himself.

Nothing.

Suddenly James appears, swarmed by the hugging crew. Thrown by the wave into the traps, he miraculously emerged unharmed. Dripping wet, he shrugs like it's no big deal. "A little bit of water. We're in the ocean. Come on, man."

As the crew give thumbs-up signs to Hillstrand, the captain is visibly shaken. "Thank you, God. . . . It felt like a train hit us. I mean, we stopped dead. That was the scaredest I've been in a long time."

Welcome to *Deadliest Catch*.

The Discovery Channel launched this series in 2005. It became one of the longest-running and most successful reality TV shows. Every year camera crews capture life aboard fishing boats in the Bering Sea during Alaska's king crab season. There is no shortage of colorful personalities. But the real star is the setting.

There's a reason they call the show *Deadliest Catch*. Day and night, the ship's crew have to fill seven-hundred-pound crab pots with bait, swing them into position over the rails, and launch them four hundred feet down, only to do the reverse hours later when the pots are hauled up full (they hope) of crabs that need to be removed and placed in the hold. All this takes place with the boat rolling on heavy seas, often in high winds. Because ice can form on deck, there is an ever-present threat the boat will become top-heavy and roll over.

Crab fishing in Alaska has long been one of the most dangerous jobs in America. From 1989 to 2005, scores of people died in the fishery. Ten boats sank. For years, crab fishing on the Bering Sea was "the deadliest job in the country—more likely to kill you than going on foot patrol in Iraq."

But it's not the weather that made crab fishing so dangerous. It's how the crabs were owned: too many boats chasing too few crabs.

For most of human history, fishing followed the same rule of capture as hunting wild animals (see Chapter 1). First come, first served. If you hauled the fish out of the ocean first, you owned it. This worked fine. With simple fishing practices, the sea's bounty was effectively limitless. In an ocean of abundance, almost any ownership rule (or no rule at all) worked fine.

Ownership design mattered more as scarcity increased and people started to compete for the same resource. And that's what happened on the high seas after World War II, with the development of flash freezing and ever-larger fishing vessels. Fish stocks that had seemed boundless began to crash—anchovies off the coast of Peru, cod off New England, king crab off Alaska.

Over the short term, as stocks declined, it made sense for each boat to catch as much of the remaining fish as quickly as possible. If not, other boats would catch those same fish instead. But every boat acting this way led to rapid destruction of fish populations. With physical possession deciding ownership, fisheries became textbook examples of the tragedy of the commons.

In 1980 the Alaska king crab fishery landed 200 million pounds. New boats arrived, eager to make their profits. Just a few years later the catch dropped by 90 percent. With the collapse of the crab population came the collapse of the local economy. As a fishery official observed, crab vessel owners couldn't make a living: "They just drove a lot of the boats to the dock, dropped the keys at the harbormaster's office, and took the next plane to Seattle."

To stop overharvesting and restore the crab fishery, the state of Alaska stepped in and abolished its unlimited rule of capture. Instead, the state set a catch limit. The goal was to fix the total catch every year at a sustainable level—the maximum harvest that still allowed crabs to reproduce a stable population. The fishery season began on a set date and shut down as soon as the limit was reached. Anyone caught catching crab after that date faced punishment.

Here is how Alaska used the ownership toolkit to conserve scarce crabs. First, in 1976, the state asserted ownership for itself through attachment. The crabs scuttling on the ocean floor were "ours because they are attached to something ours," in this case, the two-hundred-mile Exclusive Economic Zone that America claims off the Alaska coast (see Chapter 4). Alaska kicked out foreign fishing fleets. Next, Alaska designated the total allowable catch of its crabs—the season closes as soon as the catch limit is reached. Third, it set possession as the basis for ownership of those allowable crabs.

Eventually, this new system helped stabilize crab stocks. But

Alaska's approach was still terrible ownership design. Inadvertently, the state had turbocharged the race to capture, creating the conditions for *Deadliest Catch*.

Because the season ended as soon as the catch limit was reached, boats competed to catch crabs as quickly as they possibly could. The result was a dangerous race, a *Mad Max*–style free-for-all. Trawlers motored out of port the instant the season opened, even in the face of bad weather and dangerous seas. *Especially* in the face of bad weather and dangerous seas. Crews and captains worked beyond the point of exhaustion. No one could play it safe because they risked getting left behind as others caught what could have been their share of the total catch. Before anyone expected, the season would close. Sometimes in just a few days. Even a hint of caution invited commercial catastrophe.

Racing out to sea invited another catastrophe—injuries from heavy equipment on the unsteady decks, crew lost overboard, sunk ships. Versions of this frantic competition governed almost all fisheries in the United States. It became known as derby fishing—not only dangerous but also highly inefficient.

Captains spent more and more money so their boats could catch fish faster than the next vessel. Because every captain did the same, all the expense gave little advantage. Instead, the whole fleet locked itself into an unwinnable high-seas competition for better technology that drove up everyone's costs of operation, leading to less profit for the fixed number of crabs that could be caught. And to make matters worse, they caught all the crabs within the same short window. So when boats brought their catch to shore, prices were always low because of the temporary market glut from crabs landed by the others.

Catch limits helped sustain crab populations but proved disastrous for the people who caught them.

In response, Alaska tried again. Catching crabs on the Bering Sea will never be like dropping a baited line in your neighborhood pond, but thanks to smart ownership design, it's no longer the deadliest catch, either. This time around, the state looked abroad for a solution that would protect marine resources and, at the same time, make fisheries safer and more profitable. It looked to Iceland.

In the 1970s fishery managers in Iceland started with a crazy idea. They rummaged in the ownership toolkit and put together an entirely new way to claim *mine*, one specifically tailored to fisheries.

The rules of ownership steer people indirectly but effectively. Recall that when America wanted people to settle the West in the late 1800s, it modified possession—settlers became owners, but only after they had engaged in certain types of useful labor. They had to homestead 160 acres and make it productive within five years; divert water and put it to beneficial use; or find and work a mineral claim. Similarly, when Duke wanted rabid grad student fans to fill the stands, it modified first-in-time: students entered a lottery, but only after they had gone through days of Campout. In all these cases, owners realized that preexisting possession and first-in-time rules did not steer people where they wanted them to go. They needed to modify the rules.

Iceland went through the same process, creating ownership rules that would allow fishing captains to spend less money, earn more, and keep crews safer—all while ensuring robust fisheries.

In short, Iceland replaced catch limits with what came to be known as *catch shares*. Under this new system, the focus switched from exclusion to governance (see Chapter 6). The rule of capture stays in place, but you are allowed to catch fish only if you already hold a catch share (also known as an individual fishing quota, or IFQ). A single IFQ gives the holder the right to catch a specific amount of fish, such as one ton of halibut. If the season's total sustainable catch for the halibut fishery is set at one thousand tons, the state issues a thousand IFQs. To claim ownership of one ton of halibut, the vessel owner needs to have at least one IFQ. In simple terms, boats need to own an IFQ before they can fish at all.

Who gets the initial IFQs? That's a challenge. One option is for the state to auction them. But then, local fleets might be outbid by more efficient outsiders. In principle, with higher auction prices, the public reaps much of the economic benefit from fish in its waters and could use some of it to retrain laid-off locals. But in practice, resentful local fishing captains might fight back, engage in pirate halibut fishing, and even attack outsider boats. (Recall the fierce lobster gangs in Chapter 2.) So instead of auctions, Iceland used attachment to distribute IFQs initially. It attached catch shares to each boat in the existing fleet based on that boat's average catch from past seasons.

Was this distribution fair? No, not really. Newcomers and outsiders started with nothing. The state got zero auction revenue from its fisheries. And the most rapacious danger-seeking boat owners from previous years got a windfall. But attachment had a key advantage: the existing fleet accepted the new ownership regime instead of fighting it.

IFQs ended derby fishing. Boat captains owned the entire year's harvest through their IFQs before the season even opened. This meant captains could catch their fish when they wanted. If the weather was bad, the boat could stay in port until skies cleared up. If the market price of fish was low, they could wait until it went up. There was no reason to race because the total catch had already been divvied up from day one.

IFQs had another, subtler effect: it gave boat owners a reason to care about the health of the fishery as a whole. Healthier fish stocks meant more IFQs for every owner. And they mobilized the entire fleet in a common effort to guard against other pirate fishing boats taking halibut—each IFQ holder could say, rightly, *Some of those fish are mine.*

Soon enough, many boat owners realized it could be more profitable to stay in port and lease or sell their IFQs to another boat. Fewer boats were needed to catch the full share because each boat could fish for a longer time. In turn, this lowered costs in fuel, equipment, and labor. Because the boats could wait for better weather, fewer crews were put in danger. And with the catch spread out over a longer season, prices were steadier. Crews also had time to separate out female crabs, undersize crabs, and other bycatch and safely return it to the ocean. Under the catch share system, fish populations rebounded, fishing became safer, and the fleet's profits went up. It was win-win-win.

Innovative ownership worked.

Other nations took note. New Zealand and Australia adopted catch share programs after Iceland pioneered them. They caught on more slowly in the United States. The first trial in Alaska began in 1995 in the halibut fishery. Derby fishing had gotten so bad that there were only three twenty-four-hour windows of halibut fishing allowed per year. It wasn't much better for Alaskan king crabs, but crab boat owners resisted ownership innovation. Grudgingly, after waves of bankruptcies and deaths, the fleet accepted the catch share strategy in 2005, just six months after *Deadliest Catch* went on the air.

The results have been remarkable.

No more frantic free-for-all on the Bering Sea. The crab season lengthened from three days in 2004 to three months in 2006. Erik Olson, a banker who makes loans to crab vessels, described the dramatic shift: under catch shares, "You know that a fisherman is going to be allocated X percent of the crab. You can translate that into dollars, and you can get a pretty good idea of what their revenue will be. That is a huge change. It's the difference between, 'Grab a case of Red Bull, pray for good weather, and buckle up,' and, 'Now we have a business plan.'" Profits increased fourfold per vessel. And in the 2014–15 season, no one died in the entire Alaska commercial fishery, including the salmon, halibut, and other fisheries that had adopted catch shares.

But as with every ownership choice, catch shares impose trade-offs. More efficient newcomers had to buy their way in by paying off "armchair fishermen," those who got the initial IFQ windfall, then simply sold or leased them out and stayed home collecting royalties.

This was inevitable because there were far too many boats, but shrinkage in the fleet was painful for many communities. It's estimated that half the total crew lost their jobs. And wages went down for those who remained, in part because new owners had to pay armchair fishermen for IFQ leases. Instead of owning a share of the derby catch, many crew became employees paid hourly wages. The *Deadliest Catch* series has continued, but the number of active boats fell by two-thirds, and the show now edits out the boring, lower-paid routines on bigger, safer boats.

Note that both catch limits and catch shares ensure that the crab fishery survives. If your overriding goals are job protection, free entry for newcomers, and adrenaline-packed television, then stick with derby fishing. But if you value crew safety and economically sustainable fleets, then catch shares are the way to go.

Today well over half of the world's fisheries are overfished, threatening the major protein source and livelihood for large parts of the global population. Catch shares create the possibility for environmentally sustainable ownership far beyond crabbing in the Bering Sea. But they work only where states can enforce ownership. On the high seas, there are treaties for a few species, like whales and tuna, and some regional fishing agreements, but for the most part, once fleets cross out of a country's Exclusive Economic Zone, derby fishing is back on. Maybe catch shares can reach there, too, someday.

To date, catch shares have been adopted in forty countries and already account for about one-fifth of the global catch. It's no surprise the strategy has been called "the greatest unknown policy success of our time."

Cap-and-Trade for Better and Worse

This approach of reengineering ownership, used to protect fisheries through catch shares, has also proven effective in battling pollution from leaded gasoline, smog, and acid rain. The acid rain story shows how it works.

In the 1970s and '80s, coal-fired power plants in the Midwest and Southeast spewed out large amounts of sulfur-rich pollution. The jet stream carried these pollutants to the coast, falling as acid rain in New England and Canada. Lakes, forests, and streams in Maine and Vermont, nowhere near any human activity, suffered fish kills and stunted trees. The name for this problem in Germany was *Waldsterben*—"forest death," a stark but accurate description. In 1990 the U.S. Congress transformed the ownership of pollution to address the problem.

We have seen that catch shares create new ways to own fish. The government gives away—or sometimes auctions—IFQs for that year's catch. Congress adapted the same approach to create ownership rights in pollution. It sounds counterintuitive, even perverse, but the results have been dramatic.

The U.S. Environmental Protection Agency (EPA) announces how much total pollution will be allowed each year, such as one million tons of sulfur dioxide. It then creates one million pollution allowances, each allowing emission of one ton. Just as fishing boats must have an IFQ for every ton of fish they take out of the ocean, polluters must have an allowance for every ton of sulfur dioxide their chimneys put into the air. If a power plant doesn't have allowances, it cannot pollute.

For fish, the limit on total catch is set to ensure sustainable fisheries; for pollution, the goal is to reduce acid rain over time. Initially, to ensure industry support, allowances were given out to each power plant to allow it to continue emitting its then-existing level of pollution. After that, though, the total cap was lowered every year; fewer allowances were issued.

This ownership form became known as *cap-and-trade,* and here is where it gets interesting. Previously, power plants were like every other regulated polluter: they needed to come into compliance with whatever public health and environmental standards the regulator set. If their emissions limit was one thousand tons per year, they made sure not to emit over that amount—but there was no benefit to emitting even one ton less.

Cap-and-trade upended that thinking: it provided polluters a novel business opportunity.

Imagine a big power plant that has a legal limit to pollute one thousand tons. It starts with one thousand allowances, so it's business as usual for that facility. The plant managers, however, realize that they can cheaply switch to low-sulfur coal. If they do so, the plant emits only seven hundred tons. Now they are holding three hundred extra allowances they don't need. Under cap-and-trade, this newly clean plant can sell its excess allowances to polluting plants that can't cheaply switch to cleaner fuels or technology.

The genius of this approach is that pollution ownership creates a business case for reducing emissions. Reducing pollution becomes a profit center. The power plant now sells both electricity *and* sulfur dioxide allowances, which leads it to find even more ways to reduce its emissions so it can sell even more allowances.

And all this happens without the EPA having to pick winners or losers among power plants or technologies. It just estimates the overall pollution trajectory needed to reduce acid rain over time. The agency doesn't mandate what fuels to use; doesn't back one technology or another; doesn't order any particular plant to shut down. All of the conservation happens via trades in a robust market, so the most innovative power plants profit by getting cleaner and the worst plants pay for the privilege to keep polluting. We get pollution reduction for the least cost.

As with catch shares, the results have been impressive. Sulfur dioxide emissions dropped far faster than expected as power plants raced to free up allowances by adopting less-polluting fuels and better scrubber technology. Acid rain in the Northeast of America and Canada is now history.

On its face, cap-and-trade seems perfectly suited for battling not just acid rain but climate change more generally. Since the industrial revolution in the 1800s, we have increasingly relied on fossil fuels such as coal, gas, and oil for energy, leading to a rapid buildup of gases such as carbon dioxide in the atmosphere. These greenhouse gases are warming the Earth and changing its climate, driving more intense and frequent storms, raising sea levels. The most direct way to combat climate change is to reduce emissions of these gases. Since they all mix in the atmosphere, it doesn't matter where the reductions come from. From the standpoint of global climate change, reducing carbon dioxide emissions in Africa has the same benefit as reducing them in America.

Just as with acid rain, countries or states can set caps for total greenhouse gas emissions, issue allowances for the emissions, and then let companies trade the allowances to pollute. The European Union launched a program based on this principle in 2005 that now covers more than eleven thousand factories and power stations in thirty-one countries. California's trading program seeks to reduce greenhouse gas emissions by 80 percent below 1990 levels by 2050. China is in the midst of launching the largest greenhouse-gas-trading program in the world. Smart ownership design might yet save the planet.

Or it might not. With fisheries and acid rain, new ownership forms shifted behavior for the better. But there's always a risk of unintended consequences: because factories and power plants freely trade sulfur dioxide allowances, we end up with a patchwork of clean and dirty plants. But the pattern is not random. As it has turned out, the remaining dirty plants are often clustered in pollution hot spots, mostly in poorer communities of color.

And cap-and-trade can go wrong in other disastrous ways. One early cap-and-trade program for greenhouse gases resulted in what environmental groups have called "the biggest environmental scandal in history."

The negotiators of the 1997 U.N. international treaty to battle climate change, the Kyoto Protocol, adapted the approach used for fish and acid rain, but on a global scale. Designed by some of the world's leading economists, the Kyoto Protocol's program created another new type of ownership—certified emissions reductions (CERs). Just as fishing boats need IFQs to fish and power plants need allowances to emit sulfur dioxide, governments and companies need to own CERs to offset their own greenhouse gas emissions.

Projects around the world could earn CERs based on how much greenhouse gas they removed from the atmosphere. The projects could then sell these CERs to countries or companies. Growing trees capture carbon dioxide, so a forestry project in the tropics could earn CERs. It could then sell these to a refinery or cement plant in another country that needed to offset its emissions. Many economists and environmentalists thought this a terrific development. It would create a huge new market to save rainforests.

At least that was the plan.

Initially, CERs did spur some forest projects in the tropics. But they also increased activity in an unexpected quarter. A small number of companies in China and India produced a chemical used in refrigerators. Their manufacturing process created a by-product called HFC-23. This chemical has an unusual property: it is a super greenhouse gas. Just one HFC-23 molecule causes as much global warming as 11,700 molecules of carbon dioxide.

The manufacturers spotted an opportunity with CERs. Five years into the trading program, it emerged that these companies had doubled their output and had earned roughly half the world's total CERs. The market for refrigerants had not grown, though, so why had they ramped up production?

These companies had changed their business model. Their profit no longer came from producing and selling refrigerant. What they now cared about was producing and destroying the HFC-23 by-product. They duly incinerated every pound of HFC-23 they created. And for every pound of super greenhouse gas they destroyed, the companies were awarded CERs—which they then sold to polluting countries and companies in Europe and Japan. As Gerben-Jan Gerbrandy, a Dutch member of the European Parliament, explained, "It's perverse. You have companies which make a lot of money by making more of this gas, and then getting paid to destroy it."

Creating and then destroying HFC-23 generated a lot of profit—but it provided zero environmental benefit. Even worse, it was cheaper for companies to buy credits from HFC-23 destroyers than from forest builders. So very little money flowed to rainforests. By the time this scam was recognized and stopped, Chinese and Indian HFC-23 makers had earned a fortune. Billions of dollars had been wasted; the world's climate got nothing in return.

The Kyoto Protocol's trading program was designed by some very smart economists. They had intended to drive greenhouse-gas-reduction projects around the world and save forests. But a handful of Chinese and Indian refrigerant entrepreneurs proved even smarter. Ownership rules, and the profits they can generate, powerfully concentrate the mind, for good and for ill.

No doubt, CERs, IFQs, and allowances have had occasional failures—as have other novel, acronym-rich variants on environmental-resource ownership. Humility is warranted. But overall the programs have been a success. We have learned that it is possible to design ownership to motivate Catskills farmers, Bering Sea crabbers, mid-western coal plant operators, and others around the globe to protect our environment and atmosphere.

Protecting the natural world falls primarily to governments. Sometimes they get novel ownership forms wrong, but they can succeed when given the chance to experiment and try again. The ownership toolkit offers paths to avoiding species extinction, conserving forests, and keeping the air and water healthy. Humanity's best hope for survival may be to make more environmental resources—even pollution—*mine.*

Bricks and Sticks

The digital world and the natural world share a core feature. Both start from the no-ownership baseline that characterizes all new and emerging resources. As soon as the race to own the resource begins, competing stories emerge. *I'm first,* like in the fox case in Chapter 1; *I possess it,* like the parking chairs in Chapter 2; *I labored,* Disney's claim in Chapter 3. Which ownership rule seems most efficient? Fairest? Most conducive to enhancing our freedom and sustaining our joint projects?

We are now asking the same questions online. But there's an important difference between natural and virtual resources. So far governments have not been driving ownership online. Maybe they should, but they haven't. Online, it's the business community that has pushed the frontiers of ownership, relying on tools like strategic ambiguity, capturing the baseline, and opt-in versus opt-out. Companies aren't waiting for laws to be written, and they don't ask for permission. And when they tweak ownership, it's to maximize their own profit, not to serve public goals.

That's not all bad. Internet-driven innovation has been the productive engine of the modern economy for over a generation. But this dynamism comes with costs.

Anders G. da Silva experienced this trade-off in a stark way. Like millions of consumers, da Silva buys movies through his Apple iTunes account. To his surprise one day, he found that three movies he'd bought had disappeared from his account. He contacted Apple, looking for an explanation. He didn't like the customer service agent's answer, so he tweeted a dramatized version of his unsatisfying exchange—which promptly went viral. As he wrote:

> *Me:* Hey Apple, three movies I bought disappeared from my
> iTunes library.

Apple: Oh yes, those are not available anymore. Thank you for
        buying them. Here are two movie rentals on us!
   Me: Wait . . . WHAT?? @tim_cook when did this become
        acceptable? . . .
Apple: You see, we are just a store front.
   Me: Store front?
Apple: Yeah, we take your money, but we are not responsible
        for what is sold. And, we certainly do NOT guarantee
        you get to keep anything you buy in our store front. We
        only guarantee that we get to keep your money.
   Me: I see. . . . So that "Buy" button is meaningless? It should
        maybe be called: "Feelin Lucky"?
Apple: I see you are unhappy. Have two more rentals on us.

Linn Nygaard felt the same frustration, but with Amazon instead
of Apple. An information technology consultant based in Oslo,
Nygaard is often on the road. In England on a trip, she got a Kindle.
It worked great. Over time she bought forty books. Lots to read on
a conveniently compact screen. One morning, though, she found
her account blocked. Even worse, her books had vanished from her
Kindle. Concerned, she e-mailed for help and was told Amazon and
its affiliates "reserve the right to refuse service, terminate accounts,
remove or edit content, or cancel orders at their sole discretion."

To drive the point home, Amazon added, "Please know that any
attempt to open a new account will meet with the same action." Taken
aback, Nygaard replied that she was a longtime Amazon customer in
good standing. Amazon's final reply, though, was even starker: "We
wish you luck in locating a retailer better able to meet your needs
and will not be able to offer any additional insight or action on these
matters."

A friend of Nygaard blogged about her saga, and like da Silva's
tweets, it quickly went viral. A few days later her account and books
were restored with no explanation. Amazon presumably decided to

quiet the public relations debacle. It had faced a similar uproar a few years earlier after deleting readers' purchased copies of George Orwell's dystopian novel *1984,* following a copyright dispute. Ironically, erasing *1984* was just the kind of thing the novel's Big Brother would do.

These stories go beyond digital movies and books. They now reach even into physical objects—when they're powered by online software. Arlo Gilbert owned a Revolv device, a box that controlled his home's doors, alarms, and lights. One morning he woke up and the device was dead, not just dead but "bricked." And not just Gilbert's machine. All Revolvs in the world were bricked that day.

Turns out, Google had remotely activated a kill switch on everyone's device. Why? Google had bought Revolv in 2014, when it was expanding into the "Internet of Things" market. It later decided to invest instead in a different home automation product line called Nest. What better way to boost sales of Nest than to terminate the software that powered Revolv? Deep in the terms of service for Revolv, Google had retained the right to shut it all down.

In a blog post, Gilbert asked, "Which hardware will Google choose to intentionally brick next? . . . Is your Nexus device safe? What about your Nest fire/smoke alarm? What about your Dropcam? What about your Chromecast device?" Gilbert was out of luck. He still owns the hardware, but it works only as a doorstop.

Now imagine if Amazon were a local bookstore in the same dispute with Nygaard. Surely the bookstore's employees couldn't open the door to Nygaard's home, walk into her study, and remove all the books she had bought from them. The same is true for Apple taking back movies from da Silva, or Google bricking Gilbert. Yet that's effectively what these online giants did—and had designed their ownership rights to do. The self-created power to "terminate accounts, remove or edit content" at their sole discretion is unequivocally spelled out in online contracts that no one ever reads.

Amazon, Apple, and Google are profiting from a transformation in the meaning of ownership for digital content. For most of history, we lived in a world dominated by farms, horses, hammers, and bread. In that world, ownership mostly referred to tangible, physical things: we could stand on our land and hold on to our stuff. If you owned something, then for the most part you could exclude everyone else; you controlled the object and got to direct its fate. This exclusion intuition is how most of us thought of ownership, and how we still think of it today—what we've been calling the on-off-switch image of ownership: *It's mine. Hands off.*

Online companies know this. They count on that on-off response as they evoke our visceral and indeed instinctual feelings about ownership. But it is a bait-and-switch.

Website marketplaces show us the little shopping cart icon, so we will assume it's just like the one at the supermarket. We "put things" in the cart, and we head to "checkout." The online world is carefully designed to mimic the world of physical possession and to activate those impulses. Don't be fooled.

A recent survey found that 83 percent of respondents believe they own digital content just as they own a physical good—and are free to do with it what they want. They're free to loan it to friends, use it again and again, sell it, donate it, or even cut it up to make something new like a mash-up song or a collage. As a co-author of the survey explained, "There's a lot of meaning built into the phrase 'buy now.' It's not saying 'rent now.' It's not saying 'gain conditional access.' It says 'buy,' and that means something very specific to most consumers—something that, in the case of digital content, isn't true."

In most cases, your ability to reuse, sell, donate, or modify a digital product is severely limited. The on-off switch does not easily translate to the digital world. The familiar symbols of everyday possession are not meaningful online—they're vestiges of a fading system. But we are still coming to grips with this new reality. It's not just own versus rent—our old familiar choices. Instead, online, ownership feels strange and in between, more like a dimmer than a switch.

The Internet economy is routinely described with innovative superlatives—it's "unprecedented" and "unparalleled." It's easy to imagine the virtual economy as something radically new in human history. In some ways, perhaps it is. But it's not new in terms of ownership.

Lawyers sometimes describe ownership as a *bundle of sticks*. This metaphor was introduced about a century ago, and it has radically transformed the teaching and practice of law. The metaphor is useful because it helps us see ownership as a grouping of interpersonal rights that can be separated and put back together. When you say *It's mine* in reference to a resource, often that means you own a lot of the sticks that make up the full bundle: the sell stick, the rent stick, the right to mortgage, license, give away, even destroy the thing. Often, though, we split the sticks up, as for a piece of land: there may be a landowner, a bank with a mortgage, a tenant with a lease, a neighbor with a right-of-way easement, a plumber with a license to enter the land, an oil company with mineral rights. Each of these parties owns a stick in the bundle. And even the fullest ownership bundle is limited: you don't have sticks that allow you to make a nuisance of yourself, use the property to commit a crime, or discriminate in certain ways.

As da Silva, Nygaard, and Gilbert learned the hard way, when we buy online, we don't buy the full bundle, just a couple of sticks. The sellers have figured out how to hold on to the rest. When you click "buy now" on an Amazon movie, what you get is: "a non-exclusive, non-transferable, non-sublicensable, limited license, . . . for personal, non-commercial, private use."

What does that mean? Not much, after you cut through all the legalese. You definitely don't get the right to "transfer, copy, or display," except as Amazon permits; nor any right to "sell, rent, lease, distribute, or broadcast" your purchase. Amazon holds on to most of the bundle. Clicking "buy now" really gives you just a few sticks.

iTunes, Kindle, and Revolv licenses all work more or less the same way, with similar gobbledygook. The limits of your ownership are described in excruciating legal detail on a website no one ever reads and few could understand (including us, your authors).

Yet everyone clicks the "buy now" button. People want to complete their purchases and get on with their lives. Even if you did read the terms, they are complex, not open to negotiation, and everchanging. Companies generally keep the right to amend terms whenever they want without telling you. When you click to buy, often you also agree to accept without notice future changes in the scope of your ownership.

In short, today, you buy just a limited-use stick. Apple, Amazon, and Google hold the rest of the bundle. And they even keep a string attached to the stick you bought, so they can take it back if it suits their purposes. Amazon is upfront about this, if you read deeply enough into its online license agreement. When you click "buy," it agrees only that your online content will "generally continue to be available to you." Amazon makes no guarantee. Just the opposite. According to the agreement, the content "may become unavailable due to potential content provider licensing restrictions or for other reasons." What other reasons? Amazon doesn't say.

As a kicker, if Amazon shuts down Nygaard's Kindle or takes back your download of *1984,* the company "will not be liable to you"— that is, it won't owe Nygaard or you a penny. That's what it means to own an Amazon book online. And it's why Google could flip the kill switch on Gilbert's Revolv, and Apple could remove movies from da Silva's iTunes account. Don't think this is limited just to Amazon, Google, and Apple. The switch from bundle to stick is nearly universal in online ownership.

As Internet speeds increase and cloud storage becomes cheaper, we will stream more and more goods and services throughout our lives. Opaque licenses will govern not only the songs we listen to and the books we buy. They will span the entire Internet of Things, from coffee makers and thermostats to security and sound systems. Perhaps it's not so worrying if Oral-B bricks your wireless toothbrush (yes, it exists). But surprises in the ownership structure of diabetes monitors, pacemakers, and home alarms could be deadly.

Our intuitions still tell us that possessing the hardware is what matters. That's been mostly true throughout human history. But more and more, it's the software embedded in physical products that matters. In the digital economy, we hold ephemeral licenses to streams of 1s and 0s—the ghost in the machine.

Think Different(ly)

The bundle-of-sticks idea is a powerful piece of ownership design technology. The "buy now" button is just one visible example of the commercial benefits that flow from radically redesigning the bundle. The companies we interact with online are masters of ownership engineering. They profit from it. Governments let them. Perhaps, as consumers, we need to adapt Apple's old slogan, "Think different."

For starters, we need to recognize that the gap between what we feel we own and what we actually own is ever widening. And it is no accident. This is the sleight-of-hand of digital ownership: we are encouraged to think we own more than we do, the bundle rather than just a stick. When we buy online, the primitive instinctive power and scope of *mine* just don't follow.

What gets lost in this new world? One cost arises through the increasing concentration of online ownership. In olden days, physical ownership was dispersed. With books, people owned tangible copies. And multiplicity meant that memory could be preserved and diffused. Nowadays, books and movies can simply disappear. Just a few companies can own all the bundles; everyone else holds just a stick. With a press of a button somewhere in the cloud, every copy can disappear. As one commentator writes, "In the grimmest version of that narrative, we're headed toward a sort of techno-feudalism, where we all end up as serfs of these onetime Silicon Valley upstarts. In this sense, we're not looking at the end of ownership per se so much as the end of individual ownership."

A second cost can be to our freedom. Ordinary ownership of physical things automatically gives wide scope for individual choice. When you own a paperback book, you can reread it, give it away, lend it to friends, use it as a doorstop, cut it up and paste it into a scrapbook. You don't have to ask anyone's permission. If you want, you can shred your book in protest—and neither the bookseller nor the publisher can stop you. We lose much of that freedom when we click "buy now" online. Sellers can just delete your stick and brick your device if they don't like how you are behaving. Ray Bradbury anticipated exactly this dystopian world in his 1953 novel *Fahrenheit 451*—books were banned and "firemen" raced to burn the last few physical copies, leaving only the official televised version.

Techno-feudalism and lost freedom are not easy problems to solve. Sure, we could ban Amazon from using "buy now" buttons for online content and instead require a less deceptive button like "click for super-limited license." We could make online sellers notify you in all-caps text, THIS MOVIE IS NOT REALLY YOURS. NO LENDING ALLOWED. Maybe this would help. It's worth a try. But many studies have shown the limited effect of forcing information on people. We quickly learn to tune out unpleasant ownership details—in part because the digital economy brings so much immediate gratification.

There's a reason streaming services are replacing home bookshelves. While some may be nostalgic for their wall of treasured CDs, many prefer the vast library and song-recommendation engine available with a click on Spotify—both old favorites and new discoveries. We also benefit as consumers because licensing the stick can be cheaper than owning the bundle. Companies can maximize revenue by offering us just what we want right that minute. We may feel we own more, but we really don't.

Life à la Carte

There is one last stop on this frontier tour of ownership: the *sharing economy*. In a sense, the sharing economy is the flip side of digital ownership. Instead of wrongly believing we own more than we really do, in the sharing economy we intentionally want to own less. Forget the bundle of ownership. Just give us temporary use of someone else's good or service. We seek micro-ownership in exchange for micropayments. This is the world of twigs, not sticks.

"How many of you own a power drill?"

In a broad Australian accent, Rachel Botsman poses this simple question to the packed audience at a TEDx talk in Sydney.

Most of the audience's hands go up, but no one knows where this is going. Botsman makes her living thinking big thoughts and spotting emerging trends, especially on how we consume things. *Time* described her 2010 book *What's Mine Is Yours* as one of the "ten ideas that will change the world." So this simple question is clearly leading somewhere big.

"And how long will that drill be used in its lifetime?"

This question's not so easy to answer. Turns out, it's twelve to thirteen minutes.

"It's kind of ridiculous, right? Because what you need is the hole, not the drill." And given that, she asks, "Why don't you rent the drill? Or even better, rent out your own drill to other people and make some money from it?"

When you put it that way, the sharing economy seems obvious. Why didn't we think of it before?

Botsman's insight about the benefits of sharing a power drill has been true for as long as there have been power drills, so why did *Time* magazine think it was such a new, big idea that would change the world? There has been a big change, but not in the way most people think.

What's changed is not power drills. Nor is the idea of renting goods and services anything new. The big change is that smartphones and the Internet have unlocked new possibilities for micro-ownership. As a tech journalist explained, "The iPhone helped put the Internet and GPS in people's pockets. The Great Recession helped make them desperate and broke. These two developments dovetailed to sow the seeds of the sharing economy: consumers were looking for new ways to save, workers were looking for new ways to earn, and smartphones gave them both new ways to transact."

Twenty years ago renting out your power drill, spare bedroom, or car was too expensive and complicated to be practical. There was no low-cost way to communicate with potential buyers, negotiate price and terms, and collect payment. You had all kinds of assets lying around your house and parked in your driveway with value for others' use, but there was no simple way to make a deal. The Internet slashed all these costs. As one scholar put it, now we can get "slices" of things that once came only in "lumps." Suddenly new markets can arise.

The average American car is in use only 4 percent of the day. It's now possible to ask whether value can be created the other 96 percent of the time, when the car is idle. Is there a business opportunity here? Turo, Getaround, Maven, and other start-ups sure hope so—they want renters to bypass Hertz and Avis and instead take your private car out of the driveway. It's Zipcar, but for every car. As one tech reporter fantasized, "In a world where property is networked and programmable, and ultra-fast micro-payments can happen automatically, and software records and enforces who owns what, the pool of possible transactions is potentially infinite."

Getting married and don't want to own a pricey wedding dress? Log on to RentTheRunway—it has hundreds for you to choose from. Most people wear their special-occasion dresses fewer than seven times—and wedding dresses, we hope, just once. RentTheRunway tries for thirty "turns" for its dresses. Some are worn 150 times. Spending a weekend in a new city? Find a place to stay through VRBO or Airbnb. It can be cheaper than a hotel and put you in a more fun neighborhood. Not using your apartment's parking space next week? A commuter can pay for it through JustPark.

Anyone who follows business or technology news, even casually, knows this list of start-ups goes on and on—for clothes, bikes, odd jobs, groceries, electricity outlets, and more. Internet platforms are creating markets for goods and services that we owned but could not trade.

Not every idea works, of course. To return to Botsman's example about the drill hole, it turns out many do-it-yourselfers still want the power drill—as evidenced by a string of failed hole providers, including NeighborGoods, Ecomodo, Crowd Rent, Share Some Sugar, Thingloop, OhSoWe, and SnapGoods. People actually don't want to spend money, time, and hassle for a one-day rental when they can pick up a thirty-dollar drill at the local hardware store or get same-day delivery from Amazon. And more often than not, people don't want either the drill or the hole. They want the curtains hung and the IKEA dresser assembled. TaskRabbit figured out it could provide that useful combination, sending you both the drill and the person who would finish the project.

There's no shortage of names for these new markets—"collaborative consumption," the "gig economy," the "peer economy." There has been no end of breathless predictions for where it will lead: "A startling number of young people, it turns out, have begun to question one of the central tenets of American culture: ownership." And at least in theory, it's a promising development. We don't need full ownership to satisfy our wants and needs. As a *New York Times* writer notes, "Nowadays we don't really buy things. We just subscribe to online services. And how can we resist?" After all, it's the service that matters, not the thing.

The optimistic version of the sharing economy is that consumers will acquire just the amount of services they need. Nothing—no thing—is wasted.

Indeed, it may be true we are too attached to material things—as the Buddhists among us might caution. As a society, we generate and own too much stuff. Many people feel burdened by their things. How many of us have attics, basements, or even rented storage lockers full of stuff we never see? If we stop owning things that we don't use much, we won't just worry less, we will free our spirits and spark joy (per Marie Kondo). Purchasing use-on-demand may also promote a more environmentally sustainable lifestyle. "Many of us are starting to rethink what it means to own something," one commentator notes. "In turn, that's giving rise to a new social and commercial landscape in this country, and even a new way of life." To consume at our accustomed level, we can use fewer resources—say, by ridding ourselves of cars that sit idle in garages and clutter parking spaces in crowded cities.

There is something appealing to this idyllic vision, but it also misses a larger point.

The sharing economy isn't really about sharing; nor is it about the end of ownership. It's about advances in ownership technology that transform who we are as citizens and consumers—just like catch shares and FastPass+, oil unitization and dynasty trusts have changed the landscape of ownership. Going forward, the intersection of micro-ownership and smartphones may upend life as thoroughly as ownership attachment and barbed wire remodeled the Great Plains.

There will be surprising costs in the shift from owning things to streaming life. For starters, the sharing economy may turn out to encourage not Zen simplicity but even more conspicuous consumption. Think about it: you rarely see people at a big buffet with half-empty plates. Plates are piled high. As each good or service becomes cheaper, people consume greater variety—less perhaps of each thing but more overall. All that streaming of high-end dresses and handbags may be training people to value luxury over sufficiency, never quite satisfied with what they have, always ready to jump to the next, even more expensive, tier of service.

And the sharing economy does not build wealth; for most of us, it consumes wealth. People lose the discipline of saving up for big purchases, taking out loans or mortgages, paying them off, and owning equity—in their jewelry, cars, and, most of all, homes. Historically, homeownership was America's greatest source of wealth-building, for those able to buy homes (it's the largest driver of racial wealth differences). After mortgages were paid off, homes gave retired people a secure place to live or provided cash if they downsized. By contrast, renters pay month to month, and streamers day to day, accumulating nothing.

Communities also suffer if everyone streams accommodations rather than makes long-term commitments. Who organizes the local street party if its residents are just Airbnb'ers pulling wheeled suitcases from place to place? Neighbors don't go next door to get a cup of sugar from strangers or congratulate them on their child's birthday. Popular tourist destinations have seen entire neighborhoods unravel as longtime residents are replaced by investors who buy apartments with the sole purpose of short-term turnover. This transition can also drive up the price of housing, making it more difficult for people who grew up in an area to stay. Community solidarity is intangible, hard to measure, but its loss is a real cost nonetheless. In this tragedy of the commons, individual homeowners rationally choose to profit by listing on Airbnb, but collectively we all lose connection to our sense of place, to what makes us feel truly at home.

In response, some communities—like Santa Monica, California— are starting to prohibit short-term rentals, effectively banning Airbnb. By restricting willing sellers and buyers, the city is trying to prevent already high house prices from escalating further and to keep community spirit intact. But that choice also helps Santa Monica remain wealthy and white, excluding those who are neither but want a brief

sojourn by the beach. And it imposes substantial costs on local homeowners who are house rich and otherwise broke.

One way to make sense of the Airbnb ban is to see it as pushing the dimmer of ownership a little down—away from markets,
toward nonmonetary values. Santa Monica is addressing the loss of
neighborhood solidarity, but at a cost (for us, on balance, too high a
cost) to individual autonomy and racial equality. All ownership rules
involve trade-offs.

So who decides how much of our lives we will live à la carte?
The answer, as always, depends on whose hand rests on the remote
control of ownership. Should this be a choice for individual owners,
condo boards, neighborhoods, cities, or nation states? There is nothing neutral about who decides—each choice transforms the meaning
of *mine*.

Looking into the crystal ball, we can envision a world, perhaps
not too far in the future, where the full bundle of ownership is
concentrated in relatively few corporate hands and everyone else
licenses twigs of access. What would it mean to live in such a
world, where each individual's connection to goods and services is
so ephemeral?

The risk is not just that we lose touch with our neighbors and
communities. We may also lose aspects of our personhood, a connection with the sacred that many people experience through old-
fashioned ownership. We could be giving up—inadvertently, and
through a thousand clicks—the creativity, self-expression, and self-
knowledge that come from owning, personalizing, and connecting
with our most intimate objects. We move away from cherishing,
say, our parents' underlined novels and cookbooks with notes in the
margins and spills on the pages—evidence of what they thought and
cared about. Instead, we type ingredients into recipe search engines
or absentmindedly order dinner from GrubHub. And rather than
learning how to change the oil in our convertible Mustang or VW

Bug, twentieth-century automotive symbols of freedom, we Uber, consuming a rather less exalted stream of car services.

This shift matters because we exist not only as consumers. Much of our identity is bound up with the things we own. We get attached to our homes and cars, our books and clothes. As one journalist poignantly asks, "Who remembers the sound of unwrapping a new record album, the smell of a new car or the thrill of opening the front door to a newly purchased home? At different points in my life, each one stood for the joy of possession, and the sense of having really arrived."

In this grand shift from owning something—some thing—to holding just a twig in someone else's bundle, we risk losing the profound value that comes from our intimate connections to simple material possessions. Our things—like our bodies—define and constitute who we are, not just as individuals but as part of meaningful communities. In this new world, we may never cook a meal to bring to a sick neighbor, plant a garden with a friend, join together to clean up an abandoned lot, or share tools and skills to build a community playground.

In the sharing economy, we may be clicking our way to lives where physical possession really does drop below one-tenth of the law—*I'm holding it, yet it's barely mine at all.* Ownership floats free from the things we fleetingly possess. Life à la carte might be super-convenient, but do you really want to license your engagement ring and lease your dog? And how do you buy a gift for someone who can stream anything and owns nothing?

THE TODDLER'S RULES
OF OWNERSHIP

A common thread runs through *Mine!* We are surrounded by valuable stuff all the time, yet we don't just snatch what we want. We aren't thieves. And other people don't just take stuff from us. We aren't chumps.

Shared understandings of ownership make it possible for strangers to live alongside each other peaceably. Most rules can't be complex, or else we would not be able to get through a single day. Judges decide perhaps one of every million ownership conflicts, if that. All the rest, we work out among ourselves.

How is this possible?

When a semester goes well, on the last day of class, our students sometimes surprise us with a funny gift. One year students gave us a bundle of sticks—yes, actual sticks tied together in a bundle. Another year it was a stuffed fox, inspired by the classic *Pierson v. Post* case.

One of Heller's favorites was a T-shirt with a banner printed across the chest reading THE TODDLER'S RULES OF OWNERSHIP. (Many variants of the text are floating around on the Internet. We searched, but could find no author to credit. So who owns it?) Here are the rules on that T-shirt:

1. If I like it, it's mine.
2. If it's in my hand, it's mine.
3. If I can take it from you, it's mine.
4. If I had it a little while ago, it's mine.
5. If it's mine, it must never appear to be yours in any way.
6. If I'm doing or building something, all the pieces are mine.
7. If it looks just like mine, it is mine.
8. If I saw it first, it's mine.
9. If you are playing with something and you put it down, it's mine.
10. If it's broken, it's yours.

These rules are funny because they ring so true. It's no coincidence that *mine* is one of the very first words toddlers speak. From a young age, kids have a strong drive to possess and a surprisingly clear sense of what ownership means. Zoom-zooming the toy truck is fine, but if you whack your sister with it, the truck is not yours anymore. Toddlers are experts at negotiating the spaces between the rules. So are we all. And that has to be the case for us to get through everyday life.

When valuable resources emerge—and they do all the time—ownership is always up for grabs. Whether it's access to Supreme Court seats, streaming HBO shows, drones hovering above your house, rides on a breaking wave, or a parking spot on a snowy street, people assert competing claims. Often the ownership maxims that frame this book carry the day. But there's always another story, threatening to turn ownership upside down. *First come, last served. Possession is one-tenth of the law. I reap what you sow.* And sometimes even the Toddler's Rules prevail.

This tension is where things get interesting—both for people seeking profit and for those aiming to advance the public good.

The toddler's view of Disney World is: *I got in line before you, so I ride before you. No cutting.* But Disney has engineered a fast path to the front for the super-wealthy. The toddler's view of iTunes is: *I put* Dora the Explorer *in my shopping cart, Mum clicked "buy now," so it's mine. No take-backs.* But Apple has attached a string that lets it retrieve the show. Owners are always tweaking ownership to steer us this way or that—whether it's to ensure rabid fans for Duke basketball, scoop up our genetic code for 23andMe, or encourage safer and more sustainable crabbing on the Bering Sea.

Remember the Knee Defender story that opened this book? In the time it took us to write this manuscript, airplane seating has changed. Airlines are now ripping out built-in entertainment screens, making tray tables into even more intense sites for ownership contests: you need that "media device support" so you can stream your own content. American Airlines decreased seat recline from a restful four inches to a symbolic two; Delta is following suit. Spirit and other discount airlines have gone further, "preclining" seats, fixing them at a set angle and eliminating the recline button altogether. Why? Not for a more comfortable flight experience. Preclining makes seats simpler, lighter, and thinner, and that in turn eases maintenance, saves fuel, and allows more passengers to be crammed in. It also eliminates ownership ambiguity and puts the Knee Defender out of business. The only price: most passengers are a little less comfortable.

Today ownership conflicts in economy class are moving to footrests and armrests and especially to control over window shades—pitting passengers who want to stare out the window against those complaining of screen glare. The fight over the ownership baseline is like swamps versus wetlands, and redwood trees versus solar panels, but at thirty-five thousand feet.

If there is one lesson from this book, it's that *mine* reflects a choice among competing stories. There are only six simple stories everyone uses to claim everything. And which story wins is always up for grabs. Now that you can recognize the hidden rules, you can be a more effective advocate for yourself, your community, and our common good. Whether you're waiting in line, surfing the Web, or squeezed in your airplane seat, ask yourself: Whose hand is on the remote control? Who gets what and why?

Thanks

Jointly, we thank our agent Jim Levine of Levine Rostan Greenberg Literary Agency and our editor Kris Puopolo of Doubleday. Jim has stood behind *Mine!* from the first day the proposal crossed his desk, and every day since. From the book's title to its ambition—that's all Jim. Thanks as well to his team, including Mike Nardullo and Matthew Huff. Kris has steered us with a sure hand and a light touch. We lucked out when she agreed to work with us. Many thanks to the Doubleday team, including Mike Collica, Todd Doughty, Kathleen Fridella, Michael Goldsmith, Dan Meyer, Rachel Molland, Lauren Weber, Mike Windsor, and Carolyn Williams.

Carol Rose has been a mentor to us both throughout our careers. Bob Ellickson, Hanoch Dagan, and Tom Merrill taught us how to think about ownership. Rob Fischman suggested the "*Freakonomics* of ownership" premise. And, at just the right moment, Dan Ariely introduced us to Jim Levine. We are indebted to more colleagues and friends than we can mention here. Special thanks to Jamie Boyle, Ann Carlson, Glenn Cohen, Cooper Costello, Philippe Darquier, Martin Doyle, John Elkington, Jane Ginsburg, Jerry Kang, Dan Kevles, Mike McCann, Jed Purdy, Kal Raustiala, Richard Re, Buffie Scott, Chris Slobogin, Jackson Willis, Tim Wu, and to workshop participants at Colorado, Columbia, Duke, UC

Hastings, UCLA, and UCSB. Thanks also to our research assistants, Connor Clerkin, Andrew Howard, Rob Koehler, and Sara Weiss.

Personal Thanks

Thanks to my many co-authors whose ideas populate this book, especially Hanoch Dagan, my longtime collaborator in private law theory. Columbia Law School has been a great scholarly home thanks to the support of Dean Gillian Lester and my spectacular colleagues, along with generous research funding from the Marc and Eva Stern Faculty Research Fund, the Grace P. Tomei Endowment Fund, and the Henry and Lucy Moses Faculty Research Fund. A special thanks to my students with whom I field-tested much of the book's material—they are not shy about telling me when I'm off point. I am grateful for the friends who have sustained me as I write, including David Basche, Bart Gellman, Dafna Linzer, Alysia Reiner, Daniel Rothenberg, Virginia Rutter, Tamar Schapiro, and Jason Slavick, and to my parents and brothers, who taught me the meaning of *mine* from a very young age. Thanks to my co-author Jim Salzman, who has been the motor keeping this project chugging good-spiritedly along— I've had so much fun writing this together with Jim. And finally, as always and every day, I give thanks to Debora, my first reader, best critic, and true love, and to Ellie and Jonah, who make my life a joy.—*M.H.*

This book has been seven wonderful years in the making. I have enjoyed and benefited from countless brainstorming sessions with friends and strangers alike over how to think about ownership and particularly promising examples. Their enthusiasm for the topic has helped more than they know. The UCSB Bren School of Environmental Science & Management, UCLA Law School, and Duke Law School provided generous funding. This book is immeasurably better because it was a truly shared enterprise. Michael Heller's deep knowledge of property law, dedication to making each draft the very best possible, and quick wit made writing together a pleasure. A heartfelt and special thanks to my far-flung family, whose loving support and encouragement of this and other adventures, inspired and madcap alike, make me a fortunate person indeed.—*J.S.*

Notes

Many of the framing devices and some of the stories in this book were drawn from our previously published work. We have also drawn liberally on other scholars' research and on journalists' articles. Citations for these framing devices, stories, research, and articles are included in the notes. Other material not cited was generally drawn from readily accessible news sources and reference works. An expanded set of notes appears online at the book's website, www.MineTheBook.com. The online notes also include links to sources, along with suggestions for further reading on stories and scholarship related to the book.

In addition, the book's website links to photos and other illustrations keyed to the stories. Ownership gridlock prevented us from including them in the text. If you want to know what a Knee Defender looks like, go to www.MineTheBook.com.

Introduction: Who Gets What and Why

1 Toddlers in sandboxes: For some practical tips, see Melissa Dahl, "Your Toddler's Possessive Phase, Explained," *Parents,* October 4, 2017.

2 James Beach is a large guy: Alexandra Sifferlin, "Knee Defender Passenger Says He Never Reclines His Seat," *Time,* September 3, 2014. For an entertaining exploration of Knee Defender etiquette, listen to "Getting Away with It," *This American Life,* Episode 477, October 19, 2012, in which host Ira Glass travels with Ken Hegan, a six-foot-two journalist who is using a Knee Defender.

2 "stop reclining seats": The Knee Defender is sold online at Gadgetduck.com.

2 The same conflict keeps erupting: Aimee Ortiz, "Recline in Your Airplane Seat? A Debate Rages in the Skies and Online," *New York Times,* February 15, 2020.

2 "The only time it's ever": Jayme Deerwester, "'Recline to one another': Ellen DeGeneres Defends Reclining Passenger in Punching Drama," *USA Today,* February 19, 2020.

3 "The proper thing": Jessica Bursztynsky, "Delta CEO Says He Doesn't Recline His Seat—but for Those Who Do, It's 'Proper' to Ask First," CNBC.com, February 14, 2020.

3 This claim of attachment: Thomas Merrill, "Accession and Original Ownership," *Journal of Legal Analysis* 1 (2009): 462–510.

4 "No, just don't": Nick Schwartz, "Poll: Is It Acceptable to Recline Your Seat on an Airplane?" *USA Today,* February 13, 2020.

4 "What the airlines are doing": Katia Hetter, "Knee Defender Speaks Out About Airline Legroom Fight," CNN, September 5, 2014.

5 One study, though, suggests: Christopher Buccafusco and Christopher Jon Sprigman, "Who Deserves Those 4 Inches of Airplane Seat Space?," *Slate,* September 23, 2014.

5 The Knee Defender may seem: The leading modern utilitarian account linking scarcity with ownership innovation is Harold Demsetz, "Towards a Theory of Property Rights," *American Economic Review* 57 (1967): 347–59.

6 "The Greatest Discovery": For a brief account, see Tim Harford, "'The Devil's Rope': How Barbed Wire Changed America," *50 Ideas that Changed the World,* BBC World Service, August 17, 2017.

6 Glidden's invention transformed: For a scholarly treatment, see Richard Hornbeck, "Barbed Wire: Property Rights and Agricultural Development," *Quarterly Journal of Economics* 125 (2010): 767–810.

8 "a guy in New Jersey": Jenna Wortham, "No TV? No Subscription? No Problem," *New York Times,* April 6, 2013.

8 "legalish": David Thier, "How Many Are Watching 'Game of Thrones' Without Subscribing to HBO," *Forbes,* April 10, 2013. See also Kashmir Hill, "Even New York Times Is Oblivious to Fact That Sharing 'HBO Go' Passwords to Watch 'Game of Thrones' Breaks Law," *Forbes,* April 10, 2013.

9 "that's mine": Kristina Olson, "'Hey, That's My Idea!': Children's Understanding of Idea Ownership," *Psychology Today,* August 16, 2013.

9 Copyright, patent, and trademark lawyers: After surveying increasing intellectual property protections, Mark Lemley concludes "the 'propertization' of intellectual property is a very bad idea." Mark Lemley, "Romantic Authorship and the Rhetoric of Property," *Texas Law Review* 75 (1997): 902.

10 Rewarding labor often feels: For a fascinating account of innovation without ownership, see Kal Raustiala and Christopher Sprigman, *The Knockoff Economy: How Imitation Sparks Innovation* (New York: Oxford University Press, 2012).

10 "account sharing is generally": Sarah Perez, "Netflix CEO Says Account Sharing Is OK," *TechCrunch,* January 11, 2016.

11 "a terrific marketing vehicle": Greg Kumparak, "HBO Doesn't Care If You Share Your HBO Go Account . . . For Now," *TechCrunch,* January 20, 2014.

11 "We love people sharing Netflix": Richard Nieva, "Netflix Is Cool with You Sharing Your Account," CNET, January 6, 2016.

14 Amazon knows—and studies have shown: In one survey, 83 percent of online buyers wrongly believed buying digital is the same as buying the physical item. See Aaron Perzanowski and Chris Jay Hoofnagle, "What We Buy When We 'Buy Now,'" *University of Pennsylvania Law Review* 165 (2017): 317–78.

15 Even better—for the airlines: Tim Wu, "Why Airlines Want to Make You Suffer," *The New Yorker,* December 26, 2014.

18 This is a real case: Matter of McDowell, 74 Misc.2d 663 (1973). For an analogous problem, consider how ownership of dogs is split when co-owners move apart. Lauren Vinopal, "The Rise of the Dogvorce," *GQ,* January 15, 2020.

19 Coin flips work: On coin flips in court, see Adam M. Samaha, "Randomization in Adjudication," *William and Mary Law Review* 51 (2009): 1–86.

Chapter 1: First Come, Last Served

22 Welcome to the line-standing business: On the line-standing business, see Adam Liptak, "Supreme Court Spectator Line Acts as a Toll Booth," *New York Times,* April 15, 2013; Sarah Kliff, "Paid Line-Standing: The Bizarre Congressional Practice that Shocked Ocasio-Cortez, Explained," *Vox,* February 13, 2019; Joe Pinsker, "The Growing Market for Getting Paid to Wait in Line," *The Atlantic,* July 25, 2014.

23 "Let's pay the poor": Dahlia Lithwick and Mark Joseph Stern, "Not All Must Rise," *Slate,* April 27, 2015.

24 "the first Christian": Henry Wheaton, *Elements of International Law* (Boston: Little, Brown, 1855), 220.

24 "The conqueror prescribes its limits": *Johnson v. M'Intosh,* 21 U.S. 543, 589 (1823). For an in-depth exploration, see Stuart Banner, *How the Indians Lost Their Land: Law and Power on the Frontier* (Cambridge, Mass.: Harvard University Press, 2005).

25 "intended as a symbolic": Anne Platoff, "Where No Flag Has Gone Before: Political and Technical Aspects of Placing a Flag on the Moon," NASA, August 1993.

26 Today well-funded start-ups: Atossa Araxia Abrahamian, "How the Asteroid-Mining Bubble Burst," *MIT Technology Review,* June 26, 2019. On mining the moon, see Mike Wall, "Trump Signs Executive Order to Support Moon Mining, Tap Asteroid Resources," *Space,* April 6, 2020.

26 Europeans imagined Native peoples: William Cronon, *Changes in the Land: Indians, Colonists, and the Ecology of New England* (New York: Hill and Wang, 1983).

26 The little prince asks why: Antoine de Saint-Exupéry, *The Little Prince* (New York: Reynal & Hitchcock, 1943).

27 Almost all the 1.3 million lawyers: *Pierson v. Post,* 3 Cai. R. 175, 178, 181 (N.Y. 1805).

27 Here the judges split: For a powerful account of cycling between rules and standards, see Carol Rose, "Crystals and Mud in Property Law," *Stanford Law Review* 40 (1988): 577–610. In practice, law often operates in the space between ad hoc standards and rigid rules, using "informative standards" that enable people to predict the consequences of their choices and plan their lives accordingly. See Hanoch Dagan, *Reconstructing American Legal Realism & Rethinking Private Law Theory* (Oxford: Oxford University Press, 2012), 194. See also Lawrence Solum, "Legal Theory Lexicon 026: Rules, Standards, Principles, Catalogs, and Discretion," *Legal Theory Lexicon.* Solum's blog has many brief, useful entries on ownership tools.

31 Most students wouldn't want to: Ziv Carmon and Dan Ariely, "Focusing on the Forgone: How Value Can Appear So Different to Buyers and Sellers," *Journal of Consumer Research* 27 (2000): 360–70.

33 Disney may be amazing: Brooks Barnes, "Disney Tackles Major Theme Park Problem: Lines," *New York Times,* December 27, 2010. For an engaging exploration of this theme, see Nelson Schwartz, *The Velvet Rope Economy* (New York: Doubleday, 2020).

36 "Who wants a speed pass": Tara Palmeri, "Rich Manhattan Moms Hire Handicapped Tour Guides So Kids Can Cut Lines at Disney World," *New York Post,* May 14, 2013.

36 "We find it deplorable": Jeff Rossen and Josh Davis, "Undercover at Disney: 'Deplorable' Scheme to Skip Lines," *Today,* May 31, 2013; Kevin Mintz, "Disney Rides Thrill Me as a Wheelchair User. But Park Changes for Disabled Visitors Ruin the Fun," *Los Angeles Times,* December 13, 2019.

37 "Obscene": Luz Lazo and Faiz Siddiqui, "'No One Has to Pay a Toll.' Virginia Transportation Chief Defends High Tolls on I-66," *Washington Post,* December 6, 2017.

38 food trucks and carts: On Roy Choi, see Nicole Laporte, "How Roy Choi Built an Empire from One Beat-Up Taco Truck," *Fast Company,* November 18,

2014, and Raustiala and Sprigman, *Knockoff Economy,* 8–11, 184. On food cart battles for space, see Julia Moskin, "Turf War at the Hot Dog Cart," *New York Times,* June 30, 2009. On immigrant entrepreneurship, see Rachel Wharton, "Food Cart Worker's Biggest Job: Defending Vendor Rights," *New York Times,* February 3, 2020.

41 During the COVID-19 shutdown: Dahlia Lithwick and Mark Joseph Stern, "The Supreme Court Just Proved Its Secretive Rules Are Silly and Counterproductive," *Slate,* May 4, 2020.

Chapter 2: Possession Is One-Tenth of the Law

43 Enter the parking chair: Parking chairs have generated an extensive scholarly literature. For examples, see Susan S. Silbey, "J. Locke, Op. Cit.: Invocations of Law on Snowy Streets," *Journal of Comparative Law* 5 (2010): 66–91, and Richard A. Epstein, "The Allocation of the Commons: Parking on Public Roads," *Journal of Legal Studies* 31 (2002): S515–44.

43 They all know: The leading scholarly treatment on the communicative role of possession is Carol Rose, "Possession as the Origin of Property," *University of Chicago Law Review* 52 (1985): 73–88.

43 "People didn't have": Julie Xie, "Boston's Space-Saving Tradition Explained," *Boston,* January 22, 2015.

44 South Boston City councilmember: Donovan Slack, "On Parking Markers, Southie, City Dig In," *Boston Globe,* December 30, 2004.

44 In 2015, responding: Chris Sweeney, "Space Savers Are Banned in the South End," *Boston,* February 9, 2017.

44 "The space isn't your": "Walsh: Space Saver Violence, Threats Won't Be Tolerated," WCVB, January 11, 2018. Chicago's Mayor Richard Daley had a different view: "If someone spends all their time digging their car out, do not drive into that spot. This is Chicago. Fair warning." See "Standing Up for Dibs," NBC News, December 8, 2010.

45 "In a bigger-picture": Steven Holt, "The Psychology of Boston's Snow Parking Wars," *City Lab,* January 22, 2018.

46 "The useful act of shoveling": Rose, "Possession," 81.

47 And yes, we intend: James E. Krier, "Evolutionary Theory and the Origin of Property Rights," *Cornell Law Review* 95 (2009): 139–59. For an anthropologist's take, see Robert Ardrey, *The Territorial Imperative* (New York: Atheneum, 1966).

47 Possession is a primal instinct: Thomas Merrill has advanced a strong defense of an instinctive basis for the role of possession in law: "Possession as a Natural Right," *New York University Journal of Law and Liberty* 9 (2015): 345–74, and

"Ownership and Possession," in Yun-chien Chang, ed., *The Law and Economics of Possession* (Cambridge, UK: Cambridge University Press, 2015), 9–39.

47 Signaling physical control over an object: See Philippe Rochat, "Possession and Morality in Early Development," *New Directions for Child and Adolescent Development* (Summer 2011): 23–38.

47 In a now-classic experiment: Daniel Kahneman et al., "Experimental Tests of the Endowment Effect and the Coase Theorem," *Journal of Political Economy,* 98 (1990): 1325–48.

48 Chimpanzees and capuchin monkeys: Monkeys may understand ownership, but they cannot be owners. After a macaque monkey took an Internet-famous selfie, a court ruled that nonhumans cannot legally hold copyright. Sara Randazzo, "Copyright Protection for Monkey Selfie Rejected by U.S. Appeals Court," *Wall Street Journal,* April 23, 2018.

48 "endowment effect": Richard Thaler, "Toward a Positive Theory of Consumer Choice," *Journal of Economic Behavior and Organization* 1 (1980): 39–47.

48 It never happens: Researchers do remove items from strangers' carts in psychology experiments; see Jodi O'Brien, "Building and Breaching Reality," in Jodi O'Brien, ed., *The Production of Reality: Essays and Readings on Social Interaction,* 6th ed. (Thousand Oaks, Calif.: Sage Publications, 2016), 451–52; and on television prank shows, see "Butterfly Crime Scene," *Impractical Jokers, TruTV,* season 1, episode 2, December 15, 2011. On toilet paper filching, see Jordan Reynolds, "Coronavirus Panic-buyers 'Stealing from Trolleys' at Black Country Cash and Carry," *Express and Star* (Wolverhampton, UK), March 11, 2020.

50 The real rule is "Finders give it back": There are many stories like this one: Mariel Padilla, "Teenager, an Aspiring Detective, Returns $135,000 He Found," *New York Times,* May 9, 2020.

50 Back in the 1980s: Monique Cole, "The Scandal in Boulder That Won't Go Away," *High Country News,* March 10, 2008.

51 Surprisingly, a lot of landownership: For a fascinating account, see Eduardo Peñalver and Sonia K. Katyal, *Property Outlaws: How Squatters, Pirates, and Protesters Improve the Law of Ownership* (New Haven, Conn.: Yale University Press, 2010), 55–63. On the hidden social value of awarding landownership based on squatter's possession, see Hernando de Soto, *The Mystery of Capital: Why Capitalism Triumphs in the West and Fails Everywhere Else* (New York: Basic Books, 2000).

51 *adverse possession:* "Code of Hammurabi, c. 1780 BCE," trans. L. W. King (1910). According to the code, "If a chieftain or a man leave his house, garden, and field . . . and someone else takes possession of his house, garden, and field and uses it for three years: if the first owner return and claims his house,

garden, and field, it shall not be given to him, but he who has taken possession of it and used it shall continue to use it."

52   This rule explains: David W. Dunlap, "Closing for a Spell, Just to Prove It's Ours," *New York Times,* October 30, 2011.

53   "A thing which you": Oliver Wendell Holmes, Jr., "The Path of the Law," *Harvard Law Review* 10 (1897): 477.

53   Environmentalists can't win adverse possession: John Sprankling, "An Environmental Critique of Adverse Possession," *Cornell Law Review* 79 (1994): 816–84.

55   Working in the region: Michael Heller, *The Gridlock Economy: How Too Much Ownership Wrecks Markets, Stops Innovation, and Costs Lives* (New York: Basic Books, 2008), 143–56.

56   "takes root in your being": Holmes, "Path of the Law," 477.

58   "amounts to something like": Rose, "Possession," 81.

58   More often, though, scientists: Sandra Vehrencamp et al., "Negotiation of Territorial Boundaries in a Songbird," *Behavioral Ecology* 25 (November–December 2014): 1436–50; Marissa Ortega-Welch, "Learn Your Local Birds' Regional Accents," *Audubon,* April 12, 2017; Cara Giaimo, "Canada's Sparrows Are Singing a New Song. You'll Hear It Soon," *New York Times,* July 2, 2020.

58   Birds want to control: See Dale Peterson, *The Moral Lives of Animals* (New York: Bloomsbury Press, 2011), 156–72.

58   When dogs on a walk: Jason Goldman, "Defending Your Territory: Is Peeing on the Wall Just for Dogs?," *Scientific American,* March 7, 2011; Katherine Ralls, "Mammalian Scent Marking," *Science* 171 (1971): 443–49.

59   Every year at the State of the Union: On "aisle hogs," see Marin Cogan, "Saving Seats for the State of the Union," *New York Magazine,* January 20, 2015.

59   But sometimes, as the resource becomes scarcer: Ira Iosebashvili, "Phish Fans Are Friendly—Until the Tarps Come Out to Save Seats," *Wall Street Journal,* August 21, 2018. For one of hundreds of crazy stories about seat-savers, see Alfred Ng, "Gunman Fatally Shoots Pennsylvania Churchgoer After Fight over Seat at Sunday Service," *New York Daily News,* April 28, 2016.

60   You may not be surprised: Allison Carmen, "What Would Buddha Do on Southwest Airlines?," *Psychology Today,* September 22, 2014.

60   Stu Weinshanker: Dawn Gilbertson, "Is That Seat Taken? Southwest Airlines Seat-savers Drive Some Passengers Crazy," *USA Today,* December 20, 2017.

62   Is seat-saving a tool: Gyasi Ross, " 'Is There a Problem?' That Scary Brown Man and White Privilege," KUOW.org, January 9. 2015.

62   "If you want to save": Community.southwest.com, accessed May 31, 2020.

62   "It's something that": Gilbertson, "Is That Seat Taken?"

64 "the hottest issue next to": Genevieve Shaw Brown, "Travel Etiquette: Saving Seats at the Pool," ABC News, August 2, 2012.

64 Data back this up: Ibid.

65 "overwhelmingly positive": Ibid.

66 beach-spreading: Nick Corasaniti and Luis Ferré-Sadurní, "Reining In Beach-Spreading, Not to Be Confused with Manspreading," *New York Times,* August 11, 2017.

67 "you need to protect": Susannah Luthi, "With Social Distance Safety Warnings, Birx Tempers Trump's Reopening Message," *Politico,* May 22, 2020.

68 At Lunada Bay Beach, just south: Rory Carroll and Noah Smith, "California's Surf Wars: Wave 'Warlords' Go to Extreme Lengths to Defend Their Turf," *Guardian,* May 8, 2015.

68 To coordinate their attacks: Garrett Therolf, " 'Bay Boys' Surfer Gang Cannot Block Access to Upscale Beach, Coastal Commission Says," *Los Angeles Times,* February 12, 2016.

68 "The area is known": Carroll and Smith, "California's Surf Wars."

69 "It's run like an organized crime": Therolf, " 'Bay Boys' Surfer Gang."

69 "I had dreams I'd come": Carroll and Smith, "California's Surf Wars."

70 Like California surf beaches: The leading scholarly study is James M. Acheson, *The Lobster Gangs of Maine* (Hanover, N.H.: University Press of New England, 1988). For a recent account, see Jesse Dukes, "Consider the Lobstermen," *VQR* 87 (Summer 2011).

72 Negative truthful gossip: For a subtle explanation of negative truthful gossip as a tool for resource management, see Robert Ellickson, *Order Without Law: How Neighbors Settle Disputes* (Cambridge, Mass.: Harvard University Press, 1994), 213–15.

75 He studied the paths: For a superb comedic documentary on the Bonds ball fracas, see Michael Wranovics, dir., *Up for Grabs* (Los Angeles: Laemmle/Zeller Films, 2005), DVD. Paul Finkelman, a law professor who testified in the case, wrote a scholarly take in "Fugitive Baseballs and Abandoned Property: Who Owns the Home Run Ball?," *Cardozo Law Review* 23 (2002): 1609–33.

75 The law, it turned out: Meteorites are perhaps similar to baseballs in dropping great value from the sky. On meteorite law, the leading case is *Goddard v. Winchell,* 86 Iowa 71 (1892), which awarded the rock to the landowner rather than to the finder; though states are showing more variety today.

77 "It's not my ball": Jon Tayler, "Angels Fan Who Caught Albert Pujols' 600th Home Run Gives Ball Back for Free," *Sports Illustrated,* June 5, 2017. See also Amber Sutherland, "Fan Who Caught Jeter's 3,000th Ball—and Gave It Back—Has No Regrets," *New York Post,* July 11, 2011.

77 "was set upon by a gang": *Popov v. Hayashi,* 2002 WL 31833731 (Cal. Super. Ct. 2002).

79 Every ownership choice boils down: Michael Heller and Hanoch Dagan explain why property and contract law do, and should, rely on an *ex ante* approach that enhances individual autonomy, and that contains within it a commitment to relational justice and collective utility. See *The Choice Theory of Contracts* (Cambridge, UK: Cambridge University Press, 2017); "The Liberal Commons," *Yale Law Journal* 110 (2001): 549–623; and "Why Autonomy Must Be Contract's Ultimate Value," *Jerusalem Review of Legal Studies* 20 (2019): 148–71.

79 "If I had to choose only one theoretical tool": Lawrence Solum, "Legal Theory Lexicon 001: Ex Ante & Ex Post," *Legal Theory Lexicon.*

Chapter 3: I Reap What You Sow

80 King's legacy became a brand: Valerie Strauss, "53 Years Later, You Still Have to Pay to Use Martin Luther King Jr.'s Famous 'I Have a Dream' Speech," *Washington Post,* January 15, 2017; John Fund, "We Have a Brand!," *National Review,* January 4, 2015.

80 "We never even asked": Ann Hornaday, "Ava DuVernay, David Oyelowo on Breaking Martin Luther King Jr. Out of Myth and Into Life," *Washington Post,* December 26, 2014.

81 "You know, those gentlemen": Sarah Pulliam Bailey, "Martin Luther King Jr. Sermon Used in a Ram Trucks Super Bowl Commercial Draws Backlash," *Washington Post,* February 5, 2018.

81 "It is so painful": Kurt Eichenwald, "The Family Feud over Martin Luther King Jr.'s Legacy," *Newsweek,* April 3, 2014.

81 "Friends of the family": Ibid.

83 "every Man has": John Locke, *Two Treatises of Government* (1689), chap. 5, "Of Property," sec. 27.

83 Ownership of the world's previously unowned resources: Even from the "desert for labor" perspective, not everything should belong to the laborer. See Hanoch Dagan, *Property: Values and Institutions* (Oxford: Oxford University Press, 2011), 82–83.

83 "In the beginning": Locke, *Two Treatises,* chap. 5, sec. 49.

83 "The tribes of Indians": *Johnson v. M'Intosh,* 21 U.S. 543, 590 (1823).

83 For the Court: See Stuart Banner, *How the Indians Lost Their Land: Law and Power on the Frontier* (Cambridge, Mass.: Harvard University Press, 2005), 150–90.

83 Neither did the ways Native peoples farmed land: See William Cronon,

Changes in the Land: Indians, Colonists, and the Ecology of New England (New York: Hill and Wang, 1983).

84 "When white settlers": Kat Eschner, "The Little House on the Prairie Was Built on Native American Land," *Smithsonian Magazine,* February 8, 2017.

85 "Oh, come to this country": Laura Ingalls Wilder, *By the Shores of Silver Lake* (New York: Harper & Brothers, 1939), 76.

86 "inholdings": Mike Kessler, "Whose Land Is It Anyway," 5280.com, May 2016. These claims also create contests over dinosaur fossils. Do fossils belong to the mineral rights owner or to the surface rights owner? The surface owner won in Montana. See Holly Doremus, "Animal, Vegetable or Mineral?," Legal-Planet.org, May 31, 2020.

86 Throughout history, law has reinforced: What if one person rakes manure into piles on a public street, leaves to get a cart, and in the meantime someone else takes the piles? In the classic case of *Haslem v. Lockwood,* 37 Conn. 500 (1871), the court awarded the piles to the raker. Productive labor won over physical possession. Motivating people to clean up manure was a big deal in nineteenth-century life and law.

87 Very Important Babies Daycare: "Cartoon Figures Run Afoul of Law," *Chicago Tribune,* April 27, 1989.

87 "It is such a shame": Lyda Longa, "Disney Denies Bid to Keep Characters; 3 Hallandale Day-care Centers Are Given One Month to Remove Murals," *South Florida Sun-Sentinel,* May 18, 1989.

88 "As rabbits love to propagate": Corie Brown, "Walt Disney and Jim Henson," *Entertainment,* May 3, 1991.

89 "He who receives an idea": Thomas Jefferson to Isaac McPherson, August 13, 1813, Founders.archives.gov.

90 "The primary objective of copyright": *Feist Publications v. Rural Telephone Service,* 499 U.S. 340, 349–50, 360 (1991).

90 For centuries, this has been Congress's basic deal: We are telling a streamlined story here. As alternatives to patent monopolies, countries have also long offered prizes, grants, and tax credits. For a recent account, collecting sources, see Daniel Hemel and Lisa Larrimore Ouellette, "Beyond the Patents-Prizes Debate," *Texas Law Review* 92 (2015): 303–82.

90 drug-snorting Muppets: Avi Selk, "Depraved, Drug-Snorting Puppets Defile Good Name of 'Sesame Street,' Lawsuit over Trailer Claims," *Washington Post,* May 26, 2018.

91 The lobbying labor: Timothy Lee, "15 Years Ago, Congress Kept Mickey Mouse Out of the Public Domain. Will They Do It Again?" *Washington Post,* October 25, 2013; Zachary Crockett, "How Mickey Mouse Evades the Public Domain," *Priceonomics,* January 7, 2016.

91 "richest fictional billionaire": "Top-Earning Fictional Characters," *Forbes,* October 19, 2004.

92 Thousands of works: Alexandra Alter, "New Life for Old Classics, as Their Copyrights Run Out," *New York Times,* December 29, 2018.

92 "Most of twentieth-century": James Boyle, *The Public Domain: Enclosing the Commons of the Mind* (New Haven, Conn.: Yale University Press, 2008), 9.

92 Paradoxically, the orphan works problem: For an engaging account of Google's attempt to solve the orphan works problem, see James Somers, "Torching the Modern-Day Library of Alexandria," *The Atlantic,* April 20, 2017.

93 "makes books disappear": Crockett, "How Mickey Mouse Evades."

93 "The real incentive": Lee, "15 years ago."

93 Not even the Supreme Court: *Eldred v. Ashcroft,* 537 U.S. 186 (2003).

94 Sports publicity rights: Bill King, "Shifting Path for Right of Publicity," *Sports Business Journal,* August 13, 2018.

95 "the number is closed": On the *numerus clausus* puzzle, see Michael Heller, "The Boundaries of Private Property," *Yale Law Journal* 108 (1999): 1187–202; Thomas Merrill and Henry Smith, "Optimum Standardization in the Law of Property: The *Numerus Clausus* Principle," *Yale Law Journal* 110 (2000): 9–40; Hanoch Dagan, *Property: Values and Institutions* (New York: Oxford University Press, 2011), 32–57.

95 Ownership—like all technology—evolves: The leading work linking scarcity to ownership innovation is Harold Demsetz, "Towards a Theory of Property Rights," *American Economic Review* 57 (1967): 347–59.

96 They are like words: Traditionally, lawyers distinguished property from contract along exactly this dimension: Property was *in rem,* with rights valid against the world, while contract was *in personam,* binding just on the parties. Modern legal theory collapsed this distinction. Thomas Merrill and Henry Smith have sought to rehabilitate it, in articles such as "What Happened to Property in Law and Economics," *Yale Law Journal* 111 (2001): 357–98.

97 *Eyes Off the Prize:* This account is drawn substantially from Michael Heller, *The Gridlock Economy: How Too Much Ownership Wrecks Markets, Stops Innovation, and Costs Lives* (New York: Basic Books, 2008), 9–11.

98 "The open fields": James Surowiecki, "Righting Copywrongs," *The New Yorker,* January 14, 2002.

98 "Caught, now in court": Public Enemy, "Caught, Can We Get a Witness?," *It Takes a Nation of Millions to Hold Us Back,* Def Jam, Columbia Records, June 28, 1988.

98 "Public Enemy's music was affected": Kembrew McLeod, "How Copyright Law Changed Hip Hop: An Interview with Public Enemy's Chuck D and Hank Shocklee," *Stay Free!,* June 1, 2004.

99 "If you take the hip-hop": "Remixing to Protest Sample Ruling," *Wired,* September 22, 2004. Times may be changing for sampling, though. See Ben Sisario, "The 'Blurred Lines' Case Scared Songwriters. But Its Time May Be Up," *New York Times,* March 24, 2020.

99 Drug Development Gridlock: This account is drawn substantially from Heller, *Gridlock Economy,* Chapter 3.

101 wrote in *Science:* Michael Heller and Rebecca Eisenberg, "Can Patents Deter Innovation? The Anticommons in Biomedical Research," *Science* 280 (May 1998): 698–701.

101 gene-editing technologies: Jorge L. Contreras, "The Anticommons at Twenty: Concerns for Research Continue," *Science* 361 (July 2018): 335–37.

101 Innovations using these tools could save your life: Giorgia Guglielmi, "First CRISPR Test for the Coronavirus Approved in the United States," *Nature,* May 8, 2020.

103 Indeed, the Supreme Court decided: *eBay Inc. v. MercExchange, L.L.C.,* 547 U.S. 388 (2006).

104 "I was a single mom": Chavie Lieber, "Fashion Brands Steal Design Ideas All the Time. And It's Completely Legal," *Vox,* April 27, 2018.

104 "Splurge vs. Steal": For a sampling, see Carly Cardellino, "Splurge vs. Steal: Balenciaga Golden Thick Tube Ring Set," *Cosmopolitan,* April 10, 2013; Channing Hargrove, "Did Zara Knock Off These $795 Balenciaga Sneakers," *Refinery29,* September 27, 2017; and Matthew Schneier, "Did Gucci Copy 'Dapper Dan'? Or Was It 'Homage'?," *New York Times,* May 31, 2017.

105 "see ramifications": Lieber, "Fashion Brands Steal."

105 powerful alternatives: For an eye-opening read, see Kal Raustiala and Christopher Sprigman, *The Knockoff Economy: How Imitation Sparks Innovation* (New York: Oxford University Press, 2012).

105 "Copyright has an intent": Lieber, "Fashion Brands Steal."

107 Creators rely on at least four strategies: The following section draws from Raustiala and Sprigman, *Knockoff Economy,* 50–54.

107 "All comedians steal": Tony Alpsen, "10 Comedians Who Borrowed Jokes Without Making Headlines," *Vulture,* February 14, 2017.

107 "Men-Steal-ia": Colin Patrick, "A Not-So-Funny Look at 6 Comedians Accused of Plagiarism," *Mental Floss,* January 21, 2016.

108 She came out far ahead: The same holds for protecting original dance moves. Taylor Lorenz, "The Original Renegade," *New York Times,* February 18, 2020.

108 "They f*cked with us": Ryan Buxton, "Metallica Drummer Lars Ulrich Recalls Battle with Napster: 'They F—ked With Us, We'll F—k With Them,'" *Huff-Post,* September 24, 2013.

109 with the cheap fake: Raustiala and Sprigman, *Knockoff Economy,* 39–54.

109 increases the value of the original: Simona Romani, Giacomo Gistri, and Stefano Pace, "When Counterfeits Raise the Appeal of Luxury Brands," *Marketing Letters* 23 (September 2012): 807–24.

110 "always excited to see": Hilary George-Parkin, "Why Notoriously Litigious Disney Is Letting Fan Stores Thrive," *Racked,* September 5, 2017.

110 "I still don't think they're": Ibid.

110 Kristen Brown, a Bloomberg: Kristen Brown, "Deleting Your Online DNA Data Is Brutally Difficult," *Bloomberg,* June 15, 2018.

111 Today roughly two of every three: Murphy Heather, "Most White Americans' DNA Can Be Identified Through Genealogy Databases," *New York Times,* October 11, 2018.

112 "We have essentially no patents": Chris Anderson, "Elon Musk's Mission to Mars," *Wired,* October 21, 2012.

114 "a sublicensable, worldwide": AncestryDNA Terms and Conditions, accessed June 5, 2020. These terms change without notice—and that's part of our point.

114 "The average customer who": Erin Brodwin, "DNA-testing Companies Like 23andMe Sell Your Genetic Data to Drugmakers and Other Silicon Valley Startups," *Business Insider,* August 3, 2018.

115 "You can't go to them later": Molly Wood, "Who Owns the Results of Genetic Testing?," *Marketplace,* October 16, 2018. As Ancestry.com says in its terms and conditions: "You understand that by providing any DNA to us, you acquire no rights in any research or commercial products that may be developed."

116 "If people were paid": Eduardo Porter, "Your Data Is Crucial to a Robotic Age. Shouldn't You Be Paid for It?," *New York Times,* March 6, 2018.

116 Historically excluded communities: Giorgio Sirugo, Scott M. Williams, and Sarah A. Tishkoff, "The Missing Diversity in Human Genetic Studies," *Cell* 177 (March 2019): 26–30.

117 "You can't say data is valuable": Adele Peters, "This Health Startup Lets You Monetize Your DNA," *Fast Company,* December 13, 2018.

118 "nudge": Richard Thaler and Cass Sunstein, *Nudge: Improving Decisions About Health, Wealth, and Happiness* (New York: Penguin, 2009).

119 In 2018, insights: Steve Lohr, "Calls Mount to Ease Big Tech's Grip on Your Data," *New York Times,* July 25, 2019. If you want a sense of what companies know about you, see Thorin Klosowski, "Big Companies Harvest Our Data. This Is Who They Think I Am," *New York Times,* May 28, 2020.

119 "surveillance capitalism": Shoshana Zuboff, *The Age of Surveillance Capitalism: The Fight for a Human Future at the New Frontier of Power* (New York: PublicAffairs, 2019).

119 "Imagine if General Motors": Lohr, "Calls Mount."

Chapter 4: My Home Is Not My Castle

120 "Dad, there's a drone": "Hillview Man Arrested for Shooting Down Drone; Cites Right to Privacy," WDRB, July 28, 2015.

120 "Are you the son": Cyrus Farivar, "Kentucky Man Shoots Down Drone Hovering Over His Backyard," *Ars Technica,* July 29, 2015.

121 As we use the term: Our term *attachment* builds on Tom Merrill's identification of *accession* as a route to original ownership on a par with possession and labor. Thomas Merrill, "Accession and Original Ownership," *Journal of Legal Analysis* 1 (2009): 465–510. This expansive definition may discomfit lawyers accustomed to regarding accession merely as an obscure, technical doctrine.

121 Attachment is that principle: In this chapter, we focus on attachment regarding land, but the concept reaches more broadly. It explains why the Supreme Court rejected a Texas program to fund indigent legal services by collecting tiny sums of unclaimed interest on bank savings accounts. The Court ruled the account holders own the interest, however trivial, accrued on their principal. See Michael Heller and James Krier, "Deterrence and Distribution in the Law of Takings," *Harvard Law Review* 112 (1999): 997–1025.

122 "You know, when you're": "Hillview Man Arrested," WDRB.

122 "A man's house": Eduardo Peñalver, "Property Metaphors and *Kelo v. New London:* Two Views of the Castle," *Fordham Law Review* 74 (2006): 2971.

122 Some landowners asserted: Michael Heller, *Gridlock Economy: How Too Much Ownership Wrecks Markets, Stops Innovation, and Costs Lives* (New York: Basic Books, 2008), 28–30.

122 Courts quickly rejected: The most thorough, engaging exploration of this transition in airspace comes in Stuart Banner, *Who Owns the Sky?: The Struggle to Control Airspace from the Wright Brothers On* (Cambridge, Mass.: Harvard University Press, 2008).

123 Amazon, UPS, and Domino's: Colin Snow, "Amazon's Drone Delivery Plans: What's Old, What's New and When?" *Forbes,* June 17, 2019.

123 "The bottom line": Farivar, "Kentucky Man."

123 And the same is true going down: See John Sprankling, "Owning the Center of the Earth," *UCLA Law Review* 55 (2008): 979–1040.

123 Every legal system: Merrill, "Accession and Original Ownership," 465 and n6. Merrill identifies one exception to unanimity around ownership of newborn farm animals: baby swans or cygnets were split equally between the owner of the swan and cock in early English common law.

124 "Should a bull": *Mánava Dharma Sástra; Or, The Institutes of Manu,* trans. Sir William Jones (Madras: Higginbotham, 1863), 237.

124 "a reward to planned production": Felix Cohen, "Dialogue on Private Property," *Rutgers Law Review* 9 (1954): 368.

125 "This, to me, is": Abigail Curtis, "Foragers, Landowners at Odds in Proposed Wild Picker Law," *Bangor Daily News,* March 29, 2017.

125 "right to roam": Katie Mingle, "Right to Roam," *99% Invisible,* episode 313. For a great read, see Ken Illgunas, *This Land Is Our Land: How We Lost the Right to Roam and How to Take It Back* (New York: Plume, 2018).

126 "The biggest problem": Curtis, "Foragers."

126 Greg Corliss was grading the driveway: Our account draws substantially from a wonderful article on the dispute by Tad Friend, "The Gold Diggers," *The New Yorker,* May 31, 1999.

128 "My culture is": Daniella Greenbaum, "Nonsensical Critics Are Accusing an 18-Year-Old Girl of Cultural Appropriation and Racism—and They're Missing Something Much Bigger," *Business Insider,* May 2, 2018.

128 Urban Outfitters won a round: For an understanding of the dispute from a Navajo perspective, see DJ Pangburn, "A Navajo Artist Breaks Down His Tribe's Urban Outfitters Lawsuit," *Vice,* August 3, 2016.

129 biopiracy: Janna Rose, "Biopiracy: When Indigenous Knowledge Is Patented For Profit," *Conversation,* March 7, 2016.

130 All they need ask is: Adaptation rights have become far more contentious in the new era of erotic fan fiction. Alexandra Alter, "A Feud in Wolf-Kink Erotica Raises a Deep Legal Question: What Do Copyright and Authorship Mean in the Crowdsourced Realm Known as the Omegaverse?," *New York Times,* May 23, 2020.

130 "has built into its very operation": Merrill, "Accession," 499.

130 With land, the trend: Ibid., 493.

131 Charlie Pitigliano's grandfather: Bettina Boxall, "Overpumping of Central Valley Groundwater Creating a Crisis, Experts Say," *Los Angeles Times,* March 18, 2015.

132 "I understand that": Scott Shafer and Jeremy Raff, "California's Central Valley: 'More Than Just Farmers on Tractors,'" KQED, August 25, 2014.

132 "You don't want to": Ibid.

133 "it was like living": Stuart Eskenazi, "The Great Sucking Sound," *Houston Press,* November 19, 1998. Nestlé is involved in a similar battle in Florida. Julie Creswell, "Where Mermaids Play, a Nasty Water Fight," *New York Times,* March 8, 2020.

133 "In my furthest dreams": Eskenazi, "Great Sucking Sound."

134 "is now formed into": Francis Hargrave, *Tracts Relative to the Laws of England* (1787): 1:498.

135 "It is revolting": Oliver Wendell Holmes, "The Path of the Law," *Harvard Law Review* 10 (1897): 469

135 "protect private property": Eskenazi, "Great Sucking Sound."

136 "We're dealing with": Ibid.

136 Notice Pate's strategy here: See, for example, Eugene Volokh, "Mechanisms of the Slippery Slope," *Harvard Law Review* 116 (2003): 1026–137.

136 *tragedy of the commons:* Garrett Hardin, "The Tragedy of the Commons," *Science* 162 (December 1968): 1243–48.

137 "To save our valley": Boxall, "Overpumping of Central Valley."

138 When oil was first: Bruce Kramer and Owen Anderson, "The Rule of Capture— an Oil and Gas Perspective," *Environmental Law* 35 (2005): 899–954.

138 *unitization:* Many tools exist to fragment ownership (like subdivision rules for land), but relatively few for re-aggregating them. Assembly is the cutting edge of ownership innovation. See, for example, Michael Heller and Roderick Hills, Jr., "Land Assembly Districts," *Harvard Law Review* 121 (2008): 1465–527.

141 Linda Cherry: Andrew Rice, "A Stake in the Sand," *New York Times,* March 19, 2010.

143 Sand has become scarce: Aurora Torres et al., "The World Is Running Out of Sand," *Smithsonian,* September 8, 2017.

143 Under Florida law: *Stop the Beach Renourishment v. Florida Dept. of Environmental Protection,* 560 U.S. 702 (2010).

143 "I'm sorry, you'll": Rice, "Stake in the Sand."

144 Today, though, China: Vince Beiser, "The Secret Ingredient to China's Aggression? Sand," *New York Times,* July 31, 2018.

147 "Great Wall of Sand": "A 'Great Wall of Sand' in the South China Sea" (editorial), *Washington Post,* April 8, 2015.

147 ignore the claim: Sam LaGrone, "PACOM Harris: U.S. Would Ignore a 'Destabilizing' Chinese South China Sea Air Defense Identification Zone," *USNI News,* February 26, 2016.

147 "as its maritime empire": Geoff Ziezulewicz, "U.S. Warship Sails Contested Waters in South China Sea After White House Rejects Maritime Claims There," *Navy Times,* July 14, 2020.

147 "unless Washington plans": Mark Hanrahan, "China's Global Times: Are Paper's Warnings of War with U.S. Legitimate?," NBC News, January 13, 2017.

148 "The [rules] come with": Bernice Hirabayashi, "Cat Fight: State Supreme Court Will Decide Whether No-Pet Rules Have Teeth," *Los Angeles Times,* December 24, 1992.

150 "More than simply": *Nahrstedt v. Lakeside Village Condominium Assn.,* 8 Cal. 4th 361 (Cal. 1994).

151 Jeffrey Stambovsky decided: Bill Batson, "Nyack Sketch Log: A Legally Haunted House," *Nyack News & Views,* October 21, 2014.

152 "as a matter of law": *Stambovsky v. Ackley,* 169 A.D.2d 254, 263 (N.Y. App. Div. 1991).

152 According to ghost investigator: Batson, "Nyack Sketch Log."

152 Still today their families: Alfred Brophy, "Grave Matters: The Ancient Rights of the Graveyard," *Brigham Young University Law Review* (2006): 1479–82.

153 There's likely no better: Felicity Barringer, "Trees Block Solar Panels, and a Feud Ends in Court," *New York Times,* April 7, 2008.

153 "We're just living": Paul Rogers, "Tree Creates Green Dilemma for Home-owners," *Chicago Tribune,* February 1, 2008.

153 "I think it's": Associated Press, "In California, It's Redwoods vs. Solar Panels," NBC News, February 20, 2008.

153 British courts even developed: Sara Bronin, "Solar Rights," *Boston University Law Review* 89 (2009): 1258.

154 "would preclude development": *Hadacheck v. Sebastian,* 239 U.S. 394 (1915).

155 Nuisance law prohibits you from maintaining: Thomas Merrill, "Trespass, Nuisance, and the Costs of Determining Property Rights," *Journal of Legal Studies* 14 (1985): 13–48.

155 *law and economics* approach: Ronald Coase, "The Problem of Social Cost," *Journal of Law and Economics* 3 (1960): 1–44.

156 Asking these questions: The four-part framework we set out here was introduced in the canonical piece by Guido Calabresi and Douglas Melamed, "Property Rules, Liability Rules, and Inalienability: One View of the Cathedral," *Harvard Law Review* 85 (1972): 1089–1128.

158 we think the right outcome: Michael Heller and James Krier develop this approach, applied to public regulations, in "Deterrence and Distribution in the Law of Takings," *Harvard Law Review* 112 (1999): 997–1025.

158 trees and solar panels are a closer call: Many natural resource conflicts share this structure. Marshes are either swamps to be filled or wetlands to be protected, depending on how we set the baseline of ordinary use—and that baseline has changed over time. See *Just v. Marinette County* 201 N.W.2d 761 (Wisc. 1972). *Miller v. Schoene* 276 U.S. 272 (1928) considers an analogous nuisance conflict between innocent owners of cedar and apple trees. Frank Michelman famously analyzes the dilemma of distinguishing harms from benefits in "Property, Utility and Fairness: Comments on the Ethical Foundations of 'Just Compensation,'" *Harvard Law Review* 80 (1967): 1196–97.

159 "We are the first citizens": Rogers, "Tree Creates Green Dilemma."

159 Their case set off: For a summary of how the act works, see Scott J. Anders

et al., "California's Solar Shade Control Act: a Review of the Statutes and Relevant Cases," University of San Diego, Energy Policy Initiatives Center (March 2010).

159 Just as tall trees: Troy Rule, *Solar, Wind and Land: Conflicts in Renewable Energy Development* (New York: Routledge, 2014), 48–73.

Chapter 5: Our Bodies, Not Our Selves

161 Our Bodies, Not Our Selves: The title of this chapter pays homage to the pioneering feminist classic on women's health and sexuality from the late 1960s. Boston Women's Health Collective, *Our Bodies, Ourselves* (New York: Simon & Schuster, 1973).

161 "So far, I've never": David Porter and Carla K. Johnson, "First Case of Organ Trafficking in U.S.?," NBC News, July 24, 2009.

161 In 2009 Rosenbaum was caught: Samantha Henry, "Brooklyn Man Sentenced 2½ Years in Fed Organ Trafficking Case," NBC New York, July 11, 2012.

161 "There is only one thing": Ibid.

162 "an affront to human": Tracy Connor, "Brooklyn Black-Market Kidney Broker Pleads Guilty to Selling Israeli Organs to Desperate Americans," *New York Daily News,* October 27, 2011.

162 "simply too exploitative": Porter and Johnson, "First Case of Organ Trafficking."

162 "as from 85 fully loaded": Frank McCormick et al., "The Terrible Toll of the Kidney Shortage," *Journal of the American Society of Nephrology* 29 (2018): 2775–76; Anthony Gregory, "Why Legalizing Organ Sales Would Help Save Lives, End Violence," *The Atlantic,* November 9, 2011.

163 not in the sense: For an influential analysis, see Michael Sandel, *What Money Can't Buy: The Moral Limits of Markets* (New York: Farrar, Straus and Giroux, 2012).

163 "personhood": The canonical article elaborating this understanding is Margaret Jane Radin, "Property and Personhood," *Stanford Law Review* 34 (1982): 957–1015.

163 We can't tell you: We recognize this brief chapter wades into passionately contested terrain and cannot possibly give full airing to the arguments that frame self-ownership debates. To dig deeper, start with Sandel, *What Money Can't Buy,* and Debra Satz, *Why Some Things Should Not Be for Sale: The Moral Limits of Markets* (Oxford: Oxford University Press, 2012), and use their bibliographies to branch out. It's a worthy topic for immersion.

164 "She was 18 years old": Alex Tizon, "My Family's Slave," *The Atlantic,* June 2017.

165 between 60,000 and 400,000 enslaved people: Stef Kight, "Report: 400,000

People Are in Modern Slavery in U.S.," *Axios,* July 19, 2018. For a sobering account, see Daniel Rothenberg, *With These Hands: The Hidden World of Migrant Farmworkers Today* (Berkeley: University of California Press, 2000).

165   You may have encountered them without realizing it: See Sarah Maslin Nir, "The Price of Nice Nails," *New York Times,* May 7, 2015.

166   The Terraces lost: *Terrace v. Thompson,* 263 U.S. 197 (1923).

166   Studies have shown their mere existence: For the *Shelley* decision, see 334 U.S. 1 (1948). On the enduring effects of these private covenants, see Richard Brooks and Carol Rose, *Saving the Neighborhood: Racially Restrictive Covenants, Law, and Social Norms* (Cambridge, Mass.: Harvard University Press, 2013). For an account of the government's role, see Richard Rothstein, *The Color of Law: A Forgotten History of How Our Government Segregated America* (New York: Liveright, 2017).

167   "The position of a married woman": Melissa Homestead, *American Women Authors and Literary Property, 1822–1869* (Cambridge, UK: Cambridge University Press, 2005), 29.

167   "Man is, or should be, woman's protector": *Bradwell v. Illinois,* 83 U.S. 130, 141-42 (1872).

168   Wendy Gerrish is an accomplished: Abbie Boudreau et al., "'Premier' Donor Eggs Command High Prices for Desirable Genes," ABC News, November 5, 2015.

168   "usually based on": Ibid.

169   Now one in eight IVF: For a readable overview, see Paris Martineau, "Inside the Quietly Lucrative Business of Donating Human Eggs," *Wired,* April 23, 2019.

169   "It's like I was dating": Boudreau, "'Premier' Donor Eggs."

170   "require justification": David Tuller, "Payment Offers to Egg Donors Prompt Scrutiny," *New York Times,* May 10, 2010.

170   "Doctors don't have a cap": Boudreau, "'Premier' Donor Eggs."

171   In addition to eggs, we can sell our hair: Jana Kasperkevic, "How Much Can You Get for Selling Your Body (Parts)?," *Guardian,* January 31, 2014; Brian Grow and John Shiffman, "In the U.S. Market for Human Bodies, Almost Anyone Can Dissect and Sell the Dead," Reuters, October 24, 2017.

171   Markets in hair date back: Alex Mayyasi, "The Market for Human Hair," *Priceonomics,* December 2, 2015.

172   Even if baby sales: But see Elisabeth Landes and Richard Posner, "The Economics of the Baby Shortage," *Journal of Legal Studies* 7 (1978): 323–48.

172   "the texture of the human world": Margaret Jane Radin, "Market-Inalienability," *Harvard Law Review* 100 (1987): 1881–87.

172   Individuals are sacred: Sandel, *What Money Can't Buy,* develops this framework.

172   we call this adoption: As with egg sales, the adoption market is highly racialized, but with babies as the product. It can cost about $40,000 to adopt a

white baby, about half that for a Black baby. "Six Words: 'Black Babies Cost Less to Adopt,'" NPR, June 27, 2013.

172 The law has long framed: Clare Huntington and Elizabeth Scott, "Conceptualizing Legal Childhood in the Twenty-First Century," *Michigan Law Review* 118 (2020): 1371–1457.

176 The wealthiest patients: Brian Resnick, "The Living Cadavers: How the Poor Are Tricked into Selling Their Organs," *The Atlantic,* March 23, 2012.

176 "that human body parts": S.2048—National Organ Transplant Act, Senate Report No. 98-382 (1984), 17.

178 To sharpen this concern: For a feminist critique of egg-selling, collecting sources, see Naomi Pfeffer, "Eggs-Ploiting Women: A Critical Feminist Analysis of the Different Principles in Transplant and Fertility Tourism," *Reproductive BioMedicine Online* 23 (2011): 634–61.

180 While working on the Alaska pipeline: Rebecca Skloot, "Taking the Least of You," *New York Times Magazine,* April 16, 2006.

181 "It was very dehumanizing": Rebecca Skloot, *The Immortal Life of Henrietta Lacks* (New York: Broadway Books, 2011): 199–201.

181 Moore, however, lived: *Moore v. Regents of University of California,* 51 Cal. 3d 120, 143-146, 157-158, 170 (1990).

186 "Why Didn't She Get Alzheimer's?": Pam Belluck, "Why Didn't She Get Alzheimer's? The Answer Could Hold a Key to Fighting the Disease," *New York Times,* November 4, 2019.

187 But the Constitution nowhere defines: Where does property come from if not the Constitution? It can't just be law, because that gives the state too much power to wipe you out. In America, the answer seems rooted in jurisprudence, in the liberal values animating the institutions of property. See Hanoch Dagan and Michael Heller, "America's Property Pact" (draft on file with authors); see also Thomas W. Merrill, "The Landscape of Constitutional Property," *Virginia Law Review* 86 (2000): 885–999.

188 "Exhausted by years of infertility": Alex Kuczynski, "Her Body, My Baby," *New York Times Magazine,* November 28, 2008.

189 "We regard surrogacy as": Tamar Lewin, "Coming to U.S. for Baby, and a Womb to Carry It," *New York Times,* July 5, 2014.

189 "anyone who can afford it": Ibid.

191 "illegal, perhaps criminal": *In the Matter of Baby M,* 109 N.J. 396, 410, 440 (1988).

193 "I feel people should be": Elizabeth Landau, "What Is Virginity Worth Today?," CNN, January 22, 2009.

195 "After twelve years in the major leagues": Big Al, "Curt Flood and the Birth of the Million Dollar Baseball Player," *Bleacher Report,* October 3, 2009.

195 "A well paid slave is still a slave": Brad Snyder, *A Well-Paid Slave: Curt Flood's Fight for Free Agency in Professional Sports* (New York: Viking, 2006), 313.

195 "One way to think about slavery": Kurt Streeter, "Is Slavery's Legacy in the Power Dynamics of Sports?," *New York Times,* August 18, 2019.

195 Football, basketball, and hockey leagues: Ryan O'Hanlon, "Why Don't Soccer Stars Sign Contracts Like LeBron James and Kevin Durant?," *Ringer,* August 17, 2017; Ini-Obong Nkang, "How the Search for Football's Next Big Thing Is Fueling a Modern-Day Slave Trade," *Conversation,* August 12, 2019.

195 Flood pursued his attack: Allen Barra, "How Curt Flood Changed Baseball and Killed His Career in the Process," *The Atlantic,* July 12, 2011.

195 When National Hockey League: Tim Wu, "How to Fix Olympic Ice Hockey," *New York Times,* February 14, 2018.

195 Leagues mandate what clothes: Kelsey Kennedy, "Michael Phelps Wore Nike Instead of Under Armour on the Last Sports Illustrated Cover," *Quartz,* August 18, 2016.

196 "You can't expect people": Tom Schad, "Spencer Haywood Says He Sees 'Tinge of Slavery' with Treatment of College Players," *USA Today,* March 19, 2018.

196 "Their business model is based": Chelsea Howard, "Chris Webber, Isiah Thomas Refer to Slavery When Discussing College Athletics," *Sporting News,* February 28, 2018.

196 "It's starting to beg": Billy Witz, "N.C.A.A. Outlines Plan to Let Athletes Make Endorsement Deals," *New York Times,* April 29, 2020.

197 "They just told us": Sophie Quinton, "These Days, Even Janitors Are Being Required to Sign Non-Compete Clauses," *USA Today,* May 27, 2017.

197 About 20 percent of American workers: Evan Starr, J. J. Prescott, and Norman Bishara, "Understanding Noncompetition Agreements: The 2014 Noncompete Survey Project," *Michigan State Law Review* (2016): 369–464. For a recent analysis, collecting citations, see Karla Walter, "The Freedom to Leave," *American Progress,* January 9, 2019.

197 Jarvis Arrington worked: Billy Jean Louis, "Burger King Faces Class Action Lawsuit for 'No-Poaching' Rule," *South Florida Business Journal,* October 17, 2018.

197 You, too, may be bound: Andrew Keshner, "The No. 1 Reason You Should NOT Sign Your Employer's Non-Compete Clause," *Marketwatch,* December 14, 2019.

198 Here are some options: The theoretical framework for this section is drawn from Hanoch Dagan and Michael Heller, "Specific Performance," available

at https://ssrn.com /abstract=3647336 and from "Choice Theory: A Restate-
ment," in Hanoch Dagan and Benjamin Zipursky, eds., *Research Handbook
on Private Law Theory* (Elgar Publishing, 2021), available at https://ssrn.com/
abstract=3432743.

199 "Non-compete agreements for low-wage": Lorraine Mirabella, "Employers
     Use Non-Compete Agreements Even for Low-Wage Workers," *Baltimore Sun,*
     July 7, 2017.

200 Several studies attribute: Timothy B. Lee, "Massachusetts Just Stole an Impor-
     tant Page from Silicon Valley's Playbook," *Vox,* July 1, 2016.

Chapter 6: The Meek Shall Inherit Very Little

202 John Brown's Farm: This section is drawn substantially from Michael Heller,
     *Gridlock Economy: How Too Much Ownership Wrecks Markets, Stops Innova-
     tion, and Costs Lives* (New York: Basic Books, 2008), 121–25; it is based on
     the ownership theory developed in Hanoch Dagan and Michael Heller, "The
     Liberal Commons," *Yale Law Journal* 110 (2001): 602–11. In addition, see
     the powerful accounts by Vann R. Newkirk II, "The Great Land Robbery:
     The Shameful Story of How 1 Million Black Families Have Been Ripped
     from Their Farms," *The Atlantic,* September 2019; and Lizzie Presser, "Kicked
     Off the Land: Why So Many Black Families Are Losing Their Property," *The
     New Yorker,* July 22, 2019.

203 Here is one family's story: Emergency Land Fund, *The Impact of Heir Property
     on Black Rural Land Tenure in The Southeastern Region of the United States*
     (1980): 283–86.

204 "the worst problem": Anna Stolley Persky, "In the Cross-Heirs," *ABA Journal,*
     May 2, 2009.

205 "Many assume that not having a will": Presser, "Kicked Off the Land."

206 "are almost always white": Robert S. Brown, *Only Six Million Acres: The
     Decline of Black Owned Land in the Rural South* (Black Economic Research
     Center, 1973), 53.

206 "the leading cause": Presser, "Kicked Off the Land."

206 "forty-two per cent": Ibid.

206 "If you want to understand wealth": Presser, "Kicked Off the Land."

207 "The details are complex": Dagan and Heller, "The Liberal Commons,"
     620–22.

207 The German model helped inspire: Thomas Mitchell, "Reforming Property
     Law to Address Devastating Land Loss," *Alabama Law Review* 66 (2014):
     1–61.

208   Relatively few are left: Toni Morrison, *Song of Solomon* (New York: Alfred A. Knopf, 1977), 235.

208   A Meaningless System of Minute Partition: This section is drawn substantially from Heller, *Gridlock Economy,* 125–31.

209   "good, potentially productive": *Hearings on H.R. 11113,* 89th Congress, 2d Session, 10 (1966) (Rep. Aspinal), cited in *Hodel v. Irving,* 481 U.S. 704, 708 (1987).

209   "The administrative costs": 78 Cong. Rec. 11,728 (June 15, 1934) (Rep. Howard), cited ibid.

210   "Tract 1305 [on a Dakota Reservation] is": *Hodel* 481 U.S. at 708, 712–13.

210   Partition and lost inheritances: Dagan and Heller, "The Liberal Commons"; see also Henry E. Smith, "Exclusion Versus Governance: Two Strategies for Delineating Property Rights," *Journal of Legal Studies* 31 (2002): S453–87.

211   "that sole and despotic dominion": William Blackstone, *Commentaries on the Laws of England* (1765), bk. 2, chap. 1. A sophisticated modern statement of this view appears in Thomas Merrill, "Property and the Right to Exclude," *Nebraska Law Review* 77 (1998): 730–55.

211   *liberal commons* property: Dagan and Heller, "Liberal Commons," 609–20.

213   estate tax: In a typical example, the Missouri Supreme Court wrote, "Inheritance or will is not an absolute or natural right but one created by the laws of the sovereign power." State ex rel. *McClintock v. Guinotte,* 204 S.W. 806, 808 (1918).

213   "We also want to leave": Hearings before the House Committee on Ways and Means, 104th Congress, 1st Session, February 1, 1995, 952.

214   "the perfect poster child": This section draws from Michael Graetz and Ian Shapiro, *Death by a Thousand Cuts* (Princeton: Princeton University Press, 2005), 65.

214   "kindled voter resentment": Angelique Haugerud, *No Billionaire Left Behind* (Stanford, Calif.: Stanford University Press, 2013), 70.

214   "Thigpen's story was repeated": Josh Hoxie, "Half of Prince's $300 Million Estate Could Be Taxed. That's a Good Thing," *American Prospect,* June 8, 2016.

215   proponents of repeal were unable: David Cay Johnston, "Talk of Lost Farms Reflects Muddle of Estate Tax Debate," *New York Times,* April 8, 2001.

216   "one of the most effective": Graetz and Shapiro, *Death by a Thousand Cuts,* 13.

218   "I find it ridiculous": Anita Singh, "Julian Fellowes: Inheritance Laws Denying My Wife a Title Are Outrageous," *Telegraph,* September 13, 2011.

218   most powerful English family names: On England, see Kabir Chibber, "This Is the Proof that the 1% Have Been Running the Show for 800 Years," *Quartz,*

November 23, 2014. On Florence, see Elsa Vulliamy, "The City Where the Names of the Wealthiest Families Haven't Changed for 600 Years," *Independent,* May 30, 2016.

219   "Of all the potential perils": Joe Conason, *It Can Happen Here: Authoritarian Peril in the Age of Bush* (New York: Thomas Dunne Books, 2007), 135.

219   "The transmission from generation": Franklin Delano Roosevelt, Message to Congress on Tax Revision, June 19, 1935.

220   "Only morons pay the estate tax": Bess Levin, "Gary Cohn Thinks You'd Have to be a 'Moron' to Pay the Estate Tax," *Vanity Fair,* August 29, 2017.

222   Enter South Dakota: This section, and the quoted material in it, draws from Oliver Bullough, "The Great American Tax Haven: Why the Super-Rich Love South Dakota," *Guardian,* November 14, 2019.

222   "Aristocracy was back": Bullough, "Great American Tax Haven."

222   "To some, South Dakota is a 'fly-over' state": Ibid.

223   "The voters don't have a clue": Ibid.

224   "done a pretty good job": Ibid.

225   As baby boomers die in the coming decades: Mark Hall, "The Greatest Wealth Transfer in History: What's Happening and What Are the Implications," *Forbes,* November 11, 2019.

225   "That grown men should": John Chipman Gray, *Restraints on the Alienation of Property,* 2nd ed. (Boston: Boston Book Co., 1895), 242–47.

226   "artificial aristocracy": Thomas Jefferson to John Adams, October 28, 1813, Founders.archive.gov. See also "America's New Aristocracy," *The Economist,* January 22, 2015.

226   "honor, wealth, and power": John Adams to Thomas Jefferson, November 15, 1813, Founders.archive.gov.

227   "We don't pay taxes": "Maid Testifies Helmsley Denied Paying Taxes," *New York Times,* July 12, 1989.

227   "The dog is the only thing": "Where There's a Will, There's a Way to Stay 'Queen of Mean'" (editorial), *Chicago Sun-Times,* August 31, 2007.

227   "No more questions": Bullough, "Great American Tax Haven."

228   The bottom line: Alina Tegund, "There's More to Estate Planning Than Just the Will," *New York Times,* September 5, 2014.

229   From Shared Sacrifice to Self-Sacrifice: The private law theory animating this section is developed in Carolyn J. Frantz and Hanoch Dagan, "Properties of Marriage," *Columbia Law Review* 104 (2004): 75–133, and in Hanoch Dagan and Michael Heller, *The Choice Theory of Contracts* (Cambridge, UK: Cambridge University Press, 2017), 60–61, 121–22.

230   In a career spanning four decades: "Frederica von Stade New York Farewell

Concert," *The New Yorker,* April 22, 2010; Nimet Habachy, "Frederica von Stade's Farewell to the Opera Stage," WQXR, February 23, 2011.

230 "customers weren't expected": "La Dame aux Beaux Plombages," *Illustrated London News,* August 31, 1985.

231 For six years, she had been married: *In re Marriage of Graham,* 574 P.2d 75 (Co. 1978).

232 The court ruled for Peter Elkus: *Elkus v. Elkus,* 169 A.D.2d 134 (1st Dept, 1991).

234 This rule helps explain why: Darlena Cunha, "The Divorce Gap," *The Atlantic,* April 28, 2016.

235 Much of ownership (and contract): Ian Ayers and Robert Gertner, "Filling Gaps in Incomplete Contracts: An Economic Theory of Default Rules," *Yale Law Journal* 99 (1989): 87–130; for a brief explanation, see Lawrence Solum, "Legal Theory Lexicon: Default Rules and Completeness," *Legal Theory Blog,* September 30, 2012.

236 And all this would be available for free: Justin Elliott and Paul Kiel, "The TurboTax Trap: Inside TurboTax's 20-Year Fight to Stop Americans from Filing Their Taxes for Free," *ProPublica,* October 17, 2019.

236 Dorris married Robert: *Estate of Hanau v. Hanau,* 730 S.W.2d 663 (Tex. 1987).

237 California—also a community property state: Whenever you see the word *quasi* or *constructive,* recognize its role as a rhetorical tool in ownership debates. Lawyers use these words as "a way of pretending that whatever [words they modify depict] a state of affairs that actually exists when actually it does not." Jesse Dukeminier et al., *Property,* 9th ed. (New York: Wolters Kluwer, 2018), 37n19.

239 The mere act: On the autonomy-enhancing value of choosing among marital regimes, see Dagan and Heller, *Choice Theory of Contracts,* 121–22.

Chapter 7: The Future of Ownership—and the World

241 "greatest city in the world": Jillian Anthony et al., "50 Reasons Why NYC Is the Greatest City in the World Right Now," *Time Out,* September 18, 2018.

241 In 1990 he became commissioner: Albert Appleton, "How New York City Kept Its Drinking Water Pure—and Saved Billions of Dollars," *On the Commons,* October 24, 2012.

242 "A good environment will": Ibid.

242 "rolling Thanksgiving dinner": Gretchen Daily and Katherine Ellison, *The New Economy of Nature: The Quest to Make Conservation Profitable* (Washington, D.C.: Island Press, 2002), 74.

246 ecosystem-services ownership: James Salzman et al., "The Global Status and

Trends of Payments for Ecosystem Services," *Nature Sustainability* 1 (2018): 136.

246   Clambering around high stacks: "The Scaredest I've Been in a Long Time," *Deadliest Catch,* May 31, 2016.

247   "the deadliest job": Matt Jenkins, "The Most Cooked-Up Catch," *High Country News,* July 27, 2009.

248   "They just drove a lot": Ibid.

249   Even a hint of caution: Scott Campbell, Jr., "Making 'The Deadliest Catch' Less Deadly," *Wall Street Journal,* November 14, 2011.

252   "You know that a fisherman": Jenkins, "Most Cooked-Up Catch."

253   "the greatest unknown policy": Eric Pooley, "How Behavioral Economics Could Save Both the Fishing Industry and the Oceans," *Harvard Business Review,* January 24, 2013.

256   "the biggest environmental scandal": Christopher Booker, "The Clean Development Mechanism Delivers the Greatest Green Scam of All," *Telegraph,* August 28, 2010.

257   Five years into the trading program: Mark Schapiro, " 'Perverse' Carbon Payments Send Flood of Money to China," *Yale Environment 360,* December 13, 2010.

257   "It's perverse. You have": Schapiro, " 'Perverse' Carbon Payments."

259   "Hey Apple, three movies": Mike Masnick, "You Don't Own What You've Bought: Apple Disappears Purchased Movies," *Tech Dirt,* September 12, 2018.

260   "reserve the right to refuse": Joel Johnson, "You Don't Own Your Kindle Books, Amazon Reminds Customers," NBC News, October 24, 2012.

260   "Please know that": Ibid.

260   "We wish you luck": Suw Charman-Anderson, "Amazon Ebooks Are Borrowed, Not Bought," *Forbes,* October 23, 2012.

261   All Revolvs in the world: Cory Doctorow, "Google Reaches into Customers' Homes and Bricks Their Gadgets," *Boing Boing,* April 5, 2016.

261   "Which hardware will Google": Arlo Gilbert, "The Time That Tony Fadell Sold Me a Container of Hummus," *Arlo Gilbert,* April 3, 2016.

262   But it is a bait-and-switch: To explore this theme further, see Aaron Perzanowski and Jason Schultz, *The End of Ownership: Personal Property in the Digital Economy* (Cambridge, Mass.: MIT Press, 2016).

262   believe they own digital content: David Lazarus, "You Don't Really 'Buy' Digital Goods," *Los Angeles Times,* May 13, 2016.

262   "There's a lot of meaning": Ibid.

263   bundle of sticks: J. E. Penner, "The 'Bundle of Rights' Picture of Property," *UCLA Law Review* 43 (1996): 711–820.

263 "a non-exclusive, non-transferable": "Amazon Prime Video Terms of Use," *Prime Video,* accessed June 1, 2020.

265 "In the grimmest version": Jacob Brogan, "What's the Future of Ownership?," *Slate,* October 3, 2016.

267 "How many of you own": Rachel Botsman, "The Case for Collaborative Consumption," *TedxSydney,* May 2010.

267 "ten ideas that will": Bryan Walsh, "Today's Smart Choice: Don't Own. Share," *Time,* March 17, 2011.

268 "The iPhone helped": Ben Tarnoff, "The Future: Where Borrowing Is the Norm and Ownership Is Luxury," *Guardian,* October 17, 2016.

268 "slices": Lee Anne Fennell, *Slices and Lumps: Division and Aggregation in Law and Life* (Chicago: University of Chicago Press, 2019).

268 "In a world where": Tarnoff, "The Future."

269 failed hole providers: Sarah Kessler, "The 'Sharing Economy' Is Dead, and We Killed It," *Fast Company,* September 14, 2015.

269 "A startling number of young": Janelle Nanos, "The End of Ownership: America's New Sharing Economy," *Boston Magazine,* April 30, 2013.

269 "Nowadays we don't": Brian X. Chen, "We're Living in a Subscriptions World. Here's How to Navigate It," *New York Times,* January 15, 2020.

270 "Many of us are starting to rethink": Nanos, "End of Ownership."

273 "Who remembers the sound": Brooke Masters, "Winners and Losers in the Sharing Economy," *Financial Times,* December 28, 2017.

Index

Index

ABOUT THE AUTHORS

Michael Heller is the Lawrence A. Wien Professor of Real Estate Law and former Vice Dean for Intellectual Life at Columbia Law School. He is the author of *The Gridlock Economy: How Too Much Ownership Wrecks Markets, Stops Innovation, and Costs Lives.*

James Salzman is the Donald Bren Distinguished Professor of Environmental Law with joint appointments at the UCLA School of Law and the UCSB Bren School of Environmental Science & Management. He is the author of *Drinking Water: A History,* and his book on international environmental law is the most widely used text in the field.